P9-CLP-148

Southern Literary Studies
Louis D. Rubin, Jr., Editor

Figures of the Hero in Southern Narrative

Figures of the Hero
in Southern Narrative

Michael Kreyling

Louisiana State University Press
Baton Rouge and London

MIDDLEBURY COLLEGE LIBRARY

ABA -3559

PS
261
K74
1987

7/1987
amid

Copyright © 1987 by Louisiana State University Press
All rights reserved
Manufactured in the United States of America

Designer: Diane B. Didier
Typeface: Linotron Baskerville
Typesetter: G & S Typesetters, Inc.
Printer: Thomson-Shore, Inc.
Binder: John H. Dekker and Sons, Inc.

Chapters I, III, and V herein appeared previously, in slightly different form, in *Southern Literary Journal*, XVI (Spring, 1984), *Mississippi Quarterly*, XXXIV (Fall, 1981), and *South Atlantic Quarterly*, LXXXIV (Autumn, 1985), respectively. Grateful acknowledgment is made to Alfred A. Knopf, Inc., for granting permission to reprint excerpts from *The Moviegoer*, by Walker Percy, copyright © 1962 by Walker Percy; *The Collected Poems of William Alexander Percy*, copyright © 1943 by Leroy Pratt Percy; *Selected Poems, Third Edition, Revised and Enlarged*, by John Crowe Ransom, copyright 1927 by Alfred A. Knopf, Inc., renewed 1955 by John Crowe Ransom; and to Random House, Inc., for granting permission to reprint excerpts from *Flags in the Dust*, by William Faulkner, copyright 1929 and renewed 1957 by William Faulkner, edited by Douglas Day, copyright © 1973 by Random House, Inc.; *Go Down, Moses*, by William Faulkner, copyright 1940, 1941, 1942 by William Faulkner, copyright 1942 by Curtis Publishing Co., copyright © 1968, 1969, 1970 by Estelle Faulkner and Jill Faulkner Summers; *Light in August*, by William Faulkner, copyright 1932 and renewed 1960 by William Faulkner. Excerpts reprinted by permission of Farrar, Straus and Giroux, Inc., from: *The Last Gentleman*, copyright © 1966 by Walker Percy; *Love in the Ruins*, copyright © 1971 by Walker Percy; *The Second Coming*, copyright © 1980 by Walker Percy; and *Collected Poems 1919–1976* by Allen Tate. Copyright 1932 by Charles Scribner's Sons. Renewed © 1965 by Allen Tate.
The line quoted herein from "The Love Song of J. Alfred Prufrock," by T. S. Eliot, is reprinted by permission of Faber and Faber Ltd. from *Collected Poems 1909–1962* by T. S. Eliot.

10 9 8 7 6 5 4 3 2 1

Library of Congress Cataloging-in-Publication Data

Kreyling, Michael, 1948–
    Figures of the hero in southern narrative.

    Bibliography: p.
    Includes index.
    1. American prose literature—Southern States—History and criticism.   2. American fiction—Southern States—History and criticism.   3. Southern States in literature.   4. Heroes in literature.   5. Narration (Rhetoric)   II. Title.
PS261.K74   1987   813'.009'3275   86-20032
ISBN 0-8071-1301-8

To
C. M. K. and A. C. K.

Contents

Acknowledgments

This book turned out to be a more complicated endeavor than I had thought at the beginning. I have learned valuable lessons about the communal side of scholarship and have been helped by generous people at every step. The following is only the beginning of the thanks I owe to: Lewis Simpson, whose criticism and encouragement have been steady and deft; Louis D. Rubin, Jr., whose comments on the manuscript have helped me to tame its uncouth portions; T. D. Young and Bertram Wyatt-Brown, who read parts of the manuscript and responded with valuable suggestions; patient audiences at two meetings of the Mellon Colloquium, Tulane University, and at the English Department Symposium, Mississippi State University, who listened and followed up with constructive questions; Helen H. Tate, for kind permission to quote excerpts from Allen Tate's unfinished biography of Lee; the director, Professor Richard Ludwig, and staff of the Department of Rare Books and Special Collections, Princeton University Library, for their courtesy in aiding my research in the Allen Tate Papers; the director and staff of the Manuscript Department, William R. Perkins Library, Duke University—especially Ellen G. Gartrell, who had the card catalog drawers open and marked when I arrived; the chief, James H. Hutson, and staff of the Manuscript Division, Library of Congress, who helped in my research in the Douglas Southall Freeman Papers; the Committee on Research, Tulane University, for research support; the interlibrary Loan staff of Howard-Tilton Library, Tulane University, for their help in getting me the books I needed, and those I thought I needed; and Professor Harry Redman, Department of French and Italian, Tulane University, who helped me through the history and literature of Pierrot (all the errors are mine).

I would also like to acknowledge Elizabeth L. Carpelan of LSU Press for her meticulous editing. Uncountable thanks go to Alice Voros, administrative assistant and careful typist, not to mention shrewd reader. I wish we had another book to start on.

Figures of the Hero in Southern Narrative

Introduction

*There is the story of one's hero, and then, thanks to the
intimate connexion of things, the story of one's story.*
—Henry James
Preface to *The Ambassadors*

This is a book about southern writing, a story of the stories, limited to the genre of prose narrative. It is presented to readers
within and outside the academy who have done some thinking
about southern stories and storytelling, who are convinced that
they know the difference between southern and nonsouthern literary expressions, and who are interested in the ongoing cultural, literary, and political wrangle over the nature of the southern mind and heart. The matter of the book is approximately
thirty narrative works by southern authors or, in the related
cases of Henry James and Henry Adams, by nonsouthern writers concerned with southern forms of history and consciousness.
The design of the book is chronological. The implicit theme is,
then, developmental—the force of a heroic figural system accu-
mulates over the course of the history of southern literary self-
consciousness. I have tried to avoid concluding each section
or chapter with the thunderclap of definitive interpretation.
Rather, my intention is to suggest a structural and thematic context for the reading of southern prose narrative, and to test that
matrix in readings of narratives dating from the second decade
of the nineteenth century, when southern literature clearly de-
tached itself from other forms of writing, to the decade just past,
the 1970s, when southern writing of all forms was said to have
died. The existence of a continuity of figure and thematics along
that route is of less importance to this presentation than the im-

press of the accumulated narrative tradition upon a series of
works claiming or thought to be, in a meaningful way, southern,
especially at moments in history when southernness was thought
to constitute a real difference. My study is referential within a
southern system of author and audience; secondarily, the larger
national cultural condition does sometimes exert real pressure.

My guides for the excursion are many; they will be amply
cited along the way. A few studies that have influenced the general critical assumptions deserve mention here.

Narratives, as Frank Kermode has shown us, know more than
they say, and much of what narrative knows, encoded in structure and thematics, pertains to the cultural consciousness in
which it has its origins and ends.[1] The work of the critic of narrative, then, is to continue beyond the line of what narratives say
in quest of what they know. In a certain canny way, all readers in
the cultural circle can make the crossing; the critic tries to make
it self-consciously.

The critic of southern narrative finds a worn path, for many
have gone before and left the terrain profusely marked. But interpretation does not stop, Kermode reminds us, because reading does not stop. The "connexions," Henry James well knew,
are neverending, and readers are an obsessed lot, determined to
pursue them to the last breath. This study of southern narrative
follows one possible route of connection, the figure of the hero
and the system of thematics he centers. My goal is not to ex-
pound a position so much as to impart a feeling that the going
has been worth the time, and that tracing the figure of the hero
in southern narrative is part of an education in the "connexions"
of an episteme. There are, of course, roads not taken and the
road that goes beyond my stopping point. The reader has my
best wishes for these independent trips and is encouraged to
take along a good deal of initiative and skepticism.

In addition to the sentence from his preface to *The Ambassadors*, James contributes another that illumines the path before
us. To James, fiction was a living labyrinth in which he would be
willingly lost, but never without hope: "Nothing can exceed the

1. Frank Kermode, *The Art of Telling: Essays on Fiction* (Cambridge Mass.,
1983). The thought here is distilled, I hope correctly, from Kermode's general
attitude toward narrative.

closeness with which the whole fits again into its germ." James often used his titles as verbal emblems for the germs of his narratives. My title, though lacking Jamesian compression, stands in a similar relationship of part to whole.

Figure is a deliberate choice, for it shifts emphasis away from the "secretarial realism" of the hero (whether a character is modeled on Robert E. Lee or Jefferson Davis) toward the mythic identity of the hero.[2] This popular aspect of figure study surfaces significantly in the case of the hero as embodied in Robert E. Lee. The figural Lee concerns most southern writers more than the actual, even if the latter is their stated material. Lee the figure appeared hauntingly in southern narrative before his actual entrance into history, and has lingered on the southern retina long after his death in 1870.

Figure is also a technical term in the critical lexicon, and my usage of it in the formal sense is derived from Erich Auerbach's definition. *Figure,* he states, is a presence inscribed upon a culture's awareness, rooted in one historical event and auguring another. Auerbach emphasizes that *figure* is *not* a synonym for image or symbol; the latter describes a correspondence between the actual and the abstract, and the former is too loosely connotative. *Figure* inscribes specifically historical meaning—"*figura* is something real and historical which announces something else that is also real and historical"—and therefore (my corollary) encodes the certain authority of history to justify events and personalities that come within the figural pattern.[3] Heroes are different from you and me. The popular acceptance of Lee, for example, is assured not simply because he possessed the Carter and Lee birthright but also because he is firmly lodged in the figural pattern of the southern hero. James's Basil Ransom, the hero of *The Bostonians,* carries the southern figural pattern with him into the quite different world of the reunited nation. More than one of his fellow characters (*e.g.,* Olive Chancellor, Mrs. Luna, Miss Birdseye) sees him in his cultural figuration rather than in his actual identity. In *The Bostonians,* then, James reports on a figural conflict, not a figurative one. His characters do not

2. Kermode refers to "secretarial realism," *ibid.,* 53, 103.

3. Erich Auerbach, "Figura," in *Scenes from the Drama of European Literature,* trans. Ralph Mannheim (N.p., 1959), 29.

act "as if" the North and South were still in actual war; they are
in fact struggling for the field of meaning.

The term *figura* is nourished by deep roots in Christian her-
meneutics, for the historical Jesus is the prototype of all Western
heroic figures, and the messianic narrative is the keystone of
Western history that obtained until the modern age. The figure
of Jesus exerts cultural power even after cracks appear in the
seamless edifice of faith. Thinking in figural terms, then, entails
a view of history as finite and symmetrical, as founded in a privileged past and directed providentially and textually toward
parousia. The figure of the hero is shorthand for a theory of culture and history that transcends contingency. "The tentativeness
of events in the figural interpretation is fundamentally different
from the tentativeness of events in the modern view of historical
development. In the modern view, the provisional event is treated
as a step in an unbroken process [realism?]; in the figural system
the interpretation is always sought from above [romance?]; events
are considered not in their unbroken relation to one another,
but torn apart, individually, each in relation to something other
that is promised and not yet present."[4] My interpolations are the
signposts of one of the side trips mentioned at the outset of this
introduction. The moss-covered debate over the romantic configuration of the southern mind emerges here, contingent upon
the presence of a certain structural element, the figural, in the
narrative.

By *hero* I do not mean protagonist, for nearly every narrative
makes use of a protagonist. Nor do I mean leader or an event-
making individual—those who have been born with power, have
seized it, have had it thrust upon them. In many instances, however, the heroic figures in the narratives I discuss are indeed
leaders in the public world of power examined by such writers as
Sidney Hook and recreated for fiction.[5] By *heroism* I mean an inherent and instantaneously acknowledged capacity to render the
provisional nature of any situation or condition into part of a
consecrated pattern. This transformation occurs not only in the
plots of the various narratives but also in larger literary schemes

---

4. *Ibid.*, 58–59.
5. Sidney Hook, *The Hero in History: A Study in Limitation and Possibility* (New
York, 1943).

Jim vs. Huck for hero

of the works. As Auerbach might have expressed it, the heroic figure guarantees meaning "from above" the horizontal plane of simple contingency. Heroism is self-evident; it is not subject to appeal. To deny heroism is to deny the absolutely ordained, an act of heresy or even blasphemy against the transcendent ideals of the people for whom the hero acts. Embedded in the figure of the hero, then, is the assumption of primacy in human society, or of singleness in history—the chosen society is so ordained that heroic figures (always male) by their very presence among a people bring that people to a new degree of self-conscious unity. There can, then, be only one heroic center at a time. When several heroes compete, all but one are false, and anarchy in meaning and social organization will continue until the genuine hero is discovered and acknowledged.

The heroic model for human society is not democratic; plots that take up the conflict between democratic ideas and heroic counterpositions are numerous in southern narrative. They spring from the narrative structure, ultimately from cultural belief. Hook's *The Hero in History,* revising the elements of Carlyle's "dreamy" hero worship for a wide-awake democratic people, treats the relationship between heroism and democracy. Hook's position that the heroic and democratic concepts are fundamentally uneasy together is a point of reference throughout this study.

The romantic-democratic model of history and personality, a paradigm in which any man can become president—even a railsplitter or, *mirabile dictu,* a tanner's son from Galena, Illinois—is a profane paradigm imposed by the "unbroken process" of events. Inherent in heroic narrative is the conflict between these paradigms—either the heroic prevails (the outcome of most antebellum narratives) or it falls before a modern order universally acknowledged to be powerful but morally and culturally bankrupt (the frequent pattern after Reconstruction).

The hero in narrative is not the same as the hero in history. In narrative, the hero is not a personality so much as a set of aesthetic and cultural alternatives sensitized to historical changes but not determined by them. Consequently, the possibilities of one historical moment survive into later days; these possibilities can be useful to the artist and to the audience. Theodore Ziolkowski, whose several studies of thematics in literature explore this aspect of literary production and reception, has discussed the delicate correspondence between literature and history: "Although these stages emerge in a strict historical sequence, they do not disappear when a new stage prevails. According to a principle that might be called the Conservation of Cultural Energy, they remain in existence as fictional or intellectual possibilities."[6] The possibilities of one era might in fact be superseded by the exigencies of a new set of circumstances; yet that does not mean that they vanish. The heroic figure and the structure of narrative that accompanies him enter and exit several zones of historical relevance. The heroic never simply disappears, giving way politely to new figures called up by the age. The fiction of Walker Percy might be viewed in this light—Percy struggles to revive the heroic figure while, at the same time, being aware of the crust of barnacles on the heroic icon.

Ziolkowski has tested the theory of literary iconology by tracing the biblical pattern of narratives of the life of Jesus in literary works stretching from the late nineteenth century to the present. The iconological figure of Jesus necessitates a narrative pattern that "can be divorced or abstracted from any meaning it may once have embodied." Ziolkowski admits that we are more prepared to grant that "recognizable aesthetic shapes exist quite independently of any 'meaning' with which they are burdened . . . in such ostensibly 'value-free' media as music and painting than in literature." His conclusion is that we do recognize the abstract "shapes" of certain narratives as containing meaning. This holds for the study of southern heroic narrative as well. Aesthetic possibilities can and do exist free of the burden of meaning because they are the means by which the culture creates and maintains knowledge of itself in history. "In short," Ziolkowski writes, "a culture's choice of its representative images can tell us a great deal about the central concerns of that culture."[7]

As I have suggested apropos of figural narratives, structure is a more direct route to the central concerns of a culture than

6. Theodore Ziolkowski, *Disenchanted Images: A Literary Iconology* (Princeton, 1977), 232–33.
7. Theodore Ziolkowski, *Fictional Transfigurations of Jesus* (Princeton, 1972), 8, 10; *Disenchanted Images*, 247.

meaning because it precedes and enables meaning. Of more
primitive narratives, such as folktales, Propp states: "If one extracts all the basic forms for each [type of tale], and unites them
into one tale, such a tale will reveal that certain abstract representations lie at its core."[8] I have no such taxonomic designs on
southern narrative, but to discover the nature of the abstract
representations at the core of these writings is the objective of
my study. Focusing on the figure of the hero enables reader and
critic to produce the structure's meaning better than do dissection and reassembly. Kermode reminds us that an "important
and neglected rule about reading narratives is that once a certain kind of attention has been aroused we read according to the
values appropriate to that kind of attention whether or not there
is a series of definite gestures to prompt us; of course we may
also decide not to be docile, and evade these local and provincial
restrictions."[9] Encoded into heroic narrative is a set of gestures
that evoke in the audience a certain kind of attention, which is
related to the certain abstract representations. I will discuss both
and try to link them.

The remaining key word of the title is *narrative*. I have chosen
to use *southern narrative* rather than the more common *southern
novel* for deliberate reasons. *Novel* carries, for better or worse,
the connotation of a closed form; there are many types of novels
(for example, historical, stream-of-consciousness, novel of manners), each of which boasts an individual dynamic and a formal
history. Southern authors have written every type. To avoid
adopting a separate poetics for each type, I have simply opted
for the term *narrative*, which is more elastic and generous—all
novels are narratives, but not all narratives are novels. This
usage directs attention to structure, to what all stories have in
common in the art of telling, and devalues the content of interpretation, the so-called meaning. Critics of narrative such as
Kermode, Scholes, Todorov, Propp, Derrida, and Alter stress
the gaps and obstacles that narratives present to the reader in
quest of meaning, rather than a list of prerequisites for the genre
of novel. The more temperate of the critics of narrative also

8. V. Propp, *Morphology of the Folktale* (2nd ed.; Austin, 1968), 89.
9. Kermode, *The Art of Telling*, 57.

allow that great masses of like-minded people ("Uncle Willies," Kermode calls them) nevertheless rest confident in meaning obtained.[10]

The study of narrative is the study of the perversity of texts and the obstinacy of readers in the maintenance of communication—at least, in the possibility of communication through the written story. The word *narrative* focuses on this dynamic as it occurs in a major aspect of southern writing. Southern narrative demands a significantly active and special attention that it has not yet been given in the criticism of southern writing. And there are "definite gestures" that have also escaped notice or have been largely misconstrued. This study of southern narrative sets out to examine both the attention and the prompting gestures.

10. *Ibid.*, 8–9.

I

Literary Remains: The Hero in Antebellum Southern Narrative

> We lack a tradition in the arts; more to the point, we lack a literary tradition. We lack even a literature. We have just enough literary remains from the old regime to prove to us that, had a great literature risen, it would have been unique in modern times.
>
> —Allen Tate
> "The Profession of Letters in the South"

Antebellum southern writing has been subject to two related critical verdicts. First, the matter, tales of cavalier heroes and of plantation life, was tailored to deflect both inner and outer objections to slavery, therefore making the complete body of work nothing more than transparent propaganda. Second, the style was simply and lazily borrowed from Scott with a few unimaginative changes to fit the American locale, and Cooper did it first and better.

William Dean Howells echoed both verdicts in the early 1890s. "I know that there were before the war novelists in South Carolina, in Maryland, and in Virginia deeply imbued with what our poor Spanish friends call the Walter-Scottismo, not to say the Fenimore-Cooperismo, of an outdated fashion of the world's fiction." When this writing was not stylistically outdated, it was morally barbaric. "But that was a barbarous time when these began, and slavery not only brutalized the facts, but brutalized, if I may so express it, the point of view." Richard Watson Gilder also picked up the themes. His critical opinion of John Pendleton Kennedy's *Horse-Shoe Robinson* is handed down from the heights of Genteel moral seriousness. "It may be said, in excuse for the artificiality of this sort of writing, that it was the style of the time in which it was written, and that the scene was placed at a period when the language was supposed to be more conventional and stilted—that it was only second fiddle to Cooper's second fiddle to Scott."[1]

In our own time, the critical axes have shifted only to stress the historical realism inherent in some aspects of antebellum southern matter. J. V. Ridgely and C. Hugh Holman have concluded that only the miniature portraits of peripheral characters are worth salvaging; the romantic envelope can be discarded.[2] Recent critics argue that visions of the material culture of the antebellum South (broadly if implicitly defined as anything countering the "plantation legend") amount to a vibrant though scanted realism that proves that southern writers could observe and think as successfully as did their counterparts in the New England mainstream of American literature. Realism, construed as the amount of social and historical "life" documented in a given work, is, by silent consensus, the norm against which a literary work defines its value.

This study of the hero and his importance in the form of antebellum southern narrative proposes to adjust the prevailing critical norm by emphasizing form over matter, and by claiming for that form an importance that rebuts Howells' charge of banal and outdated imitation. We know enough about the nature of literary form never to dismiss a narrative as mere imitation. A cultural group accepts its narrative form, and rejects others, because that form alone embodies the group's nearest image of itself as its most truthful and accessible scripture. The group defines and recreates itself in the repetition of its form, confirms its understanding of the nature of things in the ritual of retelling,

1. William Dean Howells, "The Southern States in Recent American Literature: First Paper," *Literature,* September 10, 1898, p. 231; William Dean Howells, "The Southern States in Recent American Literature: Second Paper," *Literature,* September 24, 1898, p. 281; Richard Watson Gilder, "The Nationalization of Southern Literature: Part I—Before the War," *Christian Advocate,* July 3, 1890, p. 426.

2. See J. V. Ridgely, *Nineteenth-Century Southern Literature* (Lexington, Ky., 1980); and C. Hugh Holman, *The Roots of Southern Writing: Essays on the Literature of the American South* (Athens, Ga., 1972).

and advances its cause against a host of enemies and aliens in the promulgation of its story.

My own restlessness with prevailing critical statements on antebellum southern narrative springs from a conviction that the act of writing in this genre has been, and continues to be, defined much too narrowly as mere literary imitation. "*All* literature," George Steiner has written, "is language in a condition of special use."[3] Of the myriad uses literature serves, I concentrate on two: the *scriptural* (with the full load of Judeo-Christian biblical associations), by which I mean the use of the written word to unite and defend a people who come to know themselves through their sacred texts; and the *political*, by which I mean the use of the official, sanctioned work to organize the lives of society's members toward an ideal of behavior that transcends topical propaganda.

The key to this enabling structure of antebellum southern narrative is its hero. He is the linchpin of a powerful social, historical, and psychological myth, which supports the unanalyzed structures of individual and group awareness and behavior. The myth embedded in southern heroic narrative has reached outward to readers and writers for two centuries, has been embraced, rejected, and fought over. The reasons why have not been fully explored.

Any exploration of the southern hero and his narrative tradition must begin with antebellum narratives. Of the many works of fiction published between 1800 and 1860 (excluding the works of William Gilmore Simms, which will be discussed later), a few have attracted the lion's share of critical attention either because they have survived in print or because they provide particularly atrocious or elegant (depending on the critic's bias) examples of the form. For this stage of my study, I have chosen three such works: George Tucker's *The Valley of Shenandoah; or, Memories of the Graysons* (1824), Beverley Tucker's *The Partisan Leader* (1836), and William Alexander Caruthers' *Cavaliers of Virginia; or, The Recluse of Jamestown* (1834). These three works of heroic narrative are frequently mentioned in critical discussions.[4] Each

3. George Steiner, "Linguistics and Poetics," in *Extra-Territorial* (New York, 1971), 126.
4. See Jay B. Hubbell, *The South in American Literature* (Durham, 1954),

narrative features a hero in similar urgent circumstances, and from these three specimens a type can be hypothesized. As a representative segment of a tradition in its early stages, this group displays a formal continuity in the uses of heroic narrative by the southern writer and his audience.

Clearly, there are several additional candidates for discussion. John Pendleton Kennedy's *Horse-Shoe Robinson* (1835) and *Swallow Barn* (1831, revised 1851) have enjoyed their share of critical attention. What I have to say about the Tuckers' and Caruthers' heroic figures can be checked by reference to the Byronic Arthur Butler, the "Cooperismo" hero of *Horse-Shoe Robinson,* and Ned Hazard, the equally romantic southern paragon of *Swallow Barn.*

The study of southern heroic narrative frequently begins with George Tucker's *The Valley of Shenandoah.* This "melancholy history" predates the more famous excursions into heroic narrative by Simms, affording us an early view of the evolving morphology of the hero and his genre.

The hero is Edward Grayson, scion of a Virginia family of aristocratic rank and previously of comfortable, if not opulent, means. As the novel begins, the hero's father has recently died, leaving his widow and heirs the burden of mortgaged estates. The once-comfortable style of the Graysons, who had been accustomed to circulating among several of their plantations according to the seasons, is curtailed. They must now be content with one rather modest retreat. Edward, responding to hardship heroically, decides to forsake the leisure that is his birthright— he enters law school at William and Mary, hoping to recoup the Grayson fortunes at the bar.

A New Yorker, James Gildon, visits the Virginia gentry, and the first volume of the novel describes the series of stops on a tour of the Shenandoah conducted by Grayson for the edification of the outsider. Volume II tells of Gildon's growing sense of grievance against the gentry, his seduction and abandonment of

243–55; William R. Taylor, *Cavalier and Yankee: The Old South and American National Character* (New York, 1961), *passim;* and Albert J. Devlin, *Eudora Welty's Mississippi Chronicle* (Jackson, Miss., 1983), 96–106.

Grayson's sister Louisa, the hero's pursuit of the villain into Man-
hattan, and the death—at Gildon's hands—of Edward.

In *Swallow Barn,* Kennedy used the same pairing of northern
and southern representations—the cool and ironical observer
from New York, Mark Littleton, sends back dispatches on the tempestuous Virginian, Ned Hazard. One's first surmise is that Kennedy picked up the idea from reading *The Valley of Shenandoah.*
However, this literary coincidence emerges from a shared and
deep-seated cultural purpose to define the self in and through
the relation with the regional Other. Users of the North-South
narrative paradigm aim at more than topical polemics. To shore
up the proslavery argument, a charge leveled at *Swallow Barn,* is,
for instance, only part of the reason Kennedy tells this particular
story in this particular way. The matter of the plot, though it
bristles with items of historical and sociological interest, is not
merely the vehicle of momentary debate. The emerging outlines
of heroic narrative, coalescing about the figure of the hero, constitute a more complex topic.

The central elements of Edward Grayson's heroism are first
signified in his physical bearing: "In person, he was tall, thin,
with gray eyes, light hair, and a long, thin, but very pleasing visage." Simms, a few years later, would validate this heroic silhouette—erect, slender, tall, commanding of eye—by finding
the original in the Chevalier Bayard, who became instant historical corroboration for heroic civilization in the South, both Old
and New. George Tucker also found the type useful, even though
the historical and literary reverberations had not yet been given
Simms's amplification. The hero's appearance is an important
sign. George Tucker is not merely creating a matinee idol for
feminine swooning and masculine emulation. He attempts a far-
reaching formal and mythopoeic function. The hero must offer
himself for his people's affirmation, and he does so by posing for
recognition. The stock literary requirements of cavalier romance
do not alone account for the prominence of this narrative element. Max Weber suggests that the recognition of the charismatic hero (to which type the southern hero is curiously related)
is the first phase of social organization—those who share the
common recognition of the hero figure become, thereby, a social

group organized, at least rudimentarily, by their recognition. More complex social organizations (hierarchies and classes, rituals and customs) follow. "It is recognition on the part of those subject to authority which is decisive for the validity of charisma. This is freely given and guaranteed by what is held to be a 'sign' or proof, originally always a miracle, and consists in devotion to the corresponding revelation, hero worship, or absolute trust in the leader."[5] In southern heroic narrative, the appearance of the hero, in his familiar silhouette, and his instantaneous recognition by a waiting people, are essential narrative elements.

The hero's claim to superiority is often accentuated by a foil or antagonist who radiates cultural darkness against the hero's light, and the frequent first "function" (to acknowledge Propp's term) of the narrative is the physical juxtaposition of this pair. In *The Valley of Shenandoah*, James Gildon is the hero's opposite: "Gildon, without being positively short, was lower and stouter than Edward, had a full, round face, florid complexion, black eyes, and hair of the same color." The New Yorker is semiotically linked with the earth rather than the sky, with the horizontal rather than the vertical, and with darkness rather than light. Gildon's colors, red and black, are eloquent in their connotations.[6] They call to mind Hawthorne's Lord of Misrule in "My Kinsman, Major Molineux" and the Indians who danced in red and black paint before Captain John Smith. The more remote echoes reach back to Matthew (6:22−24), who describes the eye as the lamp of the body. In the evangelist's terms, Gildon's darkness is great indeed.

More obviously, Tucker selects an antagonist from an alien social and commercial organization. This does not mean simply that Gildon is a proto-Yankee. Actually, James Gildon is the son of a New York merchant; his father has exiled him to the South to scotch a romance with the daughter of a fellow merchant who has just suffered bankruptcy. Gildon represents the

5. George Tucker, *The Valley of Shenandoah; or, Memories of the Graysons* (2 vols.; 1824; rpr. Chapel Hill, 1970), I, 3; Max Weber, *The Theory of Social and Economic Organizations,* trans. A. M. Henderson and Talcott Parsons (New York, 1964), 359.

6. Propp, *Morphology of the Folktale,* 21; G. Tucker, *The Valley of Shenandoah,* I, 4.

outside group that the hero and his people identify as the enemy. Clearly, the "profane sphere," as Weber phrases it, is Gildon's universe; there, sentiment is overborne by cash. We see Gildon as despicable even before he commits the overt act that stigmatizes him. "What is despised," Weber writes, "so long as the genuinely charismatic type is adhered to, is traditional or rational everyday economizing, the attainment of a regular income by continuous economic activity devoted to this end."[7]

In these different types, George Tucker sketches a conflict more subtle than the foreordained "paces" of stereotypical young aristocrats in a cavalier romance.[8] Conflict materializes first in the juxtaposition of antithetical emblems: one upright, pacific, healthy in mind and body; the other creeping, anarchic, diabolical. The first duty of the hero, then, is to prevail against his spiritual and cultural anti-type in a contest of representations, a contest not without veiled animosities and far-reaching connotations. Every heroic gesture expresses the culture's claim to define power and reality.

Grayson's heroic manner stirs up in Gildon a storm of psychocultural resentment. The northerner, subjected to repeated gestures of Grayson's nobility, responds with thinly veiled sarcasm. To Grayson's predictable defense of slavery, for example, Gildon responds: "There is something very fascinating now confess it, Edward, in this unlimited control, let us fiery republicans say what we will. Indeed what is the love of liberty, but the love of doing what we please and, consequently, he who is proud of his own freedom, is equally gratified at controlling the freedom of others." Grayson, on behalf of his culture, dismisses this attack as "a very ingenious piece of sophistry." Shrugging off the condescension, Gildon increasingly presses Grayson to defend his assumptions. Through Gildon, Tucker touches on what W. J. Cash, more than a century later, was to name "the savage ideal": in a heroic society, freedom is "controlling the freedom of others."[9]

Gildon exposes the uncomfortable proximity to literary romance that threatens to undermine the hero's construct of self

7. Weber, *The Theory of Social and Economic Organizations,* 262.
8. Holman, *The Roots of Southern Writing,* 57.
9. G. Tucker, *The Valley of Shenandoah,* I, 60.

and culture when he makes a teasing remark about Grayson's behavior to an assembled company: "He is too much in the clouds to know what concerns such a son of the earth as I am. Whenever he formally sets out on a tour of knight-errantry, I shall accompany him, that I may catch some of the spirit of the mirror of modern chivalry."[10] Gildon's allusion to Don Quixote and his ironical acceptance of the subordinate role of Sancho Panza indicate the New Yorker's conclusion that Grayson is something other than real. He is—to anticipate Shreve's words in *Absalom, Absalom!*—theatrical, "better than Ben-Hur," and thus rendered null and void by reality. Gildon's depiction of himself as a "son of the earth" and his placement of Grayson "in the clouds," a confession that sustains the pattern of association launched by the contrasting descriptions of hero and villain at the opening of the novel, reveals that Gildon can go behind words and representations. This intellectual maneuver is denied the hero, who works in a sphere utterly devoid of irony.

The tone of this badinage, which intensifies as Volume I reaches its climax, hints at a complex sense of grievance in the alien. This feeling is evident also in a passage from the diary of John Quincy Adams, the typical Yankee of his day, on the manners of the typical "Southron" of his acquaintance, John Randolph. Adams had just returned from a session of the Supreme Court at which Randolph had held forth. "I heard him [Randolph] between three and four hours. His speech, as usual, had neither beginning, middle, nor end. Egotism, Virginian aristocracy, slave-scourging liberty, religion, literature, science, wit, fancy, generous feelings, and malignant passions constitute a chaos in his mind, from which nothing orderly can ever flow. . . . It was useless to try to call him to order; he can no more keep order than he can keep silence."[11] Adams' resentment against the illogical mind of the southerner did not turn as violent as Gildon's. It is plain, however, that animosity in such cases goes beyond hostility to the person and toward the culture for which he stands, which Adams' descendant Henry showed in his characterization of a typical southerner—Roony Lee.

10. *Ibid.*, I, 78.
11. Allan Nevins (ed.), *The Diary of John Quincy Adams, 1794–1845* (New York, 1928), 229.

The climatic scene of Volume I of *The Valley of Shenandoah* establishes the conflict of types in the realm of metaphors. (It is functionally equivalent to the Quarters scenes in *Swallow Barn*.) The final stop on the tour of the Shenandoah is a peak in the mountains above Harper's Ferry. Grayson and Gildon behold a vista rich in the symbolism of their conflict: "These grand and picturesque features of nature were rather interrupted than embellished by the arsenal of the United States, where smoke, and hammers, and workmen moving to and fro, broke in upon the repose of nature, and raised a new and uncongenial train of ideas." [12] The "new and uncongenial train of ideas," which has hitched to it a modern industrial society and commerce and the changes in human relations, is engineered by Gildon's ilk, and it is heading for a sure collision with Grayson's heroic order.

This collision occurs when Gildon seduces Louisa, the hero's sister. When Louisa tells Gildon that, after their tempestuous night, she is pregnant, the cad decamps for New York and Louisa dies, lingeringly, of shame. Gildon's New York friends reinforce his regional and cultural animosity. "Virginia dons—the better for a little currying," says one. Another adds: "These chaps have been accustomed to lord it over their slaves, that they think they are to do as they please everywhere. But I'd soon teach them the difference." [13] The voice might be John Quincy Adams' before restraint channeled his resentment into his pen rather than his fists.

Grayson heroically pursues the villain into the heart of the other's kingdom. The commercial metaphor is stamped, he thinks, on everything and everyone. He suspects his hackney driver of overcharging him. Every woman he sees appears to be a prostitute. All the locals he meets in his search for Gildon seem to be gamblers. The "cash nexus" reigns.

Increasingly alienated, the cultural hero finally tracks the villain to his lair, only to be stabbed to death on a public street in a duel. Although Gildon kills the hero, the son of the earth does not triumph, for as Grayson dies he shines forth in a heroic apotheosis that captivates the passersby who witness his last

12. G. Tucker, *The Valley of Shenandoah*, I, 303.
13. *Ibid.*, II, 261, 281.

breath.[14] The hero's image endures on the collective retina after the routine and materialistic world has exterminated him.

Away from the circle of kin and kind, the hero faces a male antagonist in a multilayered contest of melodrama and representation. Within the circle, he faces another challenge equally essential to heroic narrative and equally obscured by the barnacles of literary convention. The hero must find and wed the woman ideally suited to become the mother of heroic culture, a task as important in narrative scripture as vanquishing the villain. The sought-for heroine, traditionally the belle of southern heroic narrative, is always close to home. The obstacles to the hero's successful mating, then, are often less physical than psychological.

In *The Valley of Shenandoah*, Grayson's ideal mate is Matilda Fawkner. "She was tall and slender, had dark brown hair and eyes, and a skin that rivalled the conch shell in the fineness of its texture, and in the brilliancy of its tint." The heroine's typological similarity to the hero is a recurrent element of heroic narrative, and it suggests the vast and problematic theme of the heroine in southern narrative.[15] The mystique of the woman in the Old South (madonna, fragile vessel of great social value) influences Tucker's description of Matilda: her skin recalls the conch. And yet the southern woman is feared almost as deeply as she is venerated. Bertram Wyatt-Brown suggests that southern males were driven by a "mingled fear and love of woman": love, because in the beautiful female countenance they hoped to see the favorable image of their own honorable selves; fear, because the woman (daughter, wife, sister) might bring the clan into disgrace at any moment by producing a bastard (*vide* poor Louisa Grayson), by marrying outside the circle of kin and capital, or by witnessing the male's cowardice or immorality.[16] Southern heroic narrative, however, suggests that there is more to the mystique of the woman than social or economic factors.

The hero has to overcome his fear of the woman and the fear

14. *Ibid.*, II, 291.
15. *Ibid.*, I, 22. Many have discussed the role of the woman in southern society and her function in works of southern literature. See the recent treatment by Anne Goodwyn Jones, *Tomorrow Is Another Day: The Woman Writer in the South, 1859–1936* (Baton Rouge, 1981).
16. Bertram Wyatt-Brown, *Southern Honor: Ethics and Behavior in the Old South* (New York, 1982), 24.

of missing her, for finding and possessing her is essential to the success of his cultural quest. The importance of the ideal mate lies beyond the gratification of sentimental longings, as Scarlett O'Hara was perhaps the first southern female hero to discover. Possession of the ideal mate guarantees the transmission of the hero's identity to a future generation and symbolizes the continuity of the whole culture over time. Weber lists heredity among the several ways in which charismatic character is transmitted. Societies explain the transmission of charisma, he writes, "by the conception that charisma is a quality transmitted by heredity; thus that it is participated in by the kinsmen of its bearer, particularly by his closest relatives."[17] Heroic breeding, however, cannot be left to chance, for the continuance of a whole people rides on the offspring. In southern heroic narrative, therefore, the ideal mate is as close to the hero's type and kinship group as possible. (In narratives appearing after *The Valley of Shenandoah,* the ideal mate is often taken from the circle of first cousins.)

In heroic narrative, the ideal woman is seldom entangled in a web of everyday circumstances, biological or otherwise. Louisa Grayson, the hero's sister, falls into the biological trap and pays with her life. But she is not the heroine. Matilda Fawkner is immune to the everyday; this, as well as her physical resemblance to the hero, marks her as ideal. Marrying her, the hero marries within type—or would have, in Grayson's case, had he not been stabbed to death. By securing this match, the hero ensures cultural uniformity and reinforces the possibility of perfect repetition over time. Crossbreeding introduces change. Change is the motif of history. Southern heroic narrative, as subsequent examples will show, aims ultimately at the abolition of history and change. Frank Meriwether, Kennedy's mind of the antebellum South, is the perfect oracle of this viewpoint; he opines that we might be better off without the steamboat.

The preamble and first example in this rereading of southern heroic narrative propose a deep structure with prominent mythic and political features: a handsome male hero whose silhouette picks up resonance as the character is used; the twin challenges

17. Weber, *The Theory of Social and Economic Organizations,* 365.

of facing the villain on the field of action (which can often be a realm of static representations) and finding and wedding the female cognate; the eventual perpetuation of the hero's blessed kind in the face of history, the ultimate foe of the hero and his people. Most antebellum writers in this genre bent plausibility to the breaking point under the obligation to provide this formal narrative fulfillment and hence incurred a negative critical reputation. Seldom did they break through to the free-fire zone beyond faith and formal orthodoxy by pursuing variations upon narrative form or heroic character. Simms did; but before we consider Simms's considerable achievement from this vantage point, we should apply the critical structure to two more examples that have much to tell us about the meanings inherent in southern heroic narrative: *The Partisan Leader*, by Beverley Tucker, and *Cavaliers of Virginia*, by William Alexander Caruthers.

The Partisan Leader, "secretly" printed in 1836 and publicly in 1861, illustrates the workings of southern heroic narrative in the service of cultural civil defense. The hero of the novel is Douglas Trevor, leader of a partisan band in a fictitious guerrilla war against the forces of archvillain Martin Van Buren (fantasized as serving a fourth presidential term). Trevor's heroic quests to vanquish Van Buren's corrupt regime and to wed the ideal woman are the formal elements that, far from being simply stock literary trappings, constitute the "knowledge of the narrative" and carry what George Tucker began toward a rigid— even extremist—orthodoxy.[18]

Arthur Trevor, the hero's younger brother, appears first. The younger Trevor's debut alerts us to the familiar heroic silhouette, and the placement of his appearance in the vestibule of the narrative further reminds us that the culture's hero is its central figure and the purpose of its tales. Weber notes that "it is recognition on the part of those subject to authority which is decisive for the validity of charisma," and Wyatt-Brown adds that the hero's claim to leadership must be publicly manifested. In heroic narrative, the hero must appear and be acknowledged by the people, usually before he acts. Tucker supplies the standard portrait. "He was indeed a handsome youth, about twenty years of age,

18. Robert Alter, *The Art of Biblical Narrative* (New York, 1981), Chap. 8.

whose fair complexion and regular features made him seem
younger yet. He was tall, slightly, but eloquently formed, with a
countenance in which softness and spirit were happily blended.
His dress was plain and cheap, though not unfashionable. . . .
But, even in this plain dress, he was apparelled like a king in
comparison with the rustics that surrounded him; and his whole
air would have passed him for a gentleman, in any dress and
company, where the constituents of that character are rightly
understood." [19]

The description of Arthur Trevor triggers a series of orthodox narrative functions. The verbal portrait is pointedly addressed to a particular cultural group that can heed the "rightly
understood" set of signs emanating from the hero. This semiotic
community recognizes hierarchy as one of the articles of the
faith that moors it in the currents of history. Heroes possess un-
deniable gifts by birth and breeding, and those beneath them
who disregard these heroic *semes* or representations invite confusion. Those who might fail to meet the obligation to uphold
"family, blood, and community" by ignoring the hero suffer the
banishment of "the lowly, the alien, and the shamed." [20] The severe ethic of the hero makes its own internal tension even as it
identifies enemies without, for the hero's debut is a ceremony of
unification and a test of loyalty. Individual personality, in the
bourgeois sense, must be surrendered by "rustics," for so are we
all in the presence of the anointed. This is the meaning of the
Hugh Grayson subplot in Simms's *The Yemassee,* for example.

Individuals on the lower rungs of the social ladder need not
consciously know much about the ideal by which they are nur-
tured, but they must instinctively identify the hero who embodies that ideal and they must freely submit their single fates to
him. Recognition and submission are never omitted from the
heroic narrative structure. Tucker uses the character of Jacob
Schwartz for this obligatory function.

Schwartz is a woodsman, like Kennedy's Horse-Shoe or Simms's
Fordham, the type praised by Holman and others as a "believ-

19. Weber, *The Theory of Social and Economic Organizations,* 359; Wyatt-Brown,
Southern Honor, 14; Beverley Tucker, *The Partisan Leader* (1836; rpr. Upper
Saddle River, N.J., 1968), 5.
20. Wyatt-Brown, *Southern Honor,* 3–4.

able human being." He serves as Douglas Trevor's savvy lieutenant. Tucker gives him a noncavalier name and a recessive nature.
"He knew, and the event showed that he was right, that there
were some duties of a commander for which he was not fit; and
that there were other things to which a chief could not devote
himself, for which he was better qualified than any other."[21]
Schwartz's willing surrender of ego to the acknowledged hero argues that men, rightly constituted only in a heroic society, naturally embrace this ordained scheme and accept their roles without jealousy or rancor. The ideal society is drawn into vertical
coherence by the hero, whose virtue, sweetness, and power flow
downward and quell the anarchic natures of individual men.

Once the hero has appeared and established his order, he
must demonstrate its superiority to alien orders. In southern heroic narrative, this usually means vanquishing the minions of the
secular or historical order. In *The Partisan Leader*, Martin Van
Buren serves as the force to be overcome. A fantasy of southern
political and cultural paranoia, an American Louis XI, Tucker's
Van Buren (pawn of *demos*) has turned the White House (sacred
dwelling of Washington) into his palace, and his advisers into an
old court given over to intrigue and cynicism. The president and
his men buy loyalty with bribes of cash and office, and plot dirty
tricks to subvert the results of bona fide elections in the South.
Van Buren's maneuverings have been proven morally and culturally bankrupt in the history of all tyrants; Tucker's allusion to
Louis XI is as much history as his audience needs to take the
point. The Trevor heroic regime repudiates history and its works
of iniquity—Van Buren's perversion of the legacy of Washington,
for example—just as, in Thomas Dixon's *The Clansman* (1905),
heroic Ben Cameron leads a holy crusade against the cynical
"revolutionary," Austin Stoneman.

Van Buren's success in corrupting the eldest of the Trevor
brothers, Owen, leads us to a peripheral but corroborative aspect of the sacred character of southern heroic narrative. The
"idle life and the schemes of ambition" fostered by the Van
Buren court have distanced Owen Trevor from his childhood
home and the precepts embodied in it. He becomes an object of

21. B. Tucker, *The Partisan Leader*, 344.

pity and a lesson in the evils of personal ambition as he climbs higher and higher in Van Buren's rotten administration. The younger brother Douglas, who, like Lee, had gone home to Virginia when political trouble began to simmer, is far more admirable. Douglas, bypassing the firstborn in the familiar biblical mode of the divinely selected hero, is a man at peace within himself and a source of repose and order for those under his protection and control.[22]

A striking symbol of the defacing of natural virtue by an order hostile to the design of heroic society—a symbol working in tandem with Van Buren—is the character of Phillip Baker, a northerner whose physical deformity, like the deformity of Saul's son Ish-bosheth, disqualifies him for leadership in a contest with the splendid and divinely preferred Douglas Trevor. "His person was awkward, and disfigured by a mortal stoop. His features, at once diminutive and irregular, were either shrouded with an expression of solemn importance, or set off by a smile of yet more offensive self-complacency. His manners bore the same general character of conceit, alternately pert and grave; and his conversation wavered between resolute, though abortive, attempts at wit, and a sort of chopt logic, elaborately employed in proving, by incontestable arguments, what nobody ever pretended to deny." Baker's outward form, disfigured and grotesque, projects the inner deformity of human nature outside the sacred group. His northern society, stamped by "cupidity and . . . fanaticism," lacks the stable and symmetrical core that gives each of its members a pleasing shape and the instinct for smooth social functioning. Baker can make his way in Van Buren's corrupt Washington, but not in Virginia.[23]

Like must marry like for the timeless heroic scheme to remain intact. The men and women in the heroic altitudes of the edifice recognize appropriate mates with whom marriage will preserve the purity of the ideal and the order of the structure. Douglas Trevor loves his first cousin Delia. A kinship taboo lurks in this attraction, but the power of a doubled Trevor genetic and mythic inheritance offsets the danger of marriage between kin of close

22. *Ibid.*, 53–54.
23. *Ibid.*, 73, 40.

degree. Marriage to the hero's cognate is as essential to the narrative structure as conquest of the alien force, for it means cultural survival for those devoted to the ideal of the perfect civilization. Unless the hero makes a proper marriage, the scheme to which he gives coherence will disintegrate, succumbing to the disorderly nature of history. In short, everything permanent will evolve into something else unless the hero takes a mate with whom he can halt the metamorphosing nature of time. The nearer the hero is to his mate in type and blood, the likelier a successful denial of time.

Tucker's maneuvers around the obstacle of inbreeding underscore the value placed upon like marrying like in southern heroic narrative. Delia Trevor loves her manly cousin, Douglas, yet must suffer the attentions of the odious Baker. Douglas defends the heroine by advising Baker to remove himself permanently from Virginia. When news of the hero's honorable action reaches Delia's father, Douglas' uncle Bernard Trevor, Bernard pronounces Douglas his son. When the news of Delia's ordeal reaches Hugh Trevor, Douglas' father, Hugh makes Delia his daughter. In this curious play of cross-adoptions, the ties of blood are not distanced but redoubled. With brothers Hugh and Bernard Trevor standing as co-fathers to the lovers Delia and Douglas, the cousin bond seems less dangerous than the sibling link—even an honorary one. In fact, Bernard Trevor, pondering the intermarriage taboo, expresses the opinion that the custom of forbidding marriage between first cousins is a "superstition" not worth a sane man's time. Were Bernard equipped with an anthropologist's vocabulary, he might say that he preferred kinship endogamy. However he phrases his opinions, the crucial sign is *endo-*, the one that means return to type. Or, as Mark Littleton discovers in *Swallow Barn,* "Cousins count in Virginia."[24]

The Partisan Leader is curiously unconcluded. Douglas is left in the clutches of Van Buren and his henchmen; no rescue glows on the horizon. Despite this open-endedness, however, the novel is structurally fulfilled. How, for example, is the visionary civi-

24. *Ibid.,* 117, 94, 108; John Pendleton Kennedy, *Swallow Barn; or, a Sojourn in the Old Dominion* (Rev. ed.; New York, 1852), 23.

lization to be physically maintained, given mankind's penchant for random mating? Marriage between close genetic and caste types will keep the mythic and material resources close to home. The marital interest, then, becomes as important as the martial interest. The hero must not only conquer the foe outside the close familial bounds of his group. He must also find and wed the ideal woman inside those bounds. Douglas possesses the madonna and demonstrates his superiority to the crippled Baker and to his own unfortunate brother. To the audience for southern heroic narrative, this is enough for closure.

One additional example will further establish the significance of the two narrative functions of hero as warrior and hero as wooer. These functions are carried to a sort of loony excess in William Alexander Caruthers' *Cavaliers of Virginia*. Like *The Partisan Leader*, *Cavaliers of Virginia* uses history as a limited pretext for a story that seeks to certify an ideal civilization untainted by history or the natural order. Nathaniel Bacon is the hero of this historical romance of the Old Dominion. His rebellion serves as the historical stock onto which the heroic narrative is oddly grafted.[25]

Bacon is depicted as the vigorous and handsome young hero. His claim to leadership through possession of natural heroic traits is condoned by the author's hint that Bacon shares the blood of the epitome of the cavalier set of Jamestown, Gideon Fairfax. Bacon's parentage and marriage hopes are the major focus of the narrative, and Caruthers contorts his plot severely to bring it to the orthodox conclusion.

The ideal candidate for Bacon's bed is Virginia Fairfax. (She is not the only heroine in this genre to bear the resonant name of the colony itself.) She sums up all the qualities of woman and nation that the hero wishes to embrace and with whom he hopes to beget a civilization in his image. The problem, similar to the dilemma faced by Douglas and Delia Trevor, is that marriage to Virginia, so desirable in the visionary world, would force Natty to risk incest in the everyday world. It is rumored that the lovers

25. See Taylor, *Cavalier and Yankee*, Chap. 8, for a brief comparison of the historical Bacon and Caruthers' version.

share one or more parents, and Gideon Fairfax cryptically warns his daughter not to reciprocate Natty's attentions. In the climactic scene of Volume I, the marriage of Natty and Virginia, The Recluse, a mysterious figure who lives in a cave outside Jamestown like a Calvinist gymnosophist, halts the nuptials by charging that Natty and Virginia are siblings. The accused mother, Mrs. Fairfax, denies the allegation, but her nervous system, none too hardy, gives way under the strain. No one seems interested in her denials or requires proof from The Recluse. Mrs. Fairfax faints, murmuring, "Charles, Charles. . . ." Even though a friend, Charles Dudley, hastens to her side, we are invited to suspect that her call is addressed to The Recluse or to some remoter Charles, whose surname might be Stuart.[26]

Volume II opens with Natty rushing from the chapel into a raging storm, a convenient symbol for his state of mind. He is soon captured by Indians who have been seeking revenge on him for killing several of their warriors earlier in the story. The Indians are about to execute the hero when, in an episode patented by John Smith, the queen of the tribe, Wyanokee, intercedes and offers to take Natty as her husband.

This apparently trite episode becomes more than the well-worn fixture of romantic convention, for it complicates the marriage narrative for the hero. Natty is half-persuaded to accept conjugal life with Wyanokee. She is a queen in her world, he is a hero in his. She is beautiful, he is handsome. Marriage to Virginia seems to have been eternally ruled out. On the allegorical level, the white man's hold on Virginia as the New World site of his visionary order seems in grave jeopardy, the hero's successful access to the womb of perpetual recurrence having been denied. Ancient taboo stands in the way of the cultural ideal. The stock suspense of actual battle, between Virginia cavaliers and usurping roundheads, is a source of tension Caruthers perfunctorily resolves.

Caruthers reserves most of the narrative, then, for removing the taboo that bars Natty from marrying Virginia. Prior to Wya-

---

26. William Alexander Caruthers, *Cavaliers of Virginia; or, the Recluse of Jamestown* (2 vols; 1834; rpr. Ridgewood, N.J., 1968), I, 46, 222–24.

nokee's offer to rescue the hero, we are given an important tally on the Indian queen and the cultural madonna:

> In Wyanokee, the imagination controlled the heart—in Virginia, the heart subdued and softened the imagination.
>
> There was something touchingly beautiful in the moral development of these two young and innocent hearts. . . . As they mutually exchanged glances, something like an electric thrill passed chilly through their veins, but it was only for an instant; the reasoning faculty of the mind examined it not—they were not in a situation to examine it—imagination controlled the whole mental organization of the one and the tenderest and purest emotions of the heart that of the other.[27]

Wyanokee offers the hero natural passion uncontrolled by a cultural system known to the Western mind. Virginia, her name and figure radiating with the full wattage of the anima, presents a cultural system refined by the "tenderest and purest emotions," shorn of the natural and undomesticated. Natty dreams this dilemma into a coherent shape as he lies captive to Wyanokee's braves, and he realizes in his vision that heroic salvation cannot and will not come from marriage to the Indian queen. To wed Wyanokee would subvert heroic vision, and so Natty resolves to wed Virginia.

By working out Natty's dilemma in this particular way, with such narrative duration and a sort of nutty complexity, Caruthers contributes to the evolution of the cult of the southern heroine as madonna and implicitly testifies to his audience's preoccupation with the theme of heroic continuity. In the poem "Maid of Congaree," Simms presents a similar formulation of the imperative that faces the southern hero in his quest for a mate. He also confirms the racial tinge Caruthers supplied:

> 'Twas a Maid of Congaree,
> But no Indian maid was she,
> Large blue eyes and fair white face,
> Spoke her of the Saxon race;
> Stately in her step and mien,
> She might well have been a queen;

27. *Ibid.*, I, 130.

And a queen o'er hearts was she,
By the rolling Congaree.[28]

Virginia and all of her sisters in southern heroic narrative represent the gratification of the cultural and racial drive to abolish difference, to deny the outside world and its historical character. The incest taboo that gnaws at Natty's psyche and brings Caruthers' hero to the brink of mental and physical breakdown must be set aside, for the people's fear of homogenization, of absorption into history, is far more paralyzing.

Meanwhile, Natty is successful in routing the insurgents and their Indian mercenaries. Although he laments his massacre of the Indians, he consoles himself with the thought that regret for the passing of the lower orders is unbecoming sentimentality in a cultural hero. Wyanokee, wandering among the smoking ruins of her village, no longer elicits Natty's sympathy.

When the natural route is closed with the massacre of Wyanokee's people, the only ground for the hero's seed is the queen of his vision, Virginia. Caruthers clears away the taboo by revealing that Natty is not the son of Mrs. Fairfax, but the son of a hero of "royal line" (perhaps of the blood royal) and an English lady. Not only is the heroic route thrown open to him, it is decorated with the trappings of the English crown. Natty's heroic stature is now explained. He surpasses even the local epitome, Gideon Fairfax. Having displaced the father-chief, the hero assumes the father's position, now possessing the daughter along with the father's cultural authority.

The examples of heroic behavior found in Old South narratives were manifestations of a cultural myth that also found outlets in that society's behavior patterns and ethical systems. Its existence in these narratives has been obscured by a long-standing judgment of them as mere derivatives of Cooper or Scott, or as the jerry-built propaganda of the slavocracy. These explanations are no doubt partially true. To refute them is not the purpose of this study; rather, I wish to direct some light on a neglected area—the form of southern heroic narrative.

28. William Gilmore Simms, *Areytos; or, Songs of the South* (Charleston, 1846), 25.

The hero of southern narrative is the lens that focuses this light on the culture's semiotic system. If he and his narrative conflicts have the air of "Walter-Scottismo" imitation, that is because the writers and their audience found these types most useful in forging a foundation myth that in large measure aimed to supplant history in the southern imagination as the explanation of the nature of things. The power of directed myth to establish unity where history supplies only contingency, wished for if not actualized, was still felt a century and more later by Allen Tate, the most acute of sensors, when, mentally touring the ruins of his literary tradition, he wrote the lines that serve as the epigraph to this chapter.

II

William Gilmore Simms:
Writer and Hero

We had no Hawthorne, no Melville, no Emily Dickinson. We
had William Gilmore Simms.

—Allen Tate
"The Profession of Letters in the South"

What Tate does not say is that the American audience for a
high national literature in the nineteenth century had little of
Hawthorne, less of Melville, and almost nothing of Dickinson.
There was a surfeit of writers certainly no better, and probably a
lot worse, than Simms. But Tate considered the drowned-out or
pent-up voice to be the archetypal American literary voice. Little
wonder, then, that he regarded Simms as a sort of third prize; to
him, a great literary hush might have been better.

There have been, and still are, many cosigners to Tate's charge.
William Gilmore Simms, to the detriment of his own reputation,
wrote too much. There is something of an allegation of inconti-
nence in Trent's comment that Simms "failed to exercise proper
control on his imagination."[1] Simms's critical stock continues to
suffer, too, because he wrote so much about the manifest content
of his many books that we, like Tate, assume that there is little
more to them than what Simms says there is. It has become a
worn critical path to read Simms as historian and increasingly
cranky proslavery polemicist—as chronicler of the colonial and
revolutionary wars in the South (good), as romancer of partisans

---

1. William P. Trent, *William Gilmore Simms* (Boston, 1892), 75.

and their ladies in works of semihistory and hagiography (for-givable), as apologist for slavery (heinous).

We have, perhaps with too little reason, subscribed to Trent's opinion that Simms might have been much better had he been born in the North, where discipline was revered, work exalted, and progress in civilization an article of faith. C. Hugh Holman follows Trent's path in his essays on Simms, putting special em-phasis on the "rich context" that Simms creates for his conven-tional heroes and their trials.[2] For Holman, and for many of those who write about Simms's work, the fiction retains value only as the thorough record of a time and place. This qualified critical praise echoes Trent, who permitted Simms one "ad-mirable characteristic," thoroughness, which he found to be rare indeed among southern writers addicted to "gorgeous rhetoric" and the quick fix of a plot borrowed from Cooper or Scott.[3]

Donald Davidson, staunch defender of the southern cause against northern cultural hegemony, pleaded for a different reading of Simms. A note of partisanship and long-nursed griev-ance is the leitmotif of Davidson's argument. But that does not disqualify him from making a case for the peculiar nature of Simms's historical writing: "It is not a mere background against which historical personages like Marion and Greene make offi-cial appearances. It is the 'more veracious and philosophical mode of writing' not furnished by history as such—the rich con-text of human action that history, indeed, hardly ever touches, even when it labors most authoritatively and earnestly."[4] It is not unreasonable to suggest that Simms's handling of the so-called stock characters and narrative elements of his material—the line of goods handled by every agent for southern heroic narrative—should not be relegated to the attic of costume romance. David-son's plea for a rereading of Simms opens, albeit slightly, a new angle on heroic narrative.

Like all cultural "geniuses" (a title he came close to conferring

2. Holman, *The Roots of Southern Writing*. See the essay, "The Influence of Scott on Cooper and Simms."
3. Trent, *William Gilmore Simms*, 149, 191–92.
4. Donald Davidson, Introduction to Mary Simms Oliphant *et al.* (eds.), *The Letters of William Gilmore Simms* (5 vols.; Columbia, S.C., 1952), I, xliv.

on himself), Simms intuitively grasped the "certain abstract representations" that were inchoate in the narrative acts of articulation his culture desired or that were actually accomplished
through him and his fellow writers.[5] Simms, pursuing heroism
with greater energy than did the others, moved through and beyond the canonical form of southern heroic narrative. Carried
by a surge of narrative energy and regional identification, Simms
strove to solidify the representations and, in the process, to
create an identity between southern writers and the hero. Simms
wrote southern civilization into existence by recording the particulars of southern life and history during his lifetime. In doing
so, he certified the heroic narrative form as his culture's official
way of telling. However, with the popular figure of Porgy, drawn
from a nonheroic tradition, Simms nearly demolished the entire, carefully wrought heroic edifice.

Simms's path into the heroic is marked, at first, by his frequent
attempts to define the term *genius,* or *hero.* The two terms are
interchangeable in his lexicon. *Genius* seems to have conjured up
a loosely related congregation of feelings, narrative "spheres" or
clusters, type-scenes, figures, and functions in Simms's "more veracious and philosophical mode of writing." Drew Gilpin Faust
places Simms in the role of cultural father and artificer and ana-
lyzes the place of genius in his teeming mind. "For Simms, genius had a dual meaning: it implied special spiritual qualities dis-
tributed among all the people as well as the particular individual
who, like Simms himself, possessed an unusually rich intellectual
and moral endowment."[6] Faust views Simms as having a "dual"
relationship with his culture and his work. The genius, or hero,
wields tangible and intangible tools. He is the spirit of his people,
making his folk conscious of their corporate identity, fighting his
people's battles with literature as Green and Marion fought with
saber and rifle. The hero figure is also the autobiographical ex-
tension of the author; only the man of letters can create genius
because only he shares heroic stature. Writing about the hero is
the result of heroic traits in the writer himself; the figure of the

5. Propp, *Morphology of the Folktale,* 89.
6. Drew Gilpin Faust, *A Sacred Circle: The Dilemma of the Intellectual in the Old
South, 1840–1860* (Baltimore, 1977), 88.

hero becomes a facet of authorial design and intent. Simms set before his people a brazen serpent of communal recognition: the hero.

Simms's attachment to the concept of hero is not, as it might first appear to the skeptic, a manifestation of the warmed-over Carlylean hero worship that saturated his age. In the uneven progress of his critical reviews and essays, Simms moves toward, if he does not actually accomplish, a distinctive articulation of the genius-hero who embodies the southern tradition. In the process, Simms also uncovers the tradition's internal, fatal contradictions.

In his review essay "The Writings of James Fenimore Cooper," published in 1842, Simms gives us an early glimpse of his concept of the genius-hero. The subject of the essay is the hero figure of lone woodsman or sailor in Cooper's fiction. Simms argues that Cooper's version of the hero leaves something to be desired in his ties to a larger human group and to its culture. Cooper, Simms says, too quickly cut his losses in the genre of the "social life novel" and opted for the more spacious form of the historical romance. In the new genre, the author could roam more freely among the "resources" not yet tapped by any American writer. The figure of the hero proposed by Cooper is one of these unrefined resources. For that creation, Simms gives his rival full praise. But the figure of the hero that Simms read in Cooper encompassed no strong social element, which disturbed Simms's growing sense that the act of writing (narrative especially) performed an important sacramental function for his people.

The Cooper hero seldom indulges in social contact; most of his time is spent a decided distance away from human assemblies. Simms writes that both types of the Cooper hero, woodsman and sailor, "are permitted that degree of commerce with their fellow beings, which suffice [*sic*] to maintain in strength the sweet and sacred sources of their humanity. It is through these [connections] that they are commended to our sympathies." According to Simms, they are not heroes of the people but rather heroes without the people, imbibing natural American virtue directly from the source. In the heady times of "Young American" literary nationalism, this was a breakthrough. But Simms continued to focus on the private, unsocial turn of Cooper humanity. His heroes "all live to our eyes and thoughts, the perfect ideals of moral individuality." Although they are recommended to our sympathies, that recommendation does not admit them to our hearts: "For this [moral individuality] we admire them—love them we do not—they are objects not meant to love—they do not appeal to our affections so much as to our minds."[7]

In Simms's thinking, Cooper's isolated heroes do not create a people; they do not forge a corporate "we" through love or mutual identification. They visit communities of men infrequently and reluctantly. For all their aloofness, however, these heroes are powerfully evocative figures, the clear centers of Cooper's narratives. Their model of moral individuality in solitude clearly augurs an accompanying national cultural construction that Simms does not wholeheartedly endorse. We might read the character of Hugh Grayson in *The Yemassee* as Simms's imaginative commentary on the dangers posed by moral individuality that is unchecked by any communal devotion.

Simms is consistent in worrying the question of whether Cooper's heroes have the power to create coherence in human communities and affiliations. "He is the ideal of an abstract but innate power, which we acknowledge and perhaps fear, but cannot fathom. All is hidden within himself, and except when at work, he is nothing—he might as well be stone. Yet, around him,—such a man—a wonderful interest gathers like a halo— bright and inscrutable,—which fills us with equal curiosity and reverence. With him, a man of whom we know nothing,—whom we see now for the first time,—whom we may never see again,— whom we cannot love—whom we should never seek."[8] Cooper's hero elicits a mixed tribute. The hero's halo places him in the supernatural. He is an icon revered by a group of inferiors, a potential "us," who look to the hero for identity and direction. Yet we cannot love this hero, for he scants his social contacts and clings to his individuality. Simms sees the Cooper hero very much as D. H. Lawrence does—as a cool customer, something of an anarchist. This heroic figure might be valuable in the pinch

7. William Gilmore Simms, "The Writings of James Fenimore Cooper," in C. Hugh Holman (ed.), *Views and Reviews in American Literature History and Fiction. First Series* (Cambridge, Mass. 1962), 269, 270.
8. *Ibid.*, 271.

of circumstances; like Natty Bumppo, however, he is not interested in the long-range project of establishing a civilization capable of surviving the ordeal of history.

Simms advances his own concept of the hero in his review,
published in 1850, of John Pendleton Kennedy's biography of
William Wirt. In the eight years since his review of Cooper appeared, Simms's thinking on the hero has matured and his sense
of regional and cultural grudge has, not surprisingly, intensified.
The vital connection between genius-hero and people assumes
crucial importance. Simms successfully counters the excessive
individuality of Cooper's heroes by presenting Wirt as a man for
the people; Wirt represents the epitome of the heroic relation
with "us." Simms writes that biographies "show, perhaps, how
this thought or passion has been tutored by favorite leaders, who
represent the moods as well as the necessities of a race; how it
has wrought upon themselves, and been in turn wrought on by
them; the community and the oracle thus linked in the bonds of
a common necessity, which leaves no doubt of the sympathies of
the one being certain always for the support of the other."[9]

The hero has become, for Simms, both oracle and genius; always male, not necessarily a "crowned leader," and certainly not
a mere written document such as a charter or a constitution, he
awakens the genius of a people. The hero need not verbally for-
mulate the communal genius, for many of the moods and necessities of a people are not words but those "abstract representations." The scribe of the hero, however, does become heroic in
writing, for the heroic narrative satisfies a people's needs and
feelings just as the actual hero's gestures do. Reality, caught in
the aura of the haloed hero, merges into ideality. Simms's proper
heroic figure, as found in Kennedy's Wirt, assumes the stature of
a cultural icon. His presence ensures corporate identity and
order; he makes the people a self-conscious, functioning group.
In fact, Simms's choice of the word *race* for the people for whom
heroes exist indicates that his mind has turned to cultic and
mythic channels. "Ethnogenesis" is at hand, and Timrod's poem
can be seen as part of a larger cultural movement significantly

9. William Gilmore Simms, "Kennedy's Life of Wirt," *Southern Quarterly Review*, XVII (April, 1850), 193.

orchestrated by the writer-hero. Foremost among that group is Simms. "It is for the characteristics of the race that the man is made to speak. His reputation belongs quite as much to their sympathies as to his own will and genius. He has pronounced the decree, but it is one which he has found first written on their hearts. He leads the progress, but it is one which they have previously resolved; and thus it is that in writing the narrative of his career, you find them inseparable from it." [10]

The genius that Simms traced in the writing of others he created in the heroes of his own work. Simms used a heroic figure similar to those used by his fellow writers in the genre of southern heroic narrative. But he came closer than they did to writing through the genre—that is, he shows signs of stepping across the boundaries of the permissible for his hero. From orthodox faith in the godlike hero Singleton, Simms sails toward heresy with his depiction of Porgy and goes over the edge of the known heroic world.

The historical novel in its classical phase, according to Georg Lukacs, privileges plot and hero in order to address its audience on a particular interpretation of historical events. [11] Simms's predecessors sometimes twisted plausibility to keep the audience's attention on the triumph of the hero over historical events. Simms supplied the sometimes nutty tradition with the legitimacy of history; he discovered the origins of the hero in the life of the Chevalier Bayard. It is now a commonplace in the criticism of southern heroic narrative to find Bayard in the bloodlines of all male southern aspirants. His traits appear in the fictional Edward Grayson, Arthur Butler, Ned Hazard, and dozens more; in the flesh-and-blood Robert E. Lee and George Washington; in the names and exploits of Faulkner's Sartoris family; even in Ransom's satiric figure in "Captain Carpenter." Simms summed up the narrative practice of his forebears and fixed Bayard and his silhouette for conscious use in the tradi-

10. *Ibid.*, 195.
11. Georg Lukacs, *The Historical Novel,* trans. Hannah Mitchell and Stanley Mitchell (London, 1962). See Chap. 1, "The Classical Form of the Historical Novel."

tion: "In person, Bayard was tall, straight, and slender. His countenance was mild and gracious. His eyes were black, his nose in-
clining to aquiline, and his complexion fair." [12] The outline of
this hero is deeply engraved in the cultural mind of the Old
South: the vertical thrust of the posture, the lean body unen-
cumbered by the ills and vices of the flesh, the serene face and
eyes indicating a soul in harmony with some power and certainty
that transcends historical contingency.

There is more to the figure of the hero than a vision of fashion worked into a department store dummy. Simms interprets
Bayard's times as being rife with turmoil and change that were
reordering the relationships that had secured man in "bonds of
a common necessity." The late fifteenth and early sixteenth centuries were "a time when chivalry was at its lowest condition in
Christian Europe; when the fine affectations of the order, erring
always on the side of generosity and virtue—its strained cour-
tesies, its overwrought delicacies, its extravagant and reckless
valor—everything, in short, of that grace and magnanimity
which had constituted its essential spirit and made of it a peculiar institution—had given way to less imposing and less worthy
characteristics." The "characteristics" coming into influence at
this time were those of the ubiquitous and ever-emerging bour-
geoisie. Accompanying the rise of this class was "the growth and
centralization of the state . . . which favored the development of
large corporate entities—with each attempting to carve out an
autonomous domain of laws and authority—[and] acted to sub-
due the power of the family to affect the destiny of its members." [13] By choosing the Chevalier Bayard as the model for the
hero, and finding his virtues in every southern figure from John
Smith to Porgy, Simms makes an admirable and perhaps fated
analogy between the social and historical changes of two separate eras: the late fifteenth and mid nineteenth centuries. Seeing
the return of the late medieval age in his own century, Simms
promulgates belief in the hero's vision of the unity of history and
in the transcendent power of a race and its heroes over diversity

12. William Gilmore Simms, *The Life of The Chevalier Bayard* (New York,
1847), 400.
13. *Ibid.*, 1; Bernard Faber, *Conceptions of Kinship* (New York, 1981), 32.

and contingency. Simms was the first to exploit the full figural powers of the hero to counteract history, for he used the hero in a contest against history.

Bayard, as well as all his clones in the narratives by Simms and his cohorts, is the central type for a culture that anticipates a downward path through history. The outcome of history is, of course, always known to the authors themselves. The chivalric Middle Ages had already surrendered to the bourgeois modern age. The hero is always, therefore, an anachronism; each of his heroic gestures is in defiance of an already accomplished history. The phenomenon in the southern literary consciousness that Lewis Simpson has called "the southern repression of historical irony" is vividly present in the work Simms undertook in the cause of ordering hero and community, hero and author, author and community.[14]

The typical Simms Bayardic hero is Major Robert Singleton, hero of *The Partisan.* Singleton is a hero in times echoing those of the Chevalier, times of "the most perilous and the most brilliant crises of our fortunes." Such crises call forth the Bayardic traits in hero and in author. Both respond, Simms avers, with a character that transcends history. "History, indeed, as we style it somewhat complacently, is quite too apt to overlook the best essentials of society—such as constitute the moving impulses of men to action—in order to dilate on great events,—scenes in which men are merely massed, while a single favorite overtops all the rest, the Hero rising to the Myth, and absorbing within himself all the consideration which a more veracious and philosophical mode of writing would distribute over states and communities, and the humblest walks of life."[15] Singleton blazes into myth along the trajectory of Bayard. Simms scarcely shows his hero in actual military conflict, yet friend and foe alike respect his prowess. Singleton's heroism stems from his power to mobilize a people to self-awareness as well as to self-defense. Simms attempted to delineate the "best essentials of society . . . [that] constitute the moving impulses of men to action." He faulted

14. Lewis P. Simpson, *The Brazen Face of History: Studies in the Literary Consciousness in America* (Baton Rouge, 1980), 236.
15. William Gilmore Simms, *The Partisan. A Romance of the Revolution* (Rev. ed.; New York, 1856), xi, ix.

writers of history for narrowly focusing on events and the results
of public actions and, therefore, for failing to give adequate consideration to the ideals working toward the surface of contingency in the triumph of the hero. A significant part of Simms's
attention, then, was devoted to finding and tracing the myth
within the "mere" chain of events, however great those events
might loom in history. And that myth began and ended in the
figure of the hero.

Singleton enters Dorchester, South Carolina, in disguise. Sergeant Hastings, a redcoat of dubious character, notices "the air
of superiority which the other [Singleton] manifested, [and it]
annoyed him too greatly to give way to doubt or indetermina-
tion." Before the alien knows the hero's identity, he feels the an-
noyance of confronting the superior type. A rebel against British rule, Davis by name, is also impressed by the magnetic appeal
of the stranger. "He [Davis] had his doubts—as who could be
without them in that season of general distrust? But when he remembered the warm, manly frankness of the stranger,—his
free, bold, generous, and gentle countenance—he did not suffer
himself to doubt, for a moment more, that his secret [Davis is an
undercover agent for the rebels] would be safe in his possession."

Women are also ordered like iron filings by the hero's magnetism. Bella Humphries, the buxom daughter of the tavern
keeper, circulates around her father's taproom dissatisfied with
the crowd of "unattractive countrymen" until she comes within
Singleton's range. His "manly and handsome face and person"
cause Bella to linger at his table. There is, however, no hope for
Bella; Singleton sees at once that "she was incapable of any of
that settled and solemn feeling which belongs to love, and which
can only exist with a strongly marked character and truly elevated sentiments." In this early type-scene, Simms reminds us
that the hero's task is not only to conquer the enemy in the field
but also to obtain the ideal mate ordained by the visionary cultural order.[16]

The central figure in the visionary order is as free as possible
from human imperfection. He represents, in the mythopoeic
scheme, the struggle by which an ideally ordained vertical order

16. *Ibid.*, 30, 45, 60.

subordinates diversity and mere contingency to the gleaming ideal of the single image. In *The Partisan,* Singleton directs the defense of order against a barbarian regime of thieves, rapists, and looters. Simms pushes the story, as he does the hero, into the realm of myth; it becomes a transhistorical drama of the vertical order versus the ever-widening, ever-redefined contingent order of history. The British, in other words, are not the only enemy; in fact, they merely stand in for the actual villain.

Throughout *The Partisan* flits a more colorful and resonant villain than the British, Goggle Blonay, an ill-begotten Caliban, "blear-eyed" and scraggly haired, sired by either a Negro or an Indian who forced himself on a white woman in a moment of "diseased appetite." The chance breeding that produced Goggle suggests the nonheroic, uncontrolled way of the actual world— the chaos the hero must abolish.

Singleton and his love, his cousin Katharine Walton, "the highborn, the beautiful, the young," represent the zenith of the highly restricted kinship pattern. One evening Singleton and his page, Lance Frampton, are caught in a fierce storm as they are leaving the home of Katharine's father, the noble Colonel Walton, where the hero has been paying court to the ideal mate. In a flash of lightning they spy a weird human figure who takes a shot at them from the swamp and disappears. They give chase into the swamp, for the humanoid figure, Singleton suspects, is Goggle. Goggle dives into the muck just as Singleton, on horseback, gallops over him and halts. The hero towers over his antithesis, who wallows in the mire like some prehuman form of life. Simms explains that Goggle "hated society accordingly as he was compelled to fear it. He looked upon it as a power to be destroyed with the opportunity, as a spoil to be appropriated with the chance for its attainment; and the moods of such a nature were impatient for exercise, even upon occasions when he could hope no addition to his pleasure or his profit from their indulgence." [17] In this vivid type-scene, Simms illuminates the vertical design of the heroic cosmology. Far beneath the noble hero and heroine are the marginally human creatures whose

17. *Ibid.,* 119, 178.

controlling passions are hatred of order and resentment of the power wielded by the leaders of society. The Goggles, randomly spawned, hate the order that achieves expression in the figures of the hero and his mate. The many at the base of the pyramidal order will never be vouchsafed expression and therefore seek to destroy the social edifice that keeps them down.

Singleton, the apotheosis of the cultural ideal, is the epitome of heroism to the boy Lance, whose father has been driven mad witnessing the rape and murder of his wife by British soldiers. "Singleton became one and the same with the mind's ideal, and a lively imagination, and warm sensibilities, identified his captain, in his thought, with his only notion of a genuine hero. The more he studied him, the more complete was the resemblance. The lofty, symmetrical, strong person—the high but easy carriage— the grace of movement and attitude—the studious delicacy of speech, mingled, at the same time, with that simple adherence to propriety, which illustrates genuine manliness, were all at- tributes of Singleton and all obvious enough to his admirer." [18] It is the function of the hero to inject order where there is chaos, symmetry where there is randomness and imbalance. Lance bears a striking similarity to Walker Percy's Will Barrett in his breathless admiration for a hero who replaces the father. Figu- ratively, the hero overrides all natural fathers and unifies an en- hanced and idealized kinship group according to a new prin- ciple as strong as blood but not subject to blood's corruption. Singleton's symmetry of person and deportment abolishes the elder Frampton's madness and its causes. The heroic order de- poses the contingent, banishing unpleasantness rather than try- ing to accommodate it.

Although, in a long historical narrative segment near the end of the novel, Simms examines Gates's loss of Charleston—a string of scenes in which men are "merely massed"—he reserves the final victory in the mythopoeic plot for Singleton. Colonel Walton who, like Caruthers' Gideon Fairfax, is the chieftain of the social order in his district and father of the hero's desired Other, has been taken prisoner by the British after the Gates fi-

18. *Ibid.,* 374.

asco. Sentenced to be hanged, he is transported to Dorchester for execution. But Singleton and a few gallant men infiltrate the British-held town and rescue the colonel from the noose.

Singleton thereby triumphs in the coordinate challenge—he wins the love of his cousin in spite of her father's opposition. The kinship tie between the lovers is close, within the usually proscribed degree of cousinship, but there is little doubt in the minds of the lovers that they are destined to marry and to perpetuate the heroic order. Simms's description of the heroine stresses her likeness to Singleton. "As she approached they saw the lofty carriage, the graceful height, and the symmetrical person of our heroine—her movement bespeaking for her that degree of consideration which few ever looked upon her and withheld." [19]

Singleton does have a rival for Katharine in Major Proctor, an officer in Cornwallis' command. But the real impediment to the hero's suit is Katharine's father. Singleton must convince him to disregard his previous pledge to the British on the grounds that they have reneged on the agreement by taking up arms against the colonists. Until Singleton can force his own partisan views upon his uncle, he will not have achieved the closeness necessary to bring about his marriage to the lofty Katharine. *The Partisan* is not over until this miraculous event is concluded, until the symmetrical figures are merged.

Plot and hero reach a higher degree of complication and resolution in *The Yemassee*, in which Simms expands his study of the dynamic relationship between the genius-hero and the people he defines. In this story of the conflict between British settlers and Indians (armed by pirates and the Spanish) in early eighteenth-century South Carolina, Simms places the heroic figure and those forces and figures dedicated to the corrosion of his solidity within the same narrative frame. Here, a Goggle Blonay is not the only rival for the hero's privilege.

Gabriel Harrison, the hero, enters the novel as Singleton entered *The Partisan*, incognito, the better to manifest his heroic stature. The entrance of the hero, and his reception as such by a group that does not necessarily know him, is what Propp termed

19. *Ibid.*, 133.

a *function* in narrative: *"Function is understood as an act of a character defined from the point of view of its significance for the course of action."* Function has two inseparable aspects: what is done, the action itself; and where in the narrative sequence it takes place, its position relative to other actions. Because of the predictability with which functions appear in narrative, they *"serve as stable, constant elements in a tale."* [20] The appearance of the hero, incognito or momentarily unidentified, at the opening of the heroic narrative is an important function in the heroic form. Even before he is named, the hero exerts an ordering force on the random human community he enters.

Harrison's natural excellence, for example, shines through his alias. "The stranger was about thirty years old, with a rich European complexion, a light blue eye, and features moulded finely, so as to combine manliness with as much of beauty as might well comport with it. He was probably six feet in height, straight as an arrow, and remarkably well and closely set." [21] The tall and vertical silhouette is by now readily familiar. Harrison's "light blue eye" also accords with the pattern of the hero's appearance. Simms, however, takes Harrison further, giving him a special temperament—an "elastic" mind, wit, well-spoken, jaunty discourse, patience, and foresight approaching clairvoyance. Harrison, compared to Singleton or the heroes of Simms's fellow writers in the heroic genre, is a more thoroughly detailed example of the type, just as *The Yemassee* is a more thorough investigation of the elements of the genre.

Harrison easily proves himself superior to the villain, Chorley. In hand-to-hand combat, in speaking, in physical appearance, and in dress, the hero vanquishes the leader of the pirates. Wearing a Spanish chain and Turkish pantaloons and carrying a German rifle, Chorley is a figure of the defeat of unity. His sense of his own defeat recalls Gildon's in *The Valley of Shenandoah;* both feel a hurt deeper than any inflicted by blade or bullet. "There was some secret motive or policy, or it might be a sense of moral inferiority, in breeding or in station, which seemed to have the effect of keeping down and quelling, in some sort, the exhibi-

20. Propp, *Morphology of the Folktale*, 21.
21. William Gilmore Simms, *The Yemassee*, ed. J. V. Ridgely (New York, 1964), 51.

tions of a temper which otherwise would have prompted him
[Chorley] again to blows."[22]

Having easily proven himself the better of his foe, Harrison
further demonstrates genius by rallying the demoralized settlers
of Block House. "It is fortunate, perhaps, for mankind, that
there are some few minds always in advance, and forever preparing the way for society, even sacrificing themselves, noble,
that the species may have victory. . . . Harrison, active in perceiv-
ing, decisive in providing against events, with a sort of intuition,
had traced out a crowd of circumstances, of most imposing character and number, in the events of the time, of which few if any
in the colony besides himself, had any idea."[23] Because of his heroic clairvoyance, Harrison can anticipate contingency and vanquish history. After a long and gory series of clashes with the
Indians, he leads the destined people out of the cultural and
actual wilderness of accident and into a smooth, haloed, ordered
existence.

When Harrison is absent, order deteriorates. At one point
during his absence from Block House, the people fall into such
disarray that a mere woman, Mrs. Grayson, takes charge. Although she does quite well, she herself acknowledges that her
initiative is a breach of "good order." Only the hero's return can
revive the fortunes and coherence of the people. No lieutenant,
no matter how gifted and noble, can fill the void left by the hero.
Even the hostile pirates, under the deputy of Chorley, decay into
ineffectiveness.[24]

Left to undirected fate, the people of Block House choose
inferior men as their leaders. The garrulous and cowardly Dr.
Nichols, because he can talk more ornately than anyone else,
moves into power when Harrison is not on the scene.[25] When the
time comes for action, however, Dr. Nichols is inept. Simms, testing the limits of the genre, sees the mythic champion eventually
vulnerable to democratic suspicion, for the people easily elect
Dr. Nichols the moment they are left to themselves. That the
genius of the people might err—a lesson of "melancholy his-

22. *Ibid.*, 46, 53.
23. *Ibid.*, 64.
24. *Ibid.*, 363, 395.
25. *Ibid.*, 366, 392.

tory"—is a thought that borders on cultural heresy. Is the acclaiming of the hero by his people merely an accident of random selection? Is there nothing in his figural power that necessitates his selection above all others? Embryonic in Simms's treatment of Dr. Nichols' coup is the idea that the community harbors the potential for evolution toward a democratic model in which heroes are suspect—the model proposed by Sidney Hook in *The Hero in History*. In *The Yemassee*, Simms quickly turns away from the possible fallibility of the heroic system and its metamorphosis into an erratic democracy. Seeing mankind unheroed is seeing mankind trapped in history. Simms's vision of the historical order alongside the heroic gives *The Yemassee* its most forceful push toward the limits of the heroic genre.

In the contest to possess Bess Matthews, the ideal mate, Harrison has typical success. Although Chorley, like the stock villain of melodrama, whisks away the heroine with lust in his eye, Harrison rescues her before the fate worse than death can befall her.[26] Harrison's rivalry with Hugh Grayson is the more interesting impediment to the possession of the ideal mate.

Hugh Grayson exhibits many of the tendencies, carried to Byronic excess, that Simms had found disagreeable in Cooper's heroic figures. Grayson seems at home only in the woods, usually during violent storms, for there he can brood in solitude. He is bent upon his own individuality.

> I would be, and I am not. They keep me down—they refuse to hear—they do not heed me, and with a thought of command and a will of power in me, they yet pass me by, and I must give way to a bright wand and a gilded chain. Even here in these woods, with a poor neighborhood, and surrounded by those who are unhonoured and unknown in society, they—the slaves that they are!—they seek for artificial forms, and bind themselves with constraints that can only have a sanction in the degradation of the many. They yield up the noble and true attributes of a generous nature, and make themselves subservient to a name and a mark— thus it is that fathers enslave their children; and but for this, our lords proprietors, whom God in His mercy take to himself, have dared to say, even in this wild land not yet their own, to the people who have battled its dangers—ye shall worship after our fashion,

26. *Ibid.*, 384–85.

or your voices are unheard. Who is the tyrant in this?—not the
ruler—not the ruler—but those base spirits who let him rule,—
those weak and unworthy, who, taking care to show their weak-
nesses, have invited the oppression which otherwise could have no
head. I would my thoughts were theirs—or, and perhaps it were
better—I would their thoughts were mine.[27]

Grayson's fevered speech to his mother is a neat anti-statement to
all that the hero and his order represent—suppression of individuality, patriarchalism, rigid designations of the honored and
the unhonored, and the need for "artificial forms" for survival
in the wild. Simms plants in the character of Hugh Grayson the
seeds of the romantic rebellion against all fathers and forms that
would be a hallmark of the later stages of the nineteenth century.

Hugh's love for the ideal female is likewise violent and intense, not chastened by a view to the long-range social and cultural significance attached to mating in the heroic order. Bess,
cool but somewhat startled by Hugh's tempestuous declarations,
tells him that he represents too much passion. Harrison represents principle in her eyes and is therefore the preferable suitor.
Bess will have none of the uncontrolled appetite by which the
Goggles of the world have been spawned. She leaves Hugh with
no doubt that she prefers the other male. The ideal heroine thus
shows that she shares with the hero a consecration to the principle of the "settled and solemn" love that serves as the bedrock
of the visionary society.

Hugh, in a fit of temper in the face of these frustrations, plots
to murder Harrison. His lover's violence is associated, in the narrative, with his false hero's tendency to become subversive of the
heroic order. In his unhealthy pursuit of self, Grayson carries on
discussions with Chorley, neglects familial and communal re-
sponsibilities, and shows the reluctance to acknowledge social
ties that Simms had found so bothersome in his study of Cooper's
solitaries. Hugh Grayson is, in essence, the figural antithesis of
Harrison, an opposition suggested by their initials (G. H. is the
reverse of H. G.).

In the happy ending of *The Yemassee*, principle triumphs over
passion, the true genius-hero over the self-obsessed individual.

27. *Ibid.*, 244.

The Yemassee ultimately functions as an orthodox southern heroic narrative. At crucial points, however, counterfigures such as Dr. Nichols and Hugh Grayson strain against the margins of the genre. Simms supplies the satisfying closure called for in the orthodoxy, but not before he indicates the vulnerable areas.

Simms barges into cultural heresy with his characterization of Porgy. The portly hero makes a shambles of the heroic cosmos in *Woodcraft*. Porgy is aimed at Stowe and her infamous cohorts, and this character leads Simms and the genre into confusion. Damage to the perfection of the heroic figure and his orderly cosmos is imminent, however, in *The Partisan*, the novel of Porgy's debut, and Simms barely coaxes him back into the fold.

Porgy is a peripheral figure in *The Partisan*, along with black body servant Tom and rustic Dr. Oakenburg. Singleton does not know Porgy and comments only on his fishlike name. Lance, however, swears that Porgy, despite the unfortunate name, "rides like the devil and fights like blazes," the marks of a true gentleman.[28] One of Porgy's contributions to the novel is a supply of Falstaffian counterpoint to the chivalric Singleton and his serious page. But the Falstaffian comedy becomes a Rabelaisian subversion of the official order.

Porgy is almost totally concerned with the belly. In an exchange with the tavern keeper Humphries, Porgy elaborates upon the Rabelaisian point of view. Humphries, speaking for the orthodox system, which privileges the head, takes his obese customer to task.

> "Oh! that won't do at all, that sort of talking, lieutenant. It does seem to me as if you brought the stomach into everything, even sacred things."
>
> "Nay, nay, reverse the phrase, Humphries, and bring all sacred things into the stomach."
>
> "Well, anyhow, Lieutenant Porgy, it does seem to me that it's your greatest fault to make too much of your belly. . . ."
>
> "Well . . . The Belly *is* a great member, my friend, a very great member, and is not to be spoken of irreverently."

The lowering of the axis of human value from the head to the belly, which Mikhail Bakhtin calls "the material bodily lower stra-

28. Simms, *The Partisan*, 98.

tum," is a radical revision of the way meaning is fixed in the narrative universe.[29] This shift is made in order to subvert official, privileged control over a cultural system and to return power, if only temporarily, to those habitually subjugated by the higher orders: Goggle, Dr. Nichols, even black Hector and Tom.

Simms entertains the subversive potential in Porgy while working within a genre dedicated to the official, the stable, the unchanging, and the perennial. His doing so sparks interesting conflicts and disjunctions in any narrative in which Porgy appears. Porgy's ethics of the belly ultimately leads to the negation of the heroic order, since the belly digests all that enters it and ejects undifferentiated matter. Simms avoids the disaster of allowing his hero to be digested by the universal irony of The Belly, and he sacrifices some narrative elegance to do it. He must speak directly to the reader, arguing that what Porgy seems to be is not actually what he is. "Now, it will not do to misconceive Lieutenant Porgy. If we have said or shown anything calculated to lessen his dignity in the eyes of any of our readers, remorse must follow. Porgy might *play* the buffoon, if he pleased; but in the meantime, let it be understood, that he was born to wealth, and had received the education of a gentleman."[30]

In *Woodcraft*, revised by Simms in the aftershock of *Uncle Tom's Cabin*, young heroes of the orthodox figure oppose Porgy's claim to the center of the cultural system. Lance Frampton and Arthur Eveleigh figurally endorse the sanctioned order, while Porgy's bulging gut, spreading ominously along the horizontal, is a significant threat. Frampton, more seasoned than he was in *The Partisan*, is the image of Singleton, his heroic model, and the youth's first name concentrates the connotative power of the heroic type. Arthur Eveleigh, bearing the name of the original knight of the Round Table, is another aspirant to Porgy's position and power.[31] Despite the strong figural competition from

29. *Ibid.*, 346–47; Mikhail Bakhtin, *Rabelais and His World*, trans. Helene Iswolsky (Cambridge, Mass., 1968). See Chap. 6, "Images of the Material Bodily Lower Stratum."

30. Simms, *The Partisan*, 358.

31. William Gilmore Simms, *Woodcraft; or, Hawks About The Dovecote* (Rev. ed.; Ridgewood, N.J., 1968), 52.

the rising generation, however, Porgy is the head of the system for most of the narrative.

The heroic order of *Woodcraft* is in transition from war to peace, from martial to civilian government. Porgy is none too comfortable with the restoration of the ordinary. His character and background had furnished him with authority while Marion fought Cornwallis. But the British surrender brings an end to the life of the armed camp, and Porgy's reentry into civilian society is rough. His plantation is mortgaged to the hilt and seems sure to be seized by the villain, M'Kewn, a Tory survivor who has systematically plundered the plantations of slaves, sold them in the West Indies, and is trying to buy his way back into postwar society with the profits.

The shifting social order threatens Porgy's former status. M'Kewn commands the new order by virtue of his wealth and the mortgages he holds. Thus Simms suggests that the power of money is taking over the world of the survivors, displacing the importance of allegiance to kin or rank. In the martial order of a country at war, Porgy naturally assumed rank and responsibility. War, in fact, saved him, for it held off the creditors that were hounding him. After the hostilities end, however, Porgy continues to function under the rubric of the armed camp. He seizes authority for trying and sentencing ambushers and claims the power of the tribunal as his right by rank.

But Porgy's avoidance of civilian authority is limited. In a half-serious scene, Porgy, arrayed in full military regalia, entertains the sheriff who has come to Glen-Eberley to serve papers foreclosing on Porgy's many mortgages held by M'Kewn. Porgy and his buddies compel the sheriff to eat the writs. There is raucous laughter all around, but Porgy's well-connected town friends must hush the offended sheriff and arrange sufficient credit for Porgy so that he will never again run the risk of losing his estates. What works for the hero in war will not work in peacetime.

The hero of *Woodcraft* is self-contradictory in yet another way. The Bayardic hero fulfills the requirements of his lofty nature and godlike calling by keeping inferiors in place. Simms's characterization of Porgy argues strenuously in favor of the importance of the hero; yet Porgy's subordinate, the actual manager of

the plantation, Sergeant Millhouse, refutes his points even before he makes them. Millhouse puts the plantation on a pros-
perous footing; Porgy is relegated to a ceremonial role, surviving only as a comic relic. Clearly the mundane, but effective,
skills of Millhouse are of more use in the new order than are the
heroic offices of Porgy.[32]

Porgy in search of the ideal mate presents another thorny
problem, for there is confusion over the identity of the ideal
mate. Porgy might choose the Widow Griffen, whose life in the
pastoral forest is so beautifully simple that it brings the hero to
tears. But the pastoral life would not allow the hero to fulfill his
cultural duty and put public society in order; that life would
be a separate peace. Porgy could ally himself with the Widow
Eveleigh, who has placed her extensive and well-managed lands
at Porgy's disposal as collateral for any loans he might need. This
match would seem the correct alternative for the perpetuation
of the system. But Porgy hesitates, and Arthur, the widow's son,
puts on a Hamlet-like show of disapproval of the suitor. Ultimately, the hero remains celibate. New times are uncongenial to
the likes of Porgy. History has already changed the order of
things too drastically for the hero to recover symmetry and
stasis. Only the writer remains; only the figure and the heroic
narrative can establish order.

The hero in Simms's heroic narratives is not merely a cardboard
figure superficially changed from novel to novel by mere altera-
tion of his name and regiment. To read him in this way is to see
southern heroic narrative solely on the plane of "secretarial realism" and the clichéd plot of melodrama. The genre, as Simms
institutionalized it, is much more complex; it records the self-
remembering and self-creating drama of the southern consciousness of literature and history. The hero is the genius, in
Simms's view, of a people seeking self-knowledge and identity
through narrative myth. The genius-hero enjoys a remarkably
full knowledge of his people and bears a correspondingly heavy
duty to articulate the "certain abstract representations" by which
their narrative reassures them of selfhood. He is as fully a rep-

32. *Ibid.*, 191, 189.

resentation of a cultural group as Hawthorne's guilt-ridden Dimmesdale and Hooper are of the Puritan-American conscious- ness. Hawthorne's heroes generate the moral allegory; the south- ern hero generates the heroic narrative.

Simms understood the cultic power of the figure of the hero. In Harrison, Singleton, and other orthodox heroes, he stayed on the appointed path. With the figure of Porgy, however, Simms veered away from the sacred destination, exploring the limits of what could safely be thought and said. Porgy's potential for Rabelaisian allusion challenged the entire carefully wrought and cherished heroic cultural myth. Porgy might have been more comfortable in the genre of southwestern humor; but, as even midwesterner William Dean Howells was to say, that was scarcely literature.[33]

Simms, then, left Porgy without heirs in the heroic order. His alternative was to marry Porgy to history, for Porgy's antics posed the threat of subversion against which the whole weight of Simms's cultural myth had been massed. Perhaps by virtue of the power of the cultural pattern, the figure of Bayard appeared in flesh and blood soon after Porgy's appearance. Robert E. Lee gave heroic narrative in the South, and in the North, a second life in the remainder of the century following the war.

33. Howells, "The Southern States in Recent American Literature: First Paper," 231.

III

Nationalizing the Southern Hero: Figural Reconstruction

The name of *American*, which belongs to you in your national capacity, must always exalt the just pride of patriotism, more than any appellation derived from local discriminations. With slight shades of difference, you have the same religion, manners, habits and political principles.

—M. L. Weems
Life of George Washington

Parson Weems had made Washington the republican saint and hero for the youth of the early national era, and the same figure returned, with its national capacity for abolishing difference, in the aftermath of our second revolution. After the Civil War, the broken national texts had to be reassembled, and the figure of the southern hero carried renewed significance. Grant's rise to power and the presidency was slowed and eventually reversed not only by his unsavory reputation and his foot-shooting talent for surrounding himself with indictable subordinates. There was, in addition, the old cavalier in Lexington, Virginia, around whom grew a university, a cult of biographers and fund raisers, a social fraternity, and ultimately a chapel in which Lee himself is the recumbent deity. These two antagonists, Grant and Lee, gravitated in the national mind toward irreconcilable poles in a cultural debate over which would be our national hero, the model for our male youth (and for the suitors of our daughters), and the bonding figure in our narratives.

Defeat had done nothing to weaken Lee's chances of being chosen. The historical fact of the defeat and surrender of the

Army of Northern Virginia is even today debatable. The actual history of the hero takes second place to the needs and preferences of a culture's idea of itself. In 1885, Charles Dudley Warner, visiting the Cotton Exposition in New Orleans, reported to the readers of *Harper's New Monthly Magazine* on what he had discovered there: a new "American historic consciousness" that grew ever stronger as myth was reconciled to fact. "I have believed that for the past ten years there has been growing in this country a stronger feeling of nationality—a distinct American historic consciousness—and nowhere else has it developed more rapidly of late as at the South. I am convinced that this is a genuine development of attachment to the Union and of pride in the nation, and not in any respect a political movement for unworthy purposes."[1] Warner's cultural seismograph told him that the national plates had been in motion since the early 1870s, soon after the death of the old cavalier and the end of the conqueror-president's honeymoon. The South was at the forefront of a developing national redefinition. Warner assured his readers, accustomed to Union versions of war and Reconstruction politics, that southerners no longer thought of themselves as separate.

Warner had detected the process by which the American consciousness was becoming truly nationalized, using "the right stuff" of heroism to reorder the sacred truths, to restore one heroic icon where there were now two. He had almost invented the term before Tom Wolfe used it: "Every American must take pride in the fact that Americans have so risen superior to circumstances, and come out of trials that thoroughly threshed and winnowed soul and body in a temper so gentle and a spirit so noble. It is good stuff that can endure a test of this kind." The focal point of Warner's nationalization process was not, of course, the single combat warrior in a silver space suit.[2] But the heroic figure leading the nation through the trials of the Civil War is not essentially different: he was a male and a warrior. The nation had watched two such figures in the recent conflict. One had been elected to the presidency, but the other still claimed

1. Charles Dudley Warner, "Impressions of the South," *Harper's New Monthly Magazine*, LXXI (September, 1885), 547.
2. *Ibid.*, 548; Tom Wolfe, *The Right Stuff* (New York, 1979).

deep admiration in the mind of the nation. John Esten Cooke, an eyewitness to the old cavalier's exploits, gave these competing heroic types the symbolic instruments with which they would contest national leadership.[3]

His book is *Hammer and Rapier;* such is the aptness of Cooke's choice of symbols that no one needs to be told which identifies Lee and which Grant. And such is the ambivalent nature of the book itself that the entry for the first edition in the *National Union Catalogue Pre-1956 Imprints* identifies *Hammer and Rapier* as "1. U.S.—Hist.—Civil War—Fiction." Tulane University Library's copy, acquired in 1897, was originally catalogued under a Dewey number for U.S. history; its Library of Congress reclassification number denotes American literature.

The point is not that librarians change their minds, or even that a revisionist historian demoted *Hammer and Rapier* from history to fiction. The point is that in the process of forming an American historic consciousness, truth progresses from fact to another form that we prefer to live with. *Hammer and Rapier,* along with many works less chameleonlike in genre, such as Henry Adams' *Democracy* and Henry James's *The Bostonians,* are significant texts in the ferment that produces cultural reality. Warner detected the process and predicted its movement toward worthy synthesis in nationalism. Central to this metahistorical enterprise is the hero, the catalyst of cultural meaning.

Cooke wrote *Hammer and Rapier* in 1867, before Lee's death, before Grant's fall. But he projected, in the opposing figures and their constellated images, the cultural alternatives facing the emerging national consciousness. Lee is the incarnation of the southern hero, a cultural avatar in the flesh. In Cooke's chapter on the Confederate victory at Fredericksburg, his idea of high tide for the Army of Northern Virginia, he pauses in his historical narrative to sculpt Lee. "Lee is the model cavalier of the great Anglo-Norman race. His figure is tall and erect; his seat in the saddle perfect. His uniform is plain but neat; his equipment beyond criticism. Stately, thorough-bred, graceful in every movement, there is something in his glance, in the very carriage of his

3. See Ritchie Devon Watson, Jr., *The Cavalier in Virginia Fiction* (Baton Rouge, 1985), Chap. Four, which deals specifically with Cooke.

person, that is illustrious and imposing. He has the army-leader
look. There is not the remotest particle of ostentation, much less
of arrogance, in his bearing. This man was a gentleman you can
see, before he was a soldier." Cooke anticipates the portrait of
Lee by Douglas Southall Freeman, another Virginian, who was
also to emphasize Lee's breeding, his racial echo, and his funda-
mental identity as a gentleman. In the traditional southern hero,
these traits always frustrate analysis; the skeptic cannot find their
causes in history. As the model cavalier of a feudal, Western,
Christian era, the southern hero fixes time and his culture upon
the past. He is the model for an entire civilization that is plotted
along classical lines and designed to hold those lines against tides
of history. For example, Cooke depicts a small band of southern
soldiers as holding ground at First Manassas like Leonidas and
his three hundred at Thermopylae.[4] The Army of the Potomac
never merits such a simile.

The North, not surprisingly, is the spawn of a different world
order. The North has no cultural moorings: "The Grand Army
[at First Manassas] seemed to carry with it a great mass of
scum. Editors, idlers, Congressmen, correspondents, ladies even,
flocked to Centreville as to a festival." Its generals shuttle in and
out of command according to the demented whim of bureau-
crats. Their conduct of war is often barbaric and never accords
with classical models. Frémont shells a battlefield where parties
from both sides are collecting the wounded and burying the
dead. Burnside's bombardment of Fredericksburg is cruel and
wanton; "it affected absolutely nothing." Hooker's braggadocio is
matched by his ineptitude; he squanders a three-to-one advan-
tage and loses Chancellorsville. Lee, by contrast, never falters in
his stewardship. When he leads his troops into Pennsylvania, he
forbids reprisals for Union destruction of the Shenandoah Valley. The natives are taken aback. They will need time, Cooke explains, before they and "the world will know what it is to act as a
Christian gentleman, whatever wrongs have fired the blood—
will see the grand proportions of the Virginian, Lee, and esti-
mate him truly."[5]

4. John Esten Cooke, *Hammer and Rapier* (New York, 1870), 155, 23.
5. *Ibid.*, 17–18, 146, 209.

Cooke depicts Grant as having no connection to the heroic, Christian, classical past. Grant, like his commander in chief, was severed from the past and its models of war and leadership. (The character of Owen Trevor in *The Partisan Leader* anticipates him.) Lincoln, Cooke charges, lacked the dignity of George Washington and failed to continue the tradition of excellent men who had held the office of president. His "rude pith, and good sense" were scarcely enough to lift him above the scum. His commanding general could hardly be said to think at all.[6]

Grant is nothing more than force, an arm of muscle, without a nerve routed back to a brain. "One course alone was left to him [Grant in the Wilderness, 1864]—to take the sledge-hammer in both hands, and, leaving tricks of fence aside, advance straightforward and smash the rapier in pieces, blow by blow, shattering the arm that wielded it, to the shoulder blade." Such a rudimentary force needs no intellect and therefore never formulates a plan. The classical hero is capable of much imagination, can move in many directions other than straight ahead, can feint, parry, deflect the blows of the greater force. However, he cannot continue indefinitely. Eventually the hammer smashes the rapier and wins the war. But the hammer gains nothing of value. Even in defeat, the hero possesses his stainless rapier. It has become a powerful symbol: "It was the mirror, like its master, of antique faith and honour." Nothing of antique faith and honor attaches to or is reflected by Grant. He is the juggernaut of a mechanized, depersonalized order of mere force. Cooke explained the dynamic of Grant's leadership this way: "The question was not whether this or that brigade had fought well. What is the result? was asked. Men had ceased to be human beings; they were units; the representatives of force merely."[7]

Two clear alternatives stood before the emerging American historic consciousness in the decades of national psychic reconstruction. One was the figure of the antique hero, before the war a staple of southern narrative, now reified in the person of Lee. This heroic figure echoed his origins in classical, Christian, feudal ages. He defined men as individuals within a limited

6. *Ibid.*, 201.
7. *Ibid.*, 230, 264, 231.

range: most were beneath him in blood and rank, and only a few could rightly claim "the stubborn blood of a race of thorough-breds."[8] But a few were enough to leaven the mass, to focus a culture's ideals and aspirations, to preserve its identity in the midst of history. The other figure was faceless; the hammer, un-like the rapier, was no mirror for self-confirmation. He was cut off from the idiom of former American heroes. He spoke and thought without dignity and lacked any resonance beyond the vulgate. He was mechanized man, recognizing no individuals and acknowledging quantity only. He was force merely; he could not rise above the scum.

The undifferentiated mass of humanity plays no part in the high national culture when the prevailing ideal of that culture is Arnoldian sweetness and light. In the decades following the Civil War, the writers of the Genteel Tradition in American letters struggled to elevate the national identity. Later southern writers were not so well disposed to the salvage enterprise. Allen Tate wrote that "the genteel tradition has never done anything for letters in the South." Paul H. Buck took the opposing posi-tion, describing the "rescue" of southern writers from isolation and defeat through the popularity of the matter of the South in postbellum publications.[9]

Tate's view is often dismissed as a symptom of his unrecon-structed bias. Along with a company of Fugitives and Agrarians, he argued throughout the 1930s that the southern heritage and temperament were superior to the modern. We run the risk of superficiality if we embrace either Tate's or Buck's position with-out reflection. The situation in letters in the Genteel decades was not simply a matter of writing picturesque stories of the exotic South, selling them to Richard Watson Gilder or one of his edi-torial cohorts in New York or Boston, and gaining a national reputation as a southern writer. The overarching cause of cul-tural redefinition, for region and for nation, found one of its most interesting and difficult fields of battle in works such as Cooke's *Hammer and Rapier;* at stake were the sacred text and liturgy of images.

8. *Ibid.*, 27.
9. Paul H. Buck, *The Road to Reunion: 1865–1900* (Boston, 1937), 226.

The resulting literary situation is analogous to the situation in Orientalist scholarship that Edward Said has described. In the following excerpts, we may, with the proper caution, substitute "South" for "Orient" and "northern" or "national" for "European" or "Western." Said wrote: "The Orient was almost a European invention, and had been since antiquity a place of romance, exotic beings, haunting memories and landscapes, remarkable experiences." He further stated that Orientalism is "a way of coming to terms with the Orient that is based on the Orient's special place in European Western experience. The Orient is not only adjacent to Europe; it is also the place of Europe's greatest and richest and oldest colonies, the source of its civilizations and languages, its cultural contestant, and one of its deepest and most recurring images of the Other. In addition, the Orient has helped to define Europe (or the West) as its contrasting image, idea, personality, experience."[10]

Said provides a needed methodology for the reader of southern literature that dates from the crucial years of political reconstruction and nation building. At stake in these literary skirmishes were not only "taste" and the vague quality identified (by Gilder and others) as "artistic." A revised set of national myths, types, and heroes—an entire system of cultural referents—became the material of writers and critics as diverse as Cable, Gilder, Howells, Cooke, Henry Adams, and Henry James. The roll call could continue, for nearly every writer in the later years of the nineteenth century entered or was drawn into the battle.

Said argued that the newer culture of the Occident tried to establish itself by enforcing differences between itself and the Orient—the Other—to the detriment of the Other. Gilder, in an important essay, "The Nationalizing of Southern Literature," announced his analogous objective: the eradication of the differences between the South and the nation and the reintegration of the fallen South into the national family. Like his fellow Genteel critic Charles Dudley Warner, Gilder celebrated a national ideal freed from unworthy motives. As the wayward sister, Gilder argued, the South was compelled to demonstrate the successful purging of her rebellious and evil blood by turning out literary

10. Edward Said, *Orientalism* (New York, 1978), 1–2.

works affirming the moral and cultural primacy of the triumphant North and renouncing the poison of slavery. Gilder gave a telling example of the drive for cultural primacy. In the second part of his essay, he appealed to the emerging southern writer to submit his work to the standards of "the natural literary centers" of the nation. Toward the close of the essay, he conflated the word *natural* with *national*. The claim of cultural superiority can be clearly discerned. "The Southern intellect is for the first time in sympathy with the contemporary literature of the world. Surely, it no longer discriminates against Northern literature, either in books or in periodicals. As to the Northern—that is, the *National*—periodicals, how much of color, freshness, vivacity, and charm have been of late years added to these by Southern writers; how much more national they have hereby become all the world knows!" Once he occupied the culturally superior ground, Gilder, speaking *ex cathedra,* told the southern writer: "It is well for the North, it is well for the nation, to hear in poem and story all that the South burns to tell of her romance, her heroes, her landscapes; yes, of her lost cause, one of the greatest, most touching tragedies in the history of humanity; a tragedy that yet waits for its fitting embodiment in the fiction of America." [11] The parallel with Said's description of Western notions of the Orient is striking. This high-minded blockage of the southern literary imagination—the idealistic coercion into the romantic mode—is the pernicious legacy of the Genteel Tradition, about which Allen Tate had nothing good to say.

Of the many ways open to those who study the effects of this cultural maneuvering, the figure of the hero is most adaptable. The diverse personalities, themes, myths, and extraliterary issues that were part of this complex situation converge in an episode that connects Henry Adams, whose novel *Democracy* was published in 1880, Henry James, who was taking notes for *The Bostonians* when he came across *Democracy,* and Gilder, who serialized *The Bostonians* from February, 1885, to February, 1886, in the hope that it would offset the heavy diet of Civil War memoirs then surfeiting the readers of the *Century.* James was contem-

11. Richard Watson Gilder, "The Nationalizing of Southern Literature: Part II—After the War," *Christian Advocate,* July 10, 1890, p. 442.

plating "a very American tale, a tale very characteristic of our social conditions" when he visited the Adams home and found a
copy of *Democracy.* According to Mrs. Adams, the guest "looked
very severe and grave over it." C. Vann Woodward makes much
of the coincidence; he sees *Democracy* and *The Bostonians* as related novels that employ a "Confederate censor" who examines
the ills of Yankee civilization in the times of Grant.[12]

My own case begins with the premise that the differences between the heroes of *Democracy* and *The Bostonians* are more important than their similarities as Confederate censors. Close
reading of the two novels will show that, although Adams does
censure the politics and social conditions of the Gilded Age, he
uses a nationalized version of the southern hero, the hero of the
pure, if shattered, rapier. James, however, delivers a more ominous portrait of the southerner in the character of Basil Ransom.
What occurs in *The Bostonians*—perhaps a contributing reason
for its burgeoning into a yearlong run in the *Century*—is the pro-
liferation of the cultural warfare that Adams, Cooke, and other
Genteel, nationalizing writers wished to bring to an end. James
eventually presents us a tarnished rapier.

Charles Anderson outlined Ransom as the southern hero
over thirty years ago. Finding in this hero James's answer for the
ills of "our social conditions," Anderson states unequivocally that
Ransom's chivalry, political and social conservatism, and strong
adherence to patriarchal family order mark him as the South's
positive alternative to the confusion of modern, urban, and non-
traditional civilization.[13] Anderson regards Ransom as James's
conscious response to a realized set of social and historical circumstances. There is no essential difference between Anderson's
view of Ransom and Woodward's view of John Carrington, the
hero of *Democracy.*

More recent articles by Sara deSaussure Davis and Marcia
Jacobson have abundantly filled in the social and historical circumstances of *The Bostonians.* Davis, viewing the novel primarily

12. Irving Howe, "Introduction" to *The Bostonians,* by Henry James (New
York, 1956), x–xi; C. Vann Woodward, *The Burden of Southern History* (Rev. ed.;
Baton Rouge, 1968), 126, 134.
13. Charles R. Anderson, "James's Portrait of the Southerner," *American
Literature,* XXVII (1955), 309–31.

as a document in the history of the New England reform movement, allows scant meaning to Basil Ransom's regional prove-
nance: "A Westerner would seem equally capable of symbolizing
the uncouth 'masculinity' of Ransom." Jacobson departs somewhat from the "document in a social debate" line of interpretation and approaches the kind of interpretation essential to an
understanding of the novel and its context. She not only calls attention to Ransom's identity as a southerner but also points out
that he hails from Mississippi, not from Virginia. In the context
of the struggle to establish one "nationalized" myth of the South,
this difference is extremely important. The upper South—Virginia—is the home of such heroes as Washington and Lee, the
line from which Carrington descends. Ransom, Jacobson points
out, is from a Mississippi "one step removed from the frontier at
the time of the war. . . . [His] chivalry thinly masks an aggressive
sexuality, hinted at by his 'leonine' hair and 'sultry' accent; it is
not surprising that he virtually abducts Verena at the end of the
novel."[14]

The cultural field on which the struggle of the southern hero
took place in the final decades of the nineteenth century extends
into the present. Critics have given little or no attention to the
differences among heroes in southern narrative and thus have
missed seeing the significant cultural redefinition that was carried out in the usage of this character. The southern hero, in fiction and in Cooke's hybrid history-fiction, is an integral part of a
reinterpretation of cultural history that occurred through the
essential mediation of the southern hero and his symbolic narrative. The idea that there were two distinct cultures in America
had been accepted with little empirical evidence since the times
of Jefferson. The cultural reformers of the Genteel Tradition attempted to eradicate any differences by making the Other one
with the national self. Adams complied with the nationalizing
drive; James dissented.

The hero of *Democracy* is John Carrington, a romantic chivalric
hero similar to those created by Thomas Nelson Page (Virgin-

14. Sara deSaussure Davis, "Feminist Sources in *The Bostonians*," *American
Literature*, L (1979), 582; Marcia Jacobson, "Popular Fiction and Henry James's
Unpopular *Bostonians*," *Modern Philology*, LXXIII (February, 1976), 271.

ians all) who were to take over the popular myth a few years later. The Virginian hero is the nationalized southerner, a figure distilled from an Old South legend that is part fancy and part history. He is a theme as well as a character because he establishes, by his very appearance in a work of fiction, the Genteel Tradition's ideal of postbellum national identity: the rebel purged of his slaveholding arrogance, restored to his pastoral honor, and ready to donate the latter to a northern (national) character too deeply immured in materialistic concerns. Carrington is this southerner; Ransom is not.

Carrington is proposed by Adams as the hero to correct the deeply corrupt age of Grant. As a Virginian, he is the representative of the heritage of the colonial South, a hero of lofty ethics, probity, and self-control in his appetites for power and sexual gratification. He contrasts sharply with the villains of Grant's Capitol. Adams portrays the chief villain, Senator Silas P. Ratcliffe, as the antithesis of the Virginian in actions and in consciousness. Ratcliffe's machinations in politics and courtship show him to be a man of overpowering appetites without compensating gifts. Like Cooke's figural Grant, Adams' Ratcliffe is capable of only one direction of movement: forward, toward the object of his desire.

In several telling scenes we can see hero and villain in figural contrast, which accentuates the particular cultural values attached to each. Each scene involves power manifested in speech rather than in physical action. Schooling himself to declare his love for Madeleine Lee, the woman desired by both men, Carrington tours the Arlington cemetery with her sister, Sybil. Carrington's effectiveness in speech has been his most attractive trait throughout his competition with Ratcliffe for the affections of the lovely widow. In an earlier scene, Carrington's stories of Washington, the saint of Mount Vernon, enthrall his audience and keep Ratcliffe dumb. In his crucial approach to the heroine, Carrington once again relies upon his powers of speech.

Sybil is moved to tears by his narrative of the harshness of the war and its aftermath. Later, when Carrington declares to Mrs. Lee that she is perfect in his eyes, Adams writes that the southerner's "tone and words pierced through all Mrs. Lee's armour as though they were pointed with most ingenious cruelty, and designed to torture her." Carrington's tone and words, the instruments of his suit, are wielded by a hero accustomed to the rapier.[15]

Ratcliffe's tactics are quite different. At a ball for visiting dignitaries, Ratcliffe advances upon Mrs. Lee. He had previously arranged to have Carrington sent to Mexico on a trumped-up diplomatic mission, and the widow is vulnerable without her protector. Ratcliffe presses her with the proposal that she join him in his rise to power in national politics. He "meant to crush her opposition by force. More and more vehement as he spoke he actually bent over her and tried to seize her hand. She drew it back as though he were a reptile."[16] A searcher for simplified Freudian symbolism would see no difference between Carrington's penetrating words and Ratcliffe's reptilian appendage. For a culture in need of corrective in 1880, however, there is a substantial difference between Carrington's knightly and upright approach to the woman and Ratcliffe's essentially Grant-like war of attrition.

Carrington, the bearer of the culture and gentlemanly control of the Lee dynasty of Virginia, is a hero in a mode approved by Adams and the nationalizers. In one of the first hagiographic biographies of Lee, Thomas Nelson Page emphasized his hero's temperate self-control and made an article of faith of the general's famous directive to the Army of Northern Virginia to abuse no one and nothing as they marched into enemy territory. Page no more than followed in Cooke's footsteps in *Hammer and Rapier*. Carrington is a creation of Adams' similar nostalgia for a heroic figure that would link the ideals of Quincy and Mount Vernon, the two cultural meccas he remembered from his childhood.[17] In creating Carrington in the image of an ideal "nationalized" southern hero, Adams became an early builder of the myth of the southern paragon in Lee's temperate, honorable, chivalric, nonaggressive mold. Many writers were to follow this lead. Page patented the gentleman hero. Stark Young cast the

15. Henry Adams, *Democracy: An American Novel* (New York, 1880), 250–51, 262.
16. *Ibid.*, 364.
17. Thomas Nelson Page, *Robert E. Lee: The Southerner* (New York, 1908), 171; Woodward, *The Burden of Southern History*, 135.

Lee and Grant figures of *So Red the Rose* in this traditional form. Walker Percy's Lancelot complained, in one of his milder diatribes, about Lee as a cult figure.

Ratcliffe is compounded of all that the united nation must avoid. He is a surrogate for Grant, the evil genius of the age, whose invention—the war of attrition—gives its dark resonance to Ratcliffe's siege of Mrs. Lee. He treats her as Grant treated Vicksburg, as an enemy to be worn down and starved out. He represents the unbridled use of power, the flesh-and-blood forerunner of the dynamo, a personification of what the triumphant northern—national—culture feared it was or would swiftly become if there were no checks: man as mere force.

James was likely receptive to these cultural undercurrents when he "looked very severe and grave" over the pages of *Democracy*. In *The Bostonians*, this core of cultural and subconscious myth radiates from the novel's time and place and characters. It seems safe to take James at his word, then, when he said that he had no specific southern person in mind as the prototype of Basil Ransom. The way in which James composed the characters of *The Bostonians* bears repeating here. In his often-cited letter to his brother William, Henry passionately disavows any conscious attempt to use a historical person, namely, Elizabeth Peabody, as the model for the character of Miss Birdseye. "Miss Birdseye," James insists, "was evolved entirely from my moral consciousness, like every other person I have ever drawn." Miss Peabody might have been a catalyst for his imagination at some early point. But, James avers, in order to create Miss Birdseye, "I thought no more about Miss P. *at all,* but simply strove to realize my vision." [18] James's vision in *The Bostonians* is not exclusively or finally historical. In the case of the southerner Ransom, it is less closely tied to the actual world than to spheres of cultural representation. For James, the South was a region of mystery and deep expectation. We know from *The American Scene* that he cherished immense impressions of the South before he had ever set foot on its soil. Ransom is created out of subconscious experience of the cultural Other. As southerner, this character is sig-

18. Henry James to William James, February 14, [1885], in Percy Lubbock (ed.), *The Letters of Henry James* (2 vols; New York, 1920), I, 115–16.

nificantly a product of the dominant culture's need, just as the Orient was a creation of the West's need for opposition and difference. In *The Bostonians,* James shows us the southerner as product of national, willed imagination. The hero of this novel is not solely a figure of historical resonance; he is also a point of focus in an ongoing cultural process that began at least as early as 1867, when Cooke wrote *Hammer and Rapier.*

James's southern hero possesses those traits that, almost sixty years later, W. J. Cash would identify in "the savage ideal."[19] Those features of his character that, according to other critics of the novel, might be said to mark him as nationalized—an admirable chivalry toward women, strong ethical standards in personal conduct—are significantly muted or simply undercut.

Consider Ransom's chivalry toward the weaker sex. James is not completely convinced that Ransom's chivalry is either real or sincere. In Ransom's first meeting in the novel with a woman, Mrs. Luna, we see his chivalry as a highly ornamental mask behind which he can manuever and hide. When Mrs. Luna asks him whether he had known that she had just returned from Europe, Ransom, a bit nettled by the forward lady, reflected that "he might answer her that until five minutes ago he didn't know she existed; but he remembered that this was not the way in which a Southern gentleman spoke to ladies, and he contented himself with saying that she must condone his Boeotian ignorance (he was fond of an elegant phrase); that he lived in a part of the country where they didn't think much about Europe." Ransom's personal and cultural self-effacement is not humility but the positioning of a mask. Mrs. Luna, herself a proud pretender, is not fooled: "She didn't believe he had ever heard of her, Mrs. Luna, though he pretended, with his Southern chivalry, that he had."[20] The hero's chivalric mask is not an admirable social or moral façade, nor is it a substantive behavior. It conceals an aggressive desire to insult and a disturbingly manipulative temperament that becomes more visible and ominous in his dealings with the gullible Miss Birdseye.

19. W. J. Cash, *The Mind of the South* (New York, 1941), 93–94.
20. James, *The Bostonians,* 7, 9.

Miss Birdseye is immensely susceptible to the mask of chivalry. When Ransom meets her in Boston during his clandestine visit to Verena, he exploits the old reformer's disposition to trust the southern gentleman in order to pump her for information necessary to his cause: the capturing of Verena behind enemy lines. He uses his chivalry to obtain the news he desires and then to extract a promise of secrecy from Miss Birdseye. Although his "request seemed still something of a shock to the poor old lady's candor," she consents.[21] As the streetcar bearing his victim rumbles away, Ransom quite hypocritically leaves courtesy to someone else. He is just as merciless when he meets Miss Birdseye again at Marmion. He allows the dying woman to believe he is Verena while he listens to private communications. Then he disappears again behind the mask of the southern gentleman.

Miss Birdseye, however, is as determined by her peculiar "form of consciousness" as Ransom is by his. As an idealistic New Englander, she sees Ransom's pursuit of Verena as an augury of reconciliation. "She watched them a little, and it warmed her heart to see the stiff-necked young Southerner led captive by a daughter of New England trained in the right school, who would impose her opinions in their integrity."[22] Miss Birdseye's wishful interpretation is shaped by the same idealistic desire that made the national reconciliation plot so popular in postbellum fiction. It is just as unfounded. Ransom and Verena are forced into the ill-fitting costumes of the crude, unreconstructed rebel and the refined, reconstructing maiden. In this instance, James does Adams one better, for Adams skews reality into cultural reconciliation, whereas James delegates that function to a character and thereby makes the mechanism of reconciliation the subject of his fiction, not its theme.

While the tense group is still at Marmion, Ransom decides that Olive Chancellor is not entitled to his chivalry because she is neither hated nor weak; nor is chivalry in its pure form to be a bar to any of his behavior if it "should require him to give up the girl he adored." He brings upon his own head Mrs. Luna's

21. *Ibid.*, 226.
22. Henry James to Mrs. Humphrey Ward, July 26, 1899, in Lubbock (ed.), *The Letters of Henry James*, I, 324; James, *The Bostonians*, 378.

lamentation, "Ah, chivalry, chivalry!" as the two trade parting insults. Ransom is no brother to Carrington, no chivalric man for the new national type to emulate, nor does his symbolic rapier mirror antique faith and honor.[23]

Deeper in Basil's consciousness is another feature of the southern mind: the unmistakable mark of the arcadian and pagan way of thinking. Ransom's physical attributes superficially indicate this aspect of his character. Whereas the nationalized southern hero cherished the Lost Cause (Carrington, like Cooke, had been an eyewitness to the surrender and felt a religious solemnity in the desecrated Custis-Lee mansion), Ransom has cancelled most of the reverence he ever had for the ceremonial trappings of the war. Considering marriage to Olive in a brief moment, he reveals that he "had seen in his younger years one of the biggest failures that history commemorates, an immense national *fiasco*, and it had implanted in his mind a deep aversion to the ineffectual."[24] He might even marry this cold cousin whose Charles Street window opens upon an industrial wasteland that is the direct opposite of the pastoral and agrarian ideal that Ransom should, were he the truly nationalized southerner, cherish in his heroic heart. The notion of marriage with Olive, albeit briefly entertained, nevertheless shadows the popular reconciliation plot with a grotesque parody.

The often-discussed visit by Ransom and Verena to Memorial Hall at Harvard shows further his lack of reverence for the Lost Cause. He is not inspired to a partisan position as he views the memorial to the Union dead. All divisions have faded away, "and he forgot, now, the whole question of sides and parties; the simple emotion of the old fighting-time came back to him, and the monument around him seemed an embodiment of that memory; it arched over friends as well as enemies, the victims of defeat as well as the sons of triumph."[25] It is significant that James's southerner, who was appearing in the *Century* surrounded by the series "Battles and Leaders of the Civil War," remembers no names, no regiments, no battlefields, only the fighting and male

23. James, *The Bostonians*, 403, 404.
24. *Ibid.*, 17.
25. *Ibid.*, 248.

camaraderie. This is an ambivalent part of Ransom's heroism, demonstrating some generosity of spirit as well as his tendency to put the past behind him in favor of personal success. The true fraternity of the rapier would not make such adjustments.

Ransom, far from being the scrupulous and gentlemanly southern hero of the nationalized myth, is actually a disruptive consciousness at odds with this public ideal. Cash articulated the features of the southern consciousness that James found behind the mask of chivalry. For Cash, the Virginian of the Washington-Lee line was not the true southerner because he "artificialized" life. The authentic southerner is at root a romantic, a hedonist, a proud individual with a wide streak of frontier violence. The remarkable aspect of James's portrait of the southerner is not only that he anticipates Cash in many details but also that he recognizes that this southern temper hides behind the façade of the nationalized hero. A large measure of the delayed recognition of *The Bostonians*, the "justice" that, James said, came late, is due to our conflation of the nationalized myth of the southern hero with the "savage" character toward which James was working.[26] Although popular taste and critical preference had elevated the nationalized southerner, James shows us that Ransom's promotion is undeserved. He owes as much to hammer as to rapier.

This figure, as James and then Cash outlined him, was not necessarily a cultural savior. Among the salient features of typical southern character listed by Cash are pride, individualism, and a tendency to violence in the solution of problems and the fulfilling of desires. Ransom's character is replete with these traits, especially with acts of aggression that begin as manifestations of bemused contempt for the feminists and peak in his final confrontation with Olive. The first time he sees Verena's father, for instance, his temper moves toward violence. "Ransom simply loathed him, from the moment he opened his mouth; he was intensely familiar—that is, his type was; he was simply the detested carpetbagger. He was false, cunning, vulgar, ignoble; the cheapest kind of human product. That he should be the father of a delicate, pretty girl, who was apparently clever too,

26. Cash, *The Mind of the South*, 32; Henry James to William Dean Howells, August 17, 1908, in Lubbock (ed.), *The Letters of Henry James*, II, 100.

whether she had a gift or no, this was an annoying, disconcerting fact. . . . He had seen Tarrant, or his equivalent, often before; he had 'whipped' him, as he believed, controversially, again and again, at political meetings in blighted Southern towns, during the horrible period of reconstruction."[27]

In this rich passage we see James behind the heroic southern mask, showing us its workings—the "remarkable feat of objectivity" of which he boasted to Edmund Gosse—as it changes the individual into the cultural "equivalent." We also see Ransom's way of shaping experience. Verena is a "delicate, pretty girl" even though her father is a "varlet" and her mother a "white, puffy" woman.[28] In his preference for unreality and romance, Ransom avoids the possibility that there might be more evidence of the sire and dam in the offspring than meets his eye. We see Ransom's eye in active re-vision of whatever strikes it. And we see his tendency to violence sublimated into acts of speech (controversy), for he has whipped Selah Tarrant's type at political meetings in the past.

James consistently steps behind Ransom's façade in this way. Verena—whose name might be read as an anagram of "venery" (cf. Benjamin Franklin: "Rarely use venery but for health or offspring, never to dullness, weakness, or the injury of your own or another's peace or reputation")—continues to appear to Ransom as a creature from his own romantic imagination. Seeing Verena after a long absence, he paints her in the hues of a pastoral nymph: "Still, however, her glance was as pure as it was direct, and that fantastic fairness hung about her which had made an impression on him of old, and which reminded him of unworldly places—he didn't know where—convent cloisters or vales of Arcady." Ransom positions Verena in his imagination so that his abduction of her will be a classical rape with overtones of his violent breaking of another's vow of chastity. Her vapid chattering chimes in his ears like "the tone in which happy, flower-crowned maidens may have talked to sunburnt young men in the golden age." Later, beholding Verena at the Burrage soiree, he

27. Cash, *The Mind of the South*, 44, 32, 45–46; James, *The Bostonians*, 58.
28. Henry James to Edmund Gosse, August 25, 1915, in Lubbock (ed.), *The Letters of Henry James*, II, 498; James, *The Bostonians*, 58.

dismisses all claims of objectivity. Verena becomes for him the damsel, the nymph, the lady, "unconscious of the pernicious forces which were hurrying her to her ruin." And once Ransom has established Verena as a victim menaced by dragons and knaves, he must—and will—become her rescuer.[29]

By showing the autonomous power of the arcadian and chivalric myths to override reason and reality, James provides a portrait of the inner southerner not really nationalized. The southerner, for James, is not a static symbol for a certain accessible body of historical truth (as are Carrington and his ilk) but is a "form of consciousness" that is not necessarily the antidote to northern mercantilism and vulgarity. James's suspicion is vividly illustrated in Ransom's unbridled hedonism. The hero's desire is to possess Verena. As Ransom woos her we see that the placid images of hearth and family are only appearances that mask the hero's voluptuary fever. As his tendency to violence is transformed into acts of speech and talking, so also is Ransom's sexual assault and conquest of Verena rechanneled into talk.

For Cash, southern speech was the repository of the archetypal influences on the southern mind: climate, the Negro, religion. The honored forms of oratory and rhetoric became the southerner's chief means of realizing his will. For Cash's southerner, speech was not a surrogate for action but was heroic action itself. James points us to a similar attribute in Ransom. Ransom's voice occupies a good deal of James's initial description of him: "And yet the reader who likes a complete image, who desires to read with the senses as well as with the reason is entreated not to forget that [Ransom] prolonged his consonants and swallowed his vowels, that he was guilty of elisions and interpolations which were equally unexpected, and that his discourse was pervaded by something sultry and vast, something almost African in its rich, basking tone, something that suggested the teeming expanse of the cotton field."[30] James admonishes us to read *The Bostonians* with the senses as well as with the reason by listening to the southerner's voice, which carries erotic power. Sexual exhibition, possession, and conquest are carried out in

29. James, *The Bostonians*, 229, 230, 253.
30. Cash, *The Mind of the South*, 82; James, *The Bostonians*, 5.

this novel through acts of speech. With his double heritage of southern voluptuousness and potency of speech, Ransom is certain to be the victor.

Verena's first speech, the impromptu address at Miss Birdseye's, strikes Ransom as charming and attractive, but "the effect was not in what she said." The remarks, which end with the word "love," bear no rational meaning. Verena's words are an immature and incomplete erotic exhibition, "not followed by her sinking exhausted into her chair or by any of the traces of a labored climax."[31] Ransom is interested and Olive is stunned by Verena's guileless performance. Here the plot of the senses (not the plot of the reason) is begun in earnest: Who shall be the rightful user of venery/Verena?

Olive takes possession first, but in his conversation with Verena in Chapter 12—after Olive has proposed a vow of maidenhood to Verena—Ransom succeeds in eliciting an invitation from her. His "familiar, friendly Southern cadence" is a potent erotic lure.[32] In fact, it is the sole erotic plume with which he might attract Verena, for he has neither money nor position.

Chapter 28, which opens with the description of Verena dressed in virginal white and standing upon a red cloth (colors sure to engage Ransom's medieval imagination), continues to trace the erotic "relations" of the pair and introduces the concentrated use of double entendre. The conversations at the Burrage apartment are lively with double meanings. Verena exclaims that Ransom is the "hardest subject" she had yet encountered among her male opponents. James calls attention to the double entendre of eroticism by putting a phrase of Verena's within quotation marks: "Mr. Ransom was 'standing out.'" Ransom easily bests Burrage in this sexual strutting. When he engages with Olive, however, the erotic play becomes more serious. His parting words to his rival, who is "panting like a hunted creature," not only carry a double meaning but add the note of taunting cruelty characteristic of Ransom's savagery: "I will ask her to come out, so that you won't see us."[33]

31. James, *The Bostonians,* 61, 63.
32. *Ibid.,* 91.
33. *Ibid.,* 278, 277, 283.

The hero's visit to Verena in New York marks a significant acceleration in their erotic relations. Chapter Thirty-three begins with Ransom's insistent "Come out with me, Miss Tarrant; come out with me. *Do* come out with me." James notes that "it had, of course, taken considerable talk to lead up to this; for the tone, even more than the words, indicated a large increase of intimacy." Ransom literally besieges Verena with talk, using satire, simile, hyperbole, and change ringing on a few points from her own feminist message. He even presses her to give him more than "this stiff little talk." Envisioning marriage to Verena, Ransom resolves that his possession of her will "strike her dumb" on the subject of women's rights. Soon his words make her blush; then they lead her into an indiscretion when she betrays the nature of her relationship with Olive. To relieve the intense pressure exerted by Ransom's voice in the closed sitting room, Verena consents to a walk in Central Park. This is Ransom's pastoral territory, and his voice jumps in power. He "said to her certain things that hummed, like memories of tunes." They argue politics and Verena encounters his archetypal southern violence in his argumentative tactics and positions: "She didn't know that being a conservative could make a person so aggressive and unmerciful." Ultimately she finds herself possessed by the voice. The more Ransom talks the more "a strange feeling came over her, a perfect willingness not to keep insisting on her side and a desire not to part from him with a mere accentuation of their differences." The "deep, sweet, distinct voice, expressing monstrous opinions," casts a "spell upon her" that results in a kind of sexual lassitude and surrender of self. She wishes to abolish the difference between herself and her suitor; she wants to be taken up into his powerfully erotic presence. The unspoken wish does not yet become the deed, however, for his enunciation of the word "loveliness" brings Verena back to her present peril. She jumps to her feet and flees the sound of Ransom's voice.[34]

James prepares for the inevitable in Book Three. Once again Ransom calls for Verena to come out to him, this time from the seaside cottage where Olive has vainly sought refuge. Every

34. *Ibid.*, 324, 327, 330, 332, 334, 335, 336, 337.

afternoon for a month his talk holds Verena in thrall. "The change that had taken place in the object of Basil Ransom's merciless devotion since the episode in New York was, briefly, just this change—that the words he had spoken to her there about her genuine vocation, as distinguished from the hollow and factitious ideal with which her family and her association with Olive Chancellor had saddled her—these words, the most affective and penetrating he had uttered, had sunk into her soul and worked and fermented there." James's use of speech as an erotic indicator also tells us that the hero's success has destroyed the erotic element in the relationship between Olive and Verena, for the two women have become speechless with each other.[35]

It is only a matter of time until Ransom's hammering shatters Verena's ramparts. When Verena hears his voice beyond the dressing room door at the Music Hall, she knows all is lost. Her independent identity, for better or worse, has been swallowed up by his "selfishness." She is overrun. Her voice, her sexuality, are totally his, and he cannot resist a vaunting word upon his victory: "'Keep your soothing words for me—you will have need of them all, in our coming time,' Ransom said, laughing." His parting shot suggests a kind of tragedy, for it hints at a sexual appetite that will consume Verena, an appetite that he feels no compunction to curb, an appetite that annihilates what it feeds upon.[36]

James's portrait of the southerner is most richly colored in the hero's overpowering eroticism, which is manifested in the use and sound of his voice. Although he uses this weapon to wrest Verena from the clutches of vulgar promoters, venal parents, insipid engagements, and a sexual liaison of questionable propriety, Ransom does not thereby leave the field as the unblemished and unqualified hero. Ransom is not only spotted with a brutal masculinity and political neanderthalism. He is also, as James portrays him, appetite without control, pride without curb, reality without dependable coordinates in the ideal. To the Bostonians who, whatever their disparate ideas on the reform of

35. *Ibid.*, 396, 416.
36. *Ibid.*, 460, 456, 461.

social ills, possess a common definition of the real and thus a basis for order, he represents the very antithesis of their tradition and society.

He is not the nationalized southern hero, that hybrid of the best of the North and the South purged of disorder and modified for national use as a paragon of unity. He is an adumbration of Cash's savage ideal; he holds in utter contempt those traits "necessary to the healthy development of any civilization."[37] As a figure in the fictional and historical narrative of the Genteel climate, Ransom taps strong subliminal energies in the conflict over a new system of cultural referents within the newly reunited nation. Basil appeals figurally to the collective unconscious of an American audience that, in buttressing a civilization shaken by civil war, had to reconcile hammer and rapier in order to forge a new national identity. Basil infiltrates the ground. In the robes of a cavalier he hides the elemental, vulgar, merciless character of all power. In the 1880s, Basil was an anomaly in popular fiction, for the machinery creating the nationalized southern hero—a figure who would be taken out of the voluptuary, cruel, hedonistic, and treasonous shadow and placed in the light of Christian, cultural idealism—was steaming along without much opposition.

The issue of the actuality of the southern hero, Carrington or Ransom, in history is secondary to the developing of an American historic consciousness by which one figure or the other would be certified regardless of empirical evidence. What Said has written about the relationships between the *real* East and the *real* West is pertinent. "The value, efficacy, strength, apparent veracity of a written statement about the Orient therefore relies very little, and cannot instrumentally depend, on the Orient as such. On the contrary, the written statement is a presence to the reader by virtue of its having excluded, displaced, made supererogatory any such *real thing* as 'the Orient.'"[38] In the supercharged literary atmosphere of the Genteel decades, an analogous interplay between real South and print South, between real

37. Cash, *The Mind of the South,* 139.
38. Said, *Orientalism,* 21.

southern character and the outsider's conception of southern character, led to the creation of written statements—texts—that must be read as maneuvers in a cultural struggle.

By developing Basil Ransom as a radical and stubborn heroic impostor, James exposes the process of cultural creation of reality. To view Ransom as succumbing to nationalization, a process of cultural definition culminating in meaning, is to scant James's achievement in *The Bostonians* and to miss the complex function of the hero in southern narrative. The work of reconstructing a single heroic type for cultural use suspended lines of demarcation between history and fiction. The hero was, and is, the central figure.

IV

Ellen Glasgow and the Dismantling of Heroic Narrative

> Dismantle: to take a mans cloake off his backe; also, to dis-
> mantle, raze, or beat downe the walls of a fortresse.
> —*Oxford English Dictionary*

The pen, it is said, is mightier than the sword. Men, it is further said, naturally claim the privilege of wielding both. In our time, the Equal Rights Amendment to the Constitution foundered on images of American women brandishing M-16's; the argument was that women by nature and by right were not equipped to handle the implements of war. For ages, male writers have made the case that the pen is also not a feminine instrument. Sandra M. Gilbert, writing on "literary paternity" in the Victorian age, has observed that Gerard Manley Hopkins identified writing with the male claim to cultural authority, which was "a concept central to that Victorian culture of which he was in this case a representative male citizen."[1]

That the patriarchs of any culture store up and wield the authority of that culture through the written word is not a new discovery. That women writers have sought this power, have been resisted, and have then employed various subversive literary strategies to dismantle the self-perpetuating structures of patriarchal authority will, likewise, surprise few. Close examination of particular cases, however, provides us with material for fruitful controversy. One case is that of Ellen Glasgow, who began

---

1. Sandra M. Gilbert and Susan Gubar, *The Madwoman in the Attic: The Woman Writer and the Nineteenth-Century Literary Imagination* (New Haven, 1979), 4.

a career as an author during the later days of Victorianism in American letters and was thus a victim of the mentality espoused by Hopkins. Glasgow faced a literary barrier doubly fortified by southern heroic narrative. That tradition in narrative, having accumulated over the century and having been sanctified in history by the Civil War and the subsequent canonization of the survivors, presented a "fortresse" forbidding indeed. Not only did this woman seek to write; she also sought to handle the sacred icons of southern civilization.

In the nineteenth century, the woman writer's challenge began, of course, when she first made private marks on a blank sheet of paper. That act, auguring treason, required no official notice or retaliation, for as long as the woman writer was content to forgo the public audience, she constituted no immediate threat. Access to an audience was controlled by a company of male sentries, known as critics and editors, who saw themselves, as did William Dean Howells, in the exclusively male roles of doctors or priests to their culture. They spoke *ex cathedra* upon questions of form and taste and even more strongly—if that be possible—on the question of female authorship itself.

Consider the case of Grace King, who preceded Glasgow in approaching the fortress of authorship in the 1880s. Her first story, "Monsieur Motte," undertaken as a response to alleged "libels" in Cable's stories about New Orleans Creoles, follows the perils and eventual rescue of its heroine, Marie Modeste, from the taint of miscegenation. She is proved white and, as a direct consequence, acquires honorary parents at the end of the story. William M. Sloane, editor of the *New Princeton Review,* responding to the success of "Monsieur Motte," requested a sequel in which Marie Modeste, saved from miscegenation but still unmarried, would be wed. King obliged with "On the Plantation," which, in her words, "brought Marie Modeste through a love story to a happy marriage in the most conventional manner."[2]

King seems not to have objected to the prescriptions of the priests and doctors. Her next major work of fiction, however, suggested to her by "the publishing autocrat" George Brett of Macmillan, was to be a "picturesque" story of Reconstruction.

2. Grace King, *Memories of a Southern Woman of Letters* (New York, 1932), 66.

King, as she tells the story, replied to Brett that she did not recol-
lect that Reconstruction was anything but a cruel imposition on a
conquered people. Nevertheless, she set about working on *The
Pleasant Ways of St. Médard* with Brett's encouragement echoing
in her ears: "Write as you know it—your own experience; and
send it to us."[3] Brett sent it back. At the turn of the century
the vogue for historical romance was at the flood, and King
had neglected to plot a romance into her own experience of
Reconstruction.

King took her complaint to a native priest, Thomas Nelson
Page. "I told him that the fault alleged was the want of a love
story in it. He brightened up. 'I know, I know,' he said. 'That was
the fault they found with one of my novels. And I had to remedy
it to get it published. Now I will tell you what to do; for I did it!
Just rip the story open and insert a love story. It is the easiest
thing to do in the world. Get a pretty girl and name her Jeanne,
that name always takes! Make her fall in love with a Federal officer and your story will be printed at once! The publishers are
right; the public wants love stories. Nothing easier than to write
them. You do it! You can do it. Don't let your story fail!'"[4] We
need little comment on Page's imagery for the act of revision, as
King remembered it; it was, perhaps, a bit too easy and cold-
blooded of Page to recommend the violation of another's text.
His advice was clearly that King submit to the voice of God mediated through His editors, who preferred women successfully
matched with men in love stories. No other outcome would
suffice.

Glasgow sought admission to the ranks of published authority
a few years after King. Julius Rowan Raper has written of Glasgow's meeting with Price Collier, a senior editor at Macmillan to
whom she had sent the manuscript of her novel *The Descendant*.
The meeting took place in New York in the early 1890s. Glasgow
was a young woman from Richmond, and Collier was an urbane
and sophisticated literary priest. Glasgow picked up the clear impression that Collier had not even read the novel he was to discuss. His central advice to Glasgow was "to stop writing, and go

3. *Ibid.*, 234.
4. *Ibid.*, 378.

back to the South and have some babies," because a woman would be judged on the quality of her babies, not on the quality of her books. Glasgow found another publisher for her novel.[5]

Collier's advice came from the same patriarchal fortress as Page's advice to King. Woman is not naturally an author, the wielder of a pen swelling with the meaning of ages, potent with the word for future generations. She is a process, biologically and authorially, to be controlled by men who design to retain their power, overtly or covertly, by blocking a woman's writing or by prescribing its form and materials.

For King, covert restriction enjoined her to supply romantic stories in which single girls were first cleansed of the stain of miscegenation, then married to men who completed their existence. If a work did not carry that neat plot or subplot, King inserted it.

Glasgow, however, preferred "blood and irony" to romance, revolt to compliance. She responded to the overt attempt to deny her authorship with a series of novels in which she dismantled the heroic narrative rather than violate her own work. Glasgow's revolt against entrenched cultural powers, which we can map in her subversions of type-character and type-scene, in verbal nuance, and in polemic, shows us a determined defense against the preemptive strike of the patriarchal guardians of authority.

Of Glasgow's twenty novels, the six she retrospectively considered a social history of Virginia from 1850 to 1914—*The Voice of the People* (1900), *The Battle-Ground* (1902), *The Deliverance* (1904), *The Romance of a Plain Man* (1909), *Virginia* (1913), and *Life and Gabriella* (1916)—contain the arduous work of dismantling the traditions of priestly power encoded in southern heroic narrative. Glasgow's attempt to throw off paternal control in this cycle of six novels—as well as in the earlier *The Descendant* (1897), in which her pattern was approximately set—suggests that southern identity and behavior (social and individual) are gender-related phenomena, like the act of authorship, and are not necessarily or wholly determined by regional consciousness or

5. Julius Rowan Raper, *Without Shelter: The Early Career of Ellen Glasgow* (Baton Rouge, 1971), 60.

history. Glasgow's revolt against the sentimental and romantic in southern writing goes beyond revision of history or the public confession of what Fred Hobson has called "the shame and guilt" school in southern apologia.[6] Glasgow works from within by undermining the historically and culturally condoned forms by which cultural truth and power are authenticated.

In the preface to *The Battle-Ground*, Glasgow took measure of the literary establishment that confronted her at the beginning of her career. "While American fiction entertained itself with an historical pageant, it occurred to me, immature as I was at this period, that it might be interesting to look beneath the costume ["cloake" or mantle] into the character of our civilization," she wrote. "I was, in my humble place and way, beginning a solitary revolt against the formal, the false, the affected, the sentimental, and the pretentious, in Southern writing." Facing this self-conscious and militant southern writer, whose sense of history ran deep, but not deeper than her ironic insight into the character of her culture, was the fortress of heroic narrative. Glasgow's efforts in the parochial (in the nonpejorative sense of the word) southern arena are synecdochically related to her artistic and intellectual engagement with her age. Raper, the most knowledgeable interpreter of Glasgow's work, has stated that "the essence of the struggle lies in shifts in the attitudes she held during those two decades [1901–1925] toward authorities of reality, writers ancient and modern who sought to impose their vision, especially their ontology, upon persons who read their words. For Glasgow's early life had created in her an ambivalence toward the most powerful controllers of the Western world picture." In a related passage, Raper wrote: "Her readings both in science and in wisdom literature reveal, even more than a disinterested pursuit of truth, a constant search for authority, a compelling need for a source of knowledge to be used, first, against the canonical arguments of her father, and later, to fill the void created when she rejected her father's traditions."[7]

6. Fred Hobson, *Tell About the South: The Southern Rage to Explain* (Baton Rouge, 1983), 5.
7. Ellen Glasgow, *The Battle-Ground* (1902; rpr. New York, 1938), x, xii; Raper, *Without Shelter*, 2, 10–11.

Glasgow's formal handling of the hero and his presumption of sexual power over women and ontological power over reality in his society was Glasgow's bracing point for her dismantling of the reality that had been transmitted through generations of southern heroic narrative. Rejecting one patriarchal form, she groped toward an alternative in her first cycle of novels. Whether she attained a new matrix for reality in *Life and Gabriella* is still debated. But debate on that novel should not begin until we see how the earlier novels gradually dismantle one ontology and leave the ground clear for an alternative.

The Descendant, a work Glasgow remembered as marking her "recoil from the uniform Southern heroes in fiction," is not a southern novel unless one adopts the rather circular argument that Glasgow, a Virginian, wrote it.[8] But it establishes vital elements in Glasgow's formal revolt. Michael Akershem, a lower-class but brilliant southern man—reminiscent of Hardy's Jude—sails to New York on the *Old Dominion* to make a life that the closed and exhausted society of Virginia will not permit. Akershem, a bastard, knows he is in a Darwinian struggle for survival, and he aims to be one of the survivors. After a few years of manual and unfulfilling labor in the Yankee metropolis, he is hired as a columnist for a reform journal called the *Iconoclast.* Through the power of his profoundly pessimistic and "modern" skepticism, radiant in a series of essays that has the intelligentsia abuzz, Akershem rapidly achieves notoriety.

Powerful in prose, Akershem is likewise powerful in passion. He becomes obsessed with Rachel Gavin, a woman from the South who has come to the city to pursue a career in painting that would not be allowed her in her native region. Michael and Rachel live together without benefit of nuptials, preferring the modern and emancipated arrangement to the sham of tradition. Even so, Rachel surrenders her career to devote full time to her role as Akershem's woman.

Eventually Akershem's passion swerves toward a society matron he has met due to his newfound fame. His power in the pages of the *Iconoclast* begins to falter as he is feted by the beau-

8. Glasgow, *The Battle-Ground,* xiii.

tiful people. As he and the journal lose prestige, the society woman snubs him. He limps back to Rachel, begs her to marry him, is crushed by her rejection. She refuses him rather caustically, commenting that marriage would be "a prosaic ending to our theories."[9] Rattled, Akershem quarrels with a younger member of the *Iconoclast* staff, kills the man, and is sentenced to ten years in prison.

As the novel ends, Akershem is out of the penitentiary, wandering the streets of New York in destitution, dying of tuberculosis. He loiters outside the apartment building where he used to live with Rachel, until she finds him and takes him in. The power that Akershem has forfeited Rachel has gained; in the intervening ten years, she has studied art in Paris, refining her talent and returning to New York as a modest but genuine success. She takes her former lover into their old apartment, proclaiming that he is now hers for all time. But time is short; Akershem is too sick to live. Their reunion is doomed.

Doomed, that is, if the reader, like the suave Price Collier, assumes that the goal of woman is to be a process that serves the specialized needs of a man. Akershem, professing scorn for conventional institutions such as marriage, nevertheless assumes that Rachel should surrender her talent, her "vision of reality," to his will. In his assumption of power over the female, Akershem is a familiar heroic figure. James's Basil Ransom is only one of his ancestors in fiction. He is, moreover, the heroic figure that Glasgow's fiction dismantles.

Although Akershem is "lithe and straight as a young pine," and although the rest of his physical description accords with the heroic silhouette, he is a bastard.[10] Controlled mating did not create him; random selection tossed him into the world. Without the protection of the tradition of the southern hero, Akershem's powerful traits turn dangerous. Simms's heroes assumed as much power, but their approved birth provided a curb for fate. Women do not fall under Akershem's spell readily. Although Rachel succumbs to his passion for her, she also falls out of love and rejects his plea for salvation by marriage. Rachel is so confident of her

9. Ellen Glasgow, *The Descendant* (1897; rpr. New York, 1900), 228.
10. *Ibid.*, 17.

talent that she does not fear the deep, as does Chopin's Edna Pontellier, or the degradation of the street, as does Crane's Maggie. Rachel's art is her primary responsibility; she chooses it over a reality imposed from the fortress. In the end, she controls the male, but significantly he is too weak for sexual or ontological imposition. "Mine for all time," Rachel murmurs; then Akershem coughs blood and slowly dies.[11]

   The Descendant is a "diploma novel" not generally regarded as one of Glasgow's successful efforts.[12] We can nevertheless see the outline of her revolt from the sentimentality of her age and from the formal narrative constraints of the literary establishment of the time. Rachel Gavin finds survival better than death as a means for revolting againt patriarchal tradition and reality; thus her character counters the examples of Edna and Maggie. Furthermore, Glasgow uses her narrative, especially the ending, to suggest an alternative relationship between hero and woman, a potentially subversive revision of the romantic denouement, in which the woman emerges unpaired and in possession of her own destiny. The hero, an excrescence, may be discarded.

   The first four novels of Glasgow's Virginia cycle elaborate her revisions of narrative tradition. *The Voice of the People* follows the lives and careers of Nicholas Burr, like Akershem a humbly born but ambitious Virginian, and Eugenia Battle, daughter of the local squire and occupant of the shrine to ideal womanhood. The vicissitudes of this central romantic relationship define a plot that Glasgow used with little variation in her cycle of novels. Humbly born man falls in love with a socially superior woman. Complications to their love arise. Sometimes these complications are overcome, and the lovers marry; sometimes the barriers prevail. In each case, the central characters represent historically established social classes: the woman the superior, landed, aristocratic class; the man the new current of political and financial power. The male also represents his gender by the force and vigor he directs upon the female, seeking her as the object of his active desire. Since he is outside the heroic order by virtue of his low social position, the male's desire is not sanctioned by tradi-

11. *Ibid.*, 275.
12. Raper, *Without Shelter*, 65.

tion and therefore can be seen without the muted sentimental glow of the heroic. With this maneuver, then, Glasgow links her revolt against the heroic tradition in southern narrative with a revolt against the fathers on a wider battleground.

Although Nicholas Burr is far below Eugenia in class, he envisions her as a goddess: "His eyes followed her as she rode serenely above him, and he thought, in his folly, of the lady in the old romance who was, to the desire of her lovers, as a 'distant flame, a sword afar off.'" Eugenia seems to love Nicholas too, for his vision of her is very flattering and his rough passion compelling, until a rumor links him with a pregnant lower-class girl. Burr knows that Eugenia's weak brother is the father of the illegitimate child, but he is too proud to plead. Eugenia marries a paragon of her traditional order, Dudley Webb, and rationalizes her rejection of Burr by telling herself, in images recalling fairy tales of banned marriages to ogres and gnomes, that marrying Burr would be marrying the type of his father—coarse, bearded, underbred. Eugenia decides that she is indeed the soul of good birth, and, heeding her "clannish soul," she chooses a man of her own type. She accepts her traditional identity: "And, above all, she was what each woman of her race had been before her—a mother from her birth." [13]

Burr keeps a celibate life, eventually becomes governor of Virginia, and stands on the brink of becoming a U.S. senator at the end of the novel, when he goes home to defend a black man accused of rape. He is killed trying to defend the accused against a lynch mob. Glasgow ushers the martyred Burr into the ranks of classic Virginian heroes—Jefferson, Madison, Marshall, and other liberal spirits of the past. Mr. and Mrs. Webb seem to concur, for the thought of Burr's integrity earlier prevented Dudley from conspiring in a cheap political trick against Burr, and the novel closes with the posed portrait of Eugenia, Dudley, and their son suffused by a light radiating from the example of Burr's heroism.

Raper, reading *The Voice of the People* with emphasis on Glasgow's formal manipulations of the romance, sensed irony in this cloying, romantic, and sentimental final scene. "The ironies

13. Ellen Glasgow, *The Voice of the People* (New York, 1900), 212–13, 180, 404.

which turn up like ghosts in this tableau . . . are quiet but mali-
cious ones: Eugenia's warm reference to Burr; Webb's always
ready, empty smile; Eugenia's (too) quick tenderness; the husband's expectation followed by the wife's ambiguously placed kiss
(almost surely on her son's lips, though just uncertain enough to
lead the romantic mind where it will); and, finally, the external
radiance picked up by Eugenia's eyes. Thus Miss Glasgow as
ironist revitalizes the romantic ending." The ironies condensed
in the final passage are indeed revitalizing; they register the shift
of power away from the heroic order. Settling for Webb, the heroine turns her back on the present and compromises her moral
stature. As a politician's wife, Eugenia must adopt hypocrisy:
"The first lesson in politics is to lie and love it; the second lesson
is to lie and live it. Oh, we've been in Congress, Dudley and I."
Above the living lie floats the rhetoric of worn-out heroic myth.
In nominating Webb for governor, one of his supporters "spoke
warmly along the old heroic lines." None of that costume rhetoric would fit Burr, who "was called ugly, but it was at least the
ugliness of individuality—the ugliness of an unpolished force,
of a raw, yet disciplined energy."[14] In politics, as in love, Burr is
the undomesticated force, and Eugenia bolts toward the silken
bonds of the tame Webb for sexual and political reasons. Webb,
the watered-down latest survivor in a line of heroes, rescues the
heroine from the ogre, and she submits to her prince and to his
control over her role as a process in service to the patriarchal
order. But the final tableau hints that the lady's revenge is coming: henceforth, her affections will be transferred from husband
to son.

   The Battle-Ground, covering the years 1850 to 1865 in Virginia,
applies irony to the familiar romantic narrative of the Civil War.
This is Glasgow's only Civil War novel, and in it she confronts the
hero and dismantles his claim to dominance by subverting character type and closing with a scene that signifies a further shift of
power and authority.

   Two families live on nearby plantations in Virginia during the
golden years before the Civil War. Major Lightfoot, master of
Chericoke, "was very tall and spare, and his eyebrows, which

---

14. Raper, *Without Shelter,* 135; Glasgow, *The Voice of the People,* 353, 301, 303.

hung thick and dark above his Roman nose, gave him an odd resemblance to a bird of prey." [15] The major is an aging Hotspur trailing suggestions of the hero of a bygone age. He is quick to explode when crossed, willful, and fiercely loyal to his region. He becomes a fire-eyed Democrat during the furor over slavery, welcomes secession, and thumps for war. His neighbor is former Virginia governor Peyton Ambler, master of Uplands. The governor represents the tradition iconologically headed by Robert E. Lee. He is temperate, deliberate, educated, a Whig in political leanings, a Unionist in political sympathies until his state secedes, then a field commander who dies in uniform. This scheme, a version of the historicopolitical allegory familiar in southern fiction after Appomattox, was particularly popular at the turn of the century.

The lovers are Dandridge Montjoy, grandson of the major, and Betty Ambler, second daughter of the governor. Dan Montjoy has the reputation of a Galahad, which he scorns, and is warmly loved by all and sundry for his generous spirit. When Montjoy returns from school, for example, the overseer rushes in from the fields to welcome him home. True to his heroic ontology, Montjoy looks about him for the ideal mate, and natural attention falls upon the Ambler sisters. He first chooses the symbolically named Virginia. The major decides that Montjoy shall indeed marry Virginia, for she is the older and therefore the proper mate. But the hero changes heart and falls in love with Betty. In a scene reminiscent of one in Tate's *The Fathers*, in which Semmes Buchan revolts from his father's wishes for him in politics, Montjoy revolts from the major's will to impose a mate on him. He leaves Chericoke, takes a job as a common stagecoach driver, and, when the war breaks out, enlists as a private in Jackson's army.

Betty pines away at home while the men are away on the field of honor. Although she has plenty of her own ideas and attitudes about life, Betty is still impressionable. A visit to Chericoke, to help Mrs. Lightfoot, leaves her alone in the room of the hero:

> She turned to the bed and picked up, one by one, the scattered books upon the little table. Among them there was a copy of the

15. Glasgow, *The Battle-Ground*, 14.

"morte d'Arthur," and as it fell open in her hand, she found a bit
of her own blue ribbon between the faded leaves. A tremor ran
through her limbs, and going to the window, she placed the book
upon the sill and read the words aloud in the fragrant stillness.
Behind her in the dim room Dan seemed to rise as suddenly as a
ghost—and that high-flown chivalry of his, which delighted in
sounding phrases as in heroic virtues, was released from the
pages of the old romance.[16]

The field of honor, however, proves to be anything but con-
gruent with the pages of the old romance. Montjoy's initiation
into the reality of battle leaves him more than a little appalled.
He feels "tremors" too, but not from Malory's story: "The sight
of the soaked shirt and the smell of blood turned Dan faint. He
felt a sudden tremor in his limbs, and his arteries throbbed dully
in his ears. 'I didn't know it was like this,' he muttered thickly.
'Why, they're no better than mangled rabbits—I didn't know it
was like this.'"[17]

Montjoy gradually sheds his heroic illusions and with them
some of his aristocratic pretensions. He befriends a mountain
dweller named Pinetop, thereby learning vividly how the other
95 percent live. He begins to read aloud from *Les Misérables*, intending to teach Pinetop to read, and draws a large audience of
illiterate soldiers in the camp. He trades his heroism of rank and
sword for a budding social conscience.

Montjoy and Pinetop part after Appomattox; the latter knows
that their mutual respect will not easily survive the reinstated social structures of peacetime. The hero returns to Chericoke,
which has been razed by the Union army. He is weak, uncertain,
and still confused over the lessons war has taught him. When he
and Betty meet, he offers to release her from her promise to
marry him, citing his loss of capital and of social position. She
archly declines his offer and begins to walk away. He calls her
back, and they embrace as he faints from a flood of emotion and
the effects of malnutrition. "Then, as she reached him, she knelt
down and drew him to her bosom, soothing him as a mother
soothes a tired child."[18]

16. *Ibid.*, 256.
17. *Ibid.*, 234–35.
18. *Ibid.*, 387.

This "Pietà" tableau, variants of which Glasgow uses in *The Descendant, The Deliverance,* and *The Romance of a Plain Man,* underscores her dismantling of the heroic order. The hero, having forfeited his sexually and socially declarative vigor and arrogance, is reduced to the dependent status of a child. The woman he once assumed to be his to control is now the authority. Betty receives and reshapes the ruins of the heroic structures; not only is the archetypal southern nation defeated on the field of honor, and the hero thus bereft of the confirmation of his image of himself at the vanguard of a worshipful society, but he is defeated in the type-scene of choosing his mate. Women take men, on women's terms.

Glasgow strips Montjoy of his heroic mantle before making him dependent in the final tableau. In the golden years before the war, Montjoy had been accustomed to the privileges of heroic status. "In another dress, with his dark hair blown backward in the wind, he might have been a cavalier fresh from the service of his lady or his king, or riding carelessly to his death for the sake of the drunken young Pretender." Raper plucked the word "drunken" from this passage as the mark of Glasgow's ironic touch. We should notice, in addition, that the cavalier guise, naturally thought to be male, is contingent upon the assent of a captive population: the women and the underclass of whites and blacks. Betty conspires to make Montjoy a hero: "Scattered visions came drifting through her mind—of herself in romantic adventures, and of Dan—always of Dan—appearing like the prince in the fairy tale, at the perilous moment."[19] It is the role, the sacred office (expected by men), of women such as Rachel Gavin, Eugenia Battle, and Betty Ambler to support the patriarchal order and reality by acts of thought and imagination.

Raper's reading of the final scene in *The Voice of the People* hinted that, with the cunning of the conquered, this support may be shifted if not totally withdrawn. Apropos of this point, Raper wrote: "In her [Glasgow's] books, the postwar South is a matriarchal society devoted to worshipping two feminine ideals, the Old South and the purity of Southern women; one in which figurehead 'colonels,' 'generals,' 'judges,' and 'governors' are

19. *Ibid.*, 104; Raper, *Without Shelter,* 156; Glasgow, *The Battle-Ground,* 92.

propped up by puritanically hard and industrious women; the war was sexual suicide for the Southern male." Raper's point is tantalizing: was the sexual suicide self-motivated, or were the women present in some way, as Wyatt-Brown has speculated, to coerce the men into a war that would surely end male hegemony over reality, culture, and the women themselves?[20] By dismantling the hero and the configuration of reality promulgated by his narrative, Glasgow explores the intricacies of this situation. Montjoy is not killed (as is Betty's father, for example) but he does, like the phoenix, die that he might rise again—not as the head of the woman, but as an appendage, an accessory.

It is one thing to take the stock characters and scenes of the Civil War romance and season them with irony; it is another to suggest the dismantling of the structures of political and cultural authority embedded in them. Perhaps, sensing that she had done something such as this, Glasgow—looking back from the vantage of 1938—felt justified in writing that *The Battle-Ground* was not a romance.[21] It is yet another thing to pursue the heroic ontology and its servant narrative beyond the costume drama of the Civil War. Glasgow continued the pursuit in her next novel, *The Deliverance,* a novel of Reconstruction that carries her dismantling of the hero several steps beyond *The Battle-Ground.*

Details of *The Deliverance,* one hazards the guess, scarcely matter once the pattern is known. Christopher Blake, the hero, dominates the landscape of the tobacco country of Virginia. Carraway, a lawyer who conducts the business of the local magnate and functions intermittently as commentator on the action of the novel, describes the hero walking in the fields. He is "moulded physically in a finer shape than [the other workers], and limned in the lawyer's mental vision against a century of the brilliant if tragic history of his race . . . he seemed, indeed, as much the product of the soil on which he stood as did the great white chestnut growing beside the road. In his pose, in his walk, in the careless carriage of his head, there was something of the large freedom of the elements."[22] Blake, the surviving son of the former master of Blake Hall (which is now owned by the

20. Raper, *Without Shelter,* 169; Wyatt-Brown, *Southern Honor,* 34, 226.
21. Glasgow, *The Battle-Ground,* x.
22. Ellen Glasgow, *The Deliverance* (New York, 1904), 12.

overseer, Bill Fletcher), is reminiscent of Nicholas Burr in that both men are presented as elemental male forces habitually suited to the dominance of whatever universe the narrative sets up for them. Blake, having lost the concrete forms of his social preeminence, his house and lands, is an elemental force, a will to power over his surroundings, human and natural.

Marie, the daughter of the usurper Bill Fletcher, falls in love with Blake and he with her. "All the natural womanhood within her responded to the appeal of his superb manhood; all the fastidious refinement with which she was overlaid was alive to the rustic details which marred the finished whole."[23] There are, of course, familial and social barriers to their love. Blake hates Marie's father for "stealing" his patrimony and designs the corruption of old Fletcher's nephew, the boy on whom he plans to bestow his fortune. Blake introduces the boy to liquor, hunting, and other manly pastimes. The young man is expelled from school, becomes an alcoholic, marries beneath him, and whines about his misfortune. The relationship between nephew and uncle deteriorates to the point that the young man kills old Fletcher after the old man disinherits him. Blake, overcome with guilt, confesses to the crime to punish himself and is, like Akershem before him, sentenced to a prison term.

In prison the rude health of the white chestnut is broken. He returns to Blake Hall only after the boy, dying in Europe, confesses to the crime. Marie, herself rid of a foppish husband who died in a European asylum, deeds the Blake lands back to the Blake family. All seems to have been set aright, and we expect the happy closure of the romance plot. We get instead an ironic subversion of our expectations. Christopher, broken in health, no longer manfully potent or as elemental as his totem the chestnut tree, has lost his "naked power" to determine reality. Marie is the agent who effects the restoration of the patrimony. Like her predecessor Betty Ambler, she accepts the man as husband. The hero, recuperating in a new atmosphere, gazes with "gentle ridicule on the blithe candour in the eyes" of male ancestors' portraits.[24] No more will the male be able to control the world "with the characteristic touch of brutality."

23. *Ibid.*, 130.
24. *Ibid.*, 528–29.

Glasgow plays variations on this narrative pattern in *The Romance of a Plain Man*. The variations remove the story from the referential realism of sociopolitical history (where it was never very firmly tethered) toward the politics of sex. Ben Starr is the plain man whose life story is followed from childhood to the brink of his control over the symbol of New South financial and industrial maturity, the Great South Midland and Atlantic Railroad. That power is originally held by George Bolingbroke, latest in a long line of powerful and well-born Virginians who control Starr's world. Ben, displaying Horatio Alger–like pluck and drive, shoulders his way into Bolingbroke's affections and economic empire. Soon he becomes a more adept financier than the old man's nephew and would-be heir.

Unlike his confrere in the lower classes, Nicholas Burr, Ben Starr succeeds in the love plot of the novel. He woos and weds Sally Mickleborough, daughter of Blands and Fairfaxes, stalwart names in the list of the First Families of Virginia. At the beginning of their life together, Ben worships Sally for what he imagines is her queenly condescension in marrying him, and she is his fervent ally in ignoring the slings and arrows of her socially entrenched kin. Eventually the drive to garner all economic power causes Ben to neglect his wife; she begins to feel subordinated in his affections to money and power. To recapture her husband's attention, Sally takes up riding to hounds, a sport she had given up at her husband's request. It is an accident, suffered while she is taking a spirited mount over a jump, that brings Ben back to Sally. Whether the injury is wholly accidental is questionable:

> "Just as you like, sweetheart, but for my part, I feel easier, somehow, when you don't go out with the hounds. I'd rather you wouldn't do such rough riding."
>
> "That's because like most men you have an ideal of a 'faire ladye,'" she answered mockingly. "I'm not sure, however, that the huntress hasn't the best of it. What an empty existence the 'faire ladye' must have led!" [25]

Sally's fall is serious. The injury to her spine requires constant bedrest and around-the-clock nursing, as well as a change of cli-

25. Ellen Glasgow, *The Romance of a Plain Man* (New York, 1909), 417.

mate to southern California. The telegram offering Ben the chairmanship of the Great South Midland and Atlantic Railroad arrives at just the moment he is faced with the medical needs of his wife. He tears up the telegram, tosses it into the fire, and, in a reprise of the Pietà scene in *The Battle-Ground,* falls to his knees beside Sally's bed. The future will be hers to dictate: she can have no more children or, it seems, sexual relations. She has the man now, but on terms that strip him of any active role in her future, financial or biological.

The Romance of a Plain Man is not a successful novel. Glasgow enters the persona of a man of finance, uses peripheral characters to testify to Ben's acumen, but never shows us how he makes such startling deals. *The Romance of a Plain Man* is carried, then, not by the verisimilitude with which stock deals are described but on the less circumstantial level where power and sex are won and lost.

From the beginning of the novel this linkage is apparent. As a child, Ben asks his father who had most to do with his being born, and his father admits, "Yo' ma, I s'pose." From that initiation, the theme of sexual division of power grows until the ending. Barred as male from exercising power over life in the natural mode, Ben pursues symbolic power in money. This pursuit sets him at odds with women, especially with the woman he marries. "Yes," Sally tells Ben, "you're a man, and you couldn't be happy even with me—without something else." That something else is power. After he has financially failed once and then risen to the brink of total domination, Ben admits that he has always desired power: "The smart of my failure was still there, and I had known hours of late when my balked ambition was like a wild thing crying for freedom within me. The old lust of power, the passion for supremacy, still haunted my dreams, or came back to me at moments like this, when I drove with Sally through the restless pines, and smelt those vague, sweet scents of the spring, which stirred something primitive and male in my heart."[26] Sally, sensing that to her spouse she is just another object for "primitive and [therefore] male" domination, opts for a friendship with urbane George Bolingbroke, the surpassed nephew. With

26. *Ibid.,* 5, 336, 100.

George, at least, Sally is treated with some ceremony, if without lust. Sally and George, we are explicitly told, are not lovers. Revenge for Ben's neglect lies not in a love affair with another man, however, but in the unmanning of the culprit himself.

Curiously, the culmination of this shadow play of lust, power, and sex occurs with Sally's self-negation. She is as dead as Edna Pontellier. More or less willing the injury that negates her as mother and sexual partner, Sally also douses the central fire of Ben's existence. Henceforth he will be a sexual and financial eunuch, barred from power over the person of his wife and forced to surrender his financial base by moving to southern California. The closing tableau of *The Romance of a Plain Man,* is, then, as redolent of irony as is any in Glasgow's cycle of subversive novels.

It would be difficult to argue successfully that these five novels constitute a great artistic innovation. Glasgow plots, for the most part, with a conventional map. Love blossoms, and then complications of a social or psychological nature arise. The terms of fulfillment, however, the author subverts with a distinct touch of irony. In each case the hero is dismantled; his presumption of power over reality and women is beaten down. At the close of each of the novels, Glasgow fixes a scene that pictures the ongoing revision of the heroic order.

Virginia and *Life and Gabriella,* the final two novels of what has been called Glasgow's prewar phase, seem to step into another order of reality. Several critics have noted that these novels are closely linked as studies of a gender-conscious woman's version of reality and the social history of her specific moment. *Virginia* is a novel that purposely imposes a woman's psyche upon a region's cultural condition. *Life and Gabriella* carries the "forsaken ideal" of *Virginia* into a modern world of so-called emancipation.

Virginia is a self-conscious allegory. The central female character and the state of Virginia (synecdoche for the Old South) are identified by the same name. Glasgow's preface to the 1938 edition makes this coupling plain: "It was as if the vividness of Virginia's interior truth had brought to life every person and object, every house and street, that made up her surroundings. . . . What she was, that background and atmosphere had helped to

make her, and she, in turn, had intensified the life of the picture."[27] In short, place and persona are interchangeable; thinking of one is thinking of the other.

Virginia Pendleton has been made in the image of the patriarchal society: "By her eyes, and by an old-world charm which
she exhaled like a perfume, it was easy to discern the feminine
ideal of ages. To look at her was to think inevitably of love."
Glasgow is quick to point out, though, that the thought of love in
the mind of the male is not so chastely disembodied. Upon meeting playwright Oliver Treadwell, the hero of her dreams, Virginia
worries. "'He thinks me a simpleton, of course,' she thought,
perfectly unaware that Oliver was not thinking of her wits at all,
but of the wonderful rose-pink of her flesh." Susan Treadwell,
Virginia's friend, warns her that "Oliver isn't one bit of a hero—
not the kind of hero we used to talk about," but Virginia is beyond hearing the voice of reality. Oliver marries Virginia.[28]

After four pregnancies in five years, Virginia returns to Dinwiddie with Oliver and their three children. "She was thinner,
and there were dark circles of fatigue from the journey under
her eyes; but the Madonna dreams in her face were fulfilled, and
it seemed to Susan that she was lovelier, if anything, than before."[29] Virginia's education in dreams of youth, beauty, and service to husband and family are permanent; she is incapable of
adjusting to a new order not controlled by a husband standing in
for the patriarchal order.

Oliver, whose first realistic play is rejected, turns to writing
fluff and becomes a big success on Broadway. He falls in love
with his leading lady, tells Virginia their marriage is over, and
leaves. Virginia is shattered. Feebly she hopes that the record of
her love and devotion will bring Oliver back to her, but she finds
no vein of iron deep inside herself.

Apparently defeated, she returns to Dinwiddie and begins a
slow, isolated demise. But she does exert some late power over
the male order before she fades from memory. She claims her
own son as protector; the last line of the novel comes from him:

27. Ellen Glasgow, *Virginia* (1913; rpr. New York, 1938), xi, xii.
28. *Ibid.*, 4, 55, 22.
29. *Ibid.*, 187.

"Dearest mother, I am coming home to you!" Harry is tall, athletic, handsome, articulate (he shows promise of being the serious writer his father failed to become), apparently attractive to the young girls in England, where he attends college. But he surrenders all of that out of mother worship; he is the first appearance of the type represented by Arthur Peyton in *Life and Gabriella,* the symbol of the lifeless old order. Both have surrendered active male lives in the present for an ethereal and abstract life of service to an ideal embodied by the Madonna. John Crowe Ransom's poem "Antique Harvesters" is concerned with the process that turns living men into the musty type of Harry Treadwell or Arthur Peyton.

> Bare the arm, dainty youths, bend the knees
> Under bronze burdens. And by an autumn tone
> As by a grey, as by a green, you will have known
> Your famous Lady's image; for so have these;
> And if one say that easily will your hands
> More prosper in other lands,
>
> Angry as wasp-music be your cry then:
> "Forsake the Proud Lady, of the heart of fire,
> The look of snow, to the praise of a dwindled choir,
> Song of degenerate specters that were men?
> The sons of the fathers shall keep her, worthy of
> What these have done in love."[30]

It is this process of de-creation that Glasgow ironically places at the end of *Virginia* and reverses in *Life and Gabriella.*

The breaking of the old order, so disastrous for the idealized heroine of *Virginia,* potentially means the liberation of woman from the constricting patriarchal role that imprisons her and drains the blood from the man as well. Virginia Treadwell's capture of her own son, and his enthralled submission, is the woman's failure, as well as the culture's, to seize the chance of survival in the present and future. Deference to the past—to Virginia/*Virginia*—is a Poe-like premature burial. In *Life and Gabriella,* the final novel in her social history cycle, Glasgow attempts to take the woman out of the ruins of the antique struc-

---

30. *Ibid.,* 406; John Crowe Ransom, *Selected Poems of John Crowe Ransom* (New York, 1945), 50–51.

ture, to imagine a male both alive *and* nondominating, and to obliterate the old order with a new world.

Early in *Life and Gabriella,* Glasgow recapitulates *Virginia.* Gabriella's sister, Jane, has fled to their mother's home in Richmond after one of her husband's frequent trysts—this time with a housemaid. Although we are not told that Charley Gracey, the husband, physically abuses his wife, the biological dominion is evident in the five children young Jane brings with her. In family deliberations, the totality of male authority is made clear. Cousin Jimmy, the male whom Gabriella's mother calls for advice (a woman cannot decide for herself), jocularly transposes the facts of the situation: "What does he [the husband] mean by letting you run away from him?" The only woman who seems ready to face the issue frankly is Gabriella, who insists on hearing the whole discussion even though another uncle claims that "the less women and girls know about such matters [as male drinking and cruelty to women], the better."[31] He is flabbergasted that Gabriella stays for the discussion of particulars. She impulsively pledges her future to work for Jane's independence from her husband; we can be relatively certain that, whether she knows as much or not, Gabriella sees the domestic relationship in economic rather than sentimental terms. When Jane takes the sot back, in an orgy of forgiveness and contrition, Gabriella is disgusted.

Two men figure prominently in Gabriella's early life, Arthur Peyton and George Fowler. Peyton is the ideal of the heroic code exposed as an enervated narcissist.

> Arthur Peyton was standing in front of the fireplace, gazing abstractedly at his reflection in the French mirror. Though his chestnut hair was carefully brushed, he had instinctively lifted his hand to smooth down an imaginary lock, and while he did this, he frowned slightly as if at a recollection that had ruffled his temper. His features were straight and very narrow, with the look of sensitiveness one associates with the thoroughbred, and the delicate texture of his skin emphasized this quality of high-breeding, which was the only thing that one remembered about him. In his light-gray eyes there was a sympathetic expression which invari-

31. Ellen Glasgow, *Life and Gabriella: The Story of a Woman's Courage* (New York, 1916), 18, 21.

ably won the hearts of old ladies, and these old ladies were certain to say of him afterward, "such a gentleman, my dear—almost of the old school, you know, and we haven't many of them left in this hurrying age." [32]

Gabriella is engaged to Peyton; he seems to fulfill all that she could desire in a man. But Jane's trouble with her husband and Gabriella's pledge to work in a dry goods store to ransom her sister from marriage prompt her to call off the engagement. Peyton had objected to Gabriella's working for a wage, arguing that employment was an insult to a lady.

There is another man in the wings, George Fowler. When word of the broken engagement reaches him in New York, he hurries to Richmond and proposes. Breathless, Gabriella accepts George, whose sexual power eclipses the bloodless Peyton's and overrides her incipient drive for autonomy. The darker side of George's sexual magnetism, however, is an endemic male narcissism and a will to power over Gabriella that she does not anticipate. The signs of these flaws abound, but Gabriella is blind to them. Mirrors, Glasgow notes, captivate George; he never passes one without appraising himself. His pet name for Gabriella, Goosey, signals his wish to dominate her: "He liked it because it gave him a merry feeling of superiority when he said it, and Gabriella liked it for perhaps the same reason." [33]

The first issue on which they seriously clash is whether Gabriella's mother will come to live with them in New York. George is against the idea, and he tries to twist consent from Gabriella. "He was testing his power to dominate her; and never had she felt it so vividly, never had her will been so incapable of resisting him as at that instant." But she does resist, and George leaves a crushed rose geranium as a token of his frustrated will. Soon after his defeat, however, George returns and "gives in" to Gabriella's wish. But he reserves something from total defeat: "He had given in, but he knew in the very instant of his defeat that he should some day turn it to victory." [34]

32. *Ibid.*, 33.
33. *Ibid.*, 163, 108.
34. *Ibid.*, 109, 121.

The bliss of George and Gabriella rapidly cools, and Gabriella begins to rely on the vein of iron deep in her character. The turning point arrives on the night that Gabriella plans to tell George of her first pregnancy. He arrives very late, very drunk, and apparently rapes Gabriella before collapsing into unconsciousness.[35] From that moment, Gabriella writes him off; she relies on her children and her inner strength. She is so self-sufficient that when George runs off with Florrie Spencer, one of Gabriella's friends from Richmond, Gabriella smoothly dismisses her husband from her life. She can look her mother-in-law in the face and say simply that she no longer loves George.

The second half of the novel follows Gabriella on her long rise to independence in the world of women's fashion in New York. As arduous as her work is, it is not so difficult as her drive to find a feminine identity that does not depend on the proprietorship of a male superior. The dream of Arthur Peyton, seeming to offer comfortable bonds, hovers in her mind during the several years of hardship and then success in New York. The image of the hero of the past, of the well-bred but unsound aristocratic order of thoroughbred patriarchs, seems in her imagination to promise comfort and repose. In such an order she would, like Virginia, be released from all contact with reality. So, one might add, is Edna Pontellier released by suicide.

A few men come into Gabriella's life. One is Dr. French, whom she had known in Richmond. Now he is a pioneer in providing medical care to tenement dwellers. To Gabriella he seems to be a "priest—like a priest of the Middle Ages." She wants only French's friendship. Resignation to the sexual dominion of the male seems to have terminated for Gabriella when George so rudely forced himself upon her. After that night, "the ardent, if fluctuating, emotions of the lover" no longer meant anything to Gabriella; she was, in fact, relieved when his "attentions lapsed."[36]

Gabriella's escape from the sexual dominion of the male, from

35. Julius Rowan Raper, *From the Sunken Garden: The Fiction of Ellen Glasgow, 1916–1945* (Baton Rouge, 1980), 26, sees no rape in the episode. Anne Goodwyn Jones does. In *Tomorrow Is Another Day: The Woman Writer in the South,* 254, she states that George "(apparently) rapes Gabriella." Judging from Gabriella's appalled reaction, Jones's interpretation seems more likely.

36. Glasgow, *Life and Gabriella*, 316, 211–12.

the "failure of the old order to withstand the devastating advance of the new spirit," and from the clutch of the patriarchal past are conflated in her quest for an alternative to male-endorsed identity. She knows, for example, that there can be no friendship with French without her surrender of physical and emotional autonomy. Her refusal to see him brings the typical male assumption that there is "someone else," another man with whom he will not share the prize. So Gabriella drifts back into dreams of Arthur Peyton, into an embalmed peace.[37]

She emerges from the cocoon of dream imagery when she approaches a friend from her married years, Judge Crowborough, who makes $500,000 per year and has professed his admiration for Gabriella's pluck. She goes to his office to negotiate a loan with which to buy a controlling interest in the dress shop she has built into the best in New York. The judge agrees to lend her the capital, and Gabriella permits herself the satisfaction of thinking that she has conducted a business transaction with the judge on the level of his male peers. On the way to the door, however, the judge puts his hand on Gabriella's waist, and her illusion of equality is shattered. Gabriella reacts to this sexual paternalism and harassment with an icy disapproval that stops the elderly jurist in his tracks. "The appalling clasp," the man's assumption of proprietorship over the woman, drives Gabriella into depths of despair. No more is heard of the loan.

Glasgow's design pushes *Life and Gabriella* toward a comprehensive resolution of the intertwined issues of sex, political order, and personal happiness. Like the title character of *Virginia*, but in a new order, Gabriella carries a symbolic burden. Turning her back upon marriage, Gabriella also turns her back on the old order as personified by her mother-in-law and on men as a sexual and political ruling caste. Her redemption from solitude— Glasgow evidently does not think of narrative conclusion in terms of leaving Gabriella alone—is held by the opposing images of Arthur Peyton and Ben O'Hara. The dream image of the former enters her consciousness periodically when the burdens of the real world seem too heavy; it is the motif of escape into a tra-

37. *Ibid.*, 238–39, 329.

dition in which all options have been confronted and subdued. If Peyton is the thoroughbred, O'Hara is a mustang.

When Gabriella meets O'Hara for the first time, she does not find out his name; he accosts her on the street as she is returning from the judge's chambers. "He was doubtless devoid of those noble traditions by and through which her mother had always told her a gentleman was made out of a man—the traditions which had created Arthur and Cousin Jimmy as surely as they had created George and Charley." Instinct draws her to this unschooled male presence while vestiges of the tradition pull her away.[38]

When she finally learns O'Hara's name and that he lives downstairs, their wooing begins. O'Hara, "singing a snatch of ragtime," presents "a vivid impression of bigness, of freshness, and of gray eyes that reminded her vaguely of the colour of a storm on the sea." O'Hara's presence alerts Gabriella to the political ramifications of his character and of her attraction to him. Walking with him on the streets of New York, the woman of aristocratic tradition encounters her polar opposite. "For the first time, flowing like a current from the mind of the man beside her, there came to her an understanding of her own share in the common progress of life—for the first time she felt herself to be not merely a woman who lived in a city, but an integral part of that city, one cell among closely packed millions of cells. Something of the responsibility she felt for her own children seemed to spread out and cover the city lying there in its dimness and mystery."[39] One can read this epiphany as the realization by the new Eve, by the Miranda of a brave new world, that the city is the new Eden where her mothering achieves new definition. Gabriella's fate is still, however, to be a mother.

O'Hara, born in a cellar, raised by a ward politician, is the new Adam. Eventually, inevitably, the image of O'Hara casts out the image of Peyton: "O'Hara's image was trespassing upon the hallowed soil of her reverie." In actuality, O'Hara, like Prospero, makes things right: he buries George, who finds Gabriella in time to die in her apartment; and he takes Archibald, Gabriella's

38. *Ibid.*, 368.
39. *Ibid.*, 383, 170.

son, out of the mother's orbit and sets him on the course of becoming a red-blooded man, thus reversing the capture of young
Harry by Virginia and rewriting Ransom's poem.[40]

The momentum of the concluding pages leaves little room to
maneuver around a happy ending in which O'Hara and Gabriella
pledge their love and lives to each other. After Gabriella makes
a belated trip home to Richmond, sees its modern, hasty development, and reassures herself that Arthur Peyton represented
"distrust of life . . . profound negation of spirit," she is prepared
to accept the challenge of O'Hara. He represents "an embodied
symbol of life—that she must either take or leave completely and
without reserve or evasion."[41]

Their climactic embrace reverses the choreography of the
Pietà; neither kneels to the other. Yet Glasgow cannot escape an
ending in which the woman surrenders herself to a man who
seems to accept as his inalienable right the gift of another self.
Catching a glimpse of O'Hara in a New York railway terminal,
Gabriella feels transported: "Her face, which had been lowered,
was lifted like a flower that revives, and her feet, which had
stumbled, became the swift, flying feet of a girl. It was as if both
her spirit and her body sprang toward him." Facing him with a
look that "did not drop from his questioning gaze," Gabriella
tells O'Hara, "I wanted you." The claim is active and assertive,
yet it is his freewheeling life in the West that the two will live.
"The choice was hers that comes to all men and women sooner
or later—the choice between action and inaction, between en-
deavour and relinquishment, between affirmation and denial,
between adventure and deliberation, between youth and age."[42]
Glasgow clearly intends for Gabriella to possess the positive of
each set of alternatives; yet the reader can question whether,
amid the swelling notes of the coda, a true set of alternatives has
prevailed.

It could be argued that Glasgow does not really overturn the
patriarchal order, for in the end the male still fulfills the female
by rescuing her from mere "friendship." It could also be argued

40. *Ibid.*, 477.
41. *Ibid.*, 515, 524.
42. *Ibid.*, 528, 529.

that, although Gabriella submits, she does so with an enlightened will. The close of *Life and Gabriella,* in either case, returns to the orthodox view. The death of Gabriella's sisters in fiction—Crane's Maggie, Chopin's Edna Pontellier, Wharton's Lily Bart—argue that the alternative to being with a man is the cold comfort of the grave.

A residue of the obsolete lurks in every word we use; it is not so easy to dismiss Emerson's assertion that words are signs of natural fact. In *dismantle* lurks the natural fact of stripping, of exposing the previously private realm of mystery. As the *Oxford English Dictionary* definition states, the "cloake" that is stripped away is a "mans"; the act of dismantling, then, entails an assault upon the fatherhood of power, tradition, authorship. In these early novels of Ellen Glasgow, dismantling the heroic narrative necessitated a revolt from patriarchal hegemony in several ways. The formal exceptions and subversions found in these works give ample testimony that Glasgow's protestations of "immaturity," of relative powerlessness in her "humble" relation to the literary and cultural canons, are actually postures in an ironic obeisance before the "fortresse" of heroic narrative. Once Glasgow had her say, the hero of traditional southern narrative—like Tate's Lacy Buchan or Percy's Will Barrett—had no refuge in the crumbling heroic edifice.

V

Lee Agonistes: The Southern Hero in Midpassage

What General Lee personified was definitely gone and human existence could not very well do without it. The power, the accomplishment, of General Grant were clear, but they weren't nearly handsome enough. Men required nearly every possible detail of dignity.

—Joseph Hergesheimer
Swords and Roses

The Agrarian manifesto, *I'll Take My Stand,* was not the only instrument by which certain southern writers strove to redirect the course of American history in "midpassage." Insofar as the essays in *I'll Take My Stand* can be interpreted as a formula for programmatic change—and that is still debated—the Agrarian positions are vulnerable to rational examination (and dissection), statistical outflanking, and the dim likelihood of actual implementation. If, as Allen Tate wrote to Donald Davidson, the group was not to "have everything we write discredited with charges of medievalism and Fascism," another route into the American heart and mind would have to be discovered.[1] The Agrarians had, in fact, already found the passage and had, with one or two unlikely allies, gone a good distance along the way.

The route lay along the line of southern heroic character. To the generation of writers born near the turn of the century, this character was to be abundantly found in southern figures known

1. Allen Tate to Donald Davidson, February 23, 1936, in Thomas Daniel Young and John Tyree Fain (eds.), *The Literary Correspondence of Donald Davidson and Allen Tate* (Athens, Ga., 1974), 297.

through history and regional lore, and in figures closely allied with the epic and sanctified war. Davidson, for example, wrote his poem "Lee in the Mountains" to commemorate the greatest southern hero; he also wrote on General Kirby-Smith and the secession movement in the West. Robert Penn Warren wrote a biography of John Brown, the executed abolitionist. Andrew Nelson Lytle wrote a biography of Nathan Bedford Forrest and planned a study of the life and mind of John C. Calhoun. Gerald W. Johnson, a journalist Davidson considered one of the North Carolina apostates, wrote—for the same publisher who issued the biographies by Lytle and Tate—studies of Andrew Jackson and John Randolph of Roanoke. And such an unexpected compatriot as Lincoln Kirstein, while editor of *Hound & Horn,* caught the southern heroic fever and proposed to Tate a study of J. E. B. Stuart's artillerist, John Pelham.

We must also keep in mind that at this time (the late 1920s and early 1930s), Margaret Mitchell was stacking up manuscript in her tiny Atlanta apartment. She worked from the end of the story of Rhett and Scarlett back to the roots of what she called, in a letter to Douglas Southall Freeman, "*our* section."[2] Freeman himself, a few years older than the writers of Tate's generation, was immersed in writing *R. E. Lee: A Biography,* the first two volumes of which appeared in 1934. Tate published biographies of Stonewall Jackson and Jefferson Davis and embarked upon a biography of Lee which came to nought only after a good deal of fretful work.

In a time of crisis, a people appeals to its heroes, and those who keep the heroic images do a priestly service for their culture. They also possess power, for the heroic images can direct national action, overriding—in theory and in hope—negative circumstances and returning the people to its sense of wholeness and identity within a realizable destiny. Conscious manipulators of these icons are rightly called propagandists, and there is a fine but crucial distinction to be made between those who merely manipulate and those who—like Freeman and Tate—ponder the heroic figure with genuine and complex emotion.

2. Margaret Mitchell to Douglas Southall Freeman, October 13, 1936, in Richard Harwell (ed.), *Margaret Mitchell's "Gone With The Wind" Letters: 1936–1949* (New York, 1976), 77.

Such disparate southern writers as Freeman, Davidson, and Tate sought to prescribe exemplary cultural action and attitude through the use of, rather than submission to, history. Lewis P. Simpson has assessed the nature of this work: "Tate shared with Davidson a vision of reestablishing in modern fragmented and industrial society a sense of the value of cultural wholeness. As he affirmed the loss of the heroic in poetry, he was on the verge of joining Davidson . . . in an active engagement with modernity. This would take the form of a heroic attempt at an inquiry into the epistemological meaning of the South and of an attempted recovery of the limits and validity of the historical and mythic South as the ground of, the source of, a unified sensibility—of 'a knowledge carried to the heart.'"[3] As unlikely as it might seem, both Freeman and Tate picked up this transhistorical challenge—Freeman in *R. E. Lee* and subsequent writings about the great hero and his society, Tate in *Stonewall Jackson, Jefferson Davis,* the unfinished manuscript on Lee, and eventually his novel, *The Fathers.* Freeman's tendency to affirm the mythic and religious significance of the heroic figure differs from Tate's more critical and wary investigation. A study of the two fills in our picture of the nature and importance of the heroic in southern writing, shedding oblique light on all the southern writers of the Renascence and its aftermath.

Douglas Southall Freeman was born in Lynchburg in 1886. As a Virginian of his generation, one sensitive to the changes in the ambient pressure of the southern heroic, he saw in his adulthood the ebbing of a Confederate flood that had meant direct linkage with heroic ancestors.[4] The period of the Civil War was, for Freeman and for many others, an age entitled to the ornate rhetoric of Shakespearean history. "Auguries" abounded in the simplest incidents; armies were "hosts," and the blood that "coursed" through the veins of the living eventually "hallowed" the ground on which the dead fell. And heroic blood was a far

3. Lewis P. Simpson, Foreword to Young and Fain (eds.), *The Literary Correspondence of Davidson and Tate,* xii.
4. Douglas Southall Freeman, "Southern Perplexities: An Address for the Institute of Arts & Sciences of Columbia University [October 23, 1935]" (MS in Douglas Southall Freeman Papers, Library of Congress), 16.

richer liquid than the thin stuff to be found in latter-day men. Those times were histrionic; men stepped forward as if into a pageant, not into a trap of economic and social forces over which they had no control. Glowing significance shone from the smallest gesture.

Lee never betrayed the pledge to fill each gesture with perfect heroism and propriety. He was the classic heroic character on American soil. There was about Lee the seamless, whole, and instantaneous nature of the hero, and that quality radiated outward to bond the hero to his people and each individual beneath him to the others. There is no wonder, then, that some who revered Lee resorted to a comparison with Jesus Christ.[5] Freeman seems to have resisted deifying Lee, but the preternatural and religious aspects of his "Southern Arthur" were, in Freeman's writings, as indisputable as the dates and sites of Lee's battles.

Freeman does recognize some blemishes in the character of Lee, but neither singly nor in sum do these shortcomings mar the sainthood of the hero whose birthday is a "personal holyday" for the lucky few who partake of Virginian ancestry. According to Freeman, Americans of all sections could tap Lee's unifying heroism by acclaiming him, in the shambles of the Great Depression, as the Moses who could lead them out of the bondage of economic failure.[6]

The figures of southern heroes that Freeman sees fulfilled in Lee counsel certain virtues and attitudes, which, were we all to emulate the model, would result in the perfected human society. Lee's major virtue, the cornerstone of this social perfection, is "self-mastery"; from within the capsule of heroic selfhood, Lee controlled every facet of his life. He pledged to us the same power to triumph over the vicissitudes of history, to abolish ambiguity and contingency. Lee, for example, drew up his will twenty-four years before his death and changed not a syllable.

5. See, for one example among many, John Warwick Daniel, *Robert Edward Lee, An Oration Pronounced at the Unveiling of the Recumbent Figure at Lexington, Virginia, June 28, 1883* (Savannah, Ga., 1883).
6. Douglas Southall Freeman, "The Lengthening Shadow of Lee: An Address Before a Joint Session of the General Assembly of Virginia [January 20, 1936]" (MS in Freeman Papers), 1, 12–13.

Thus was he commander of fate. Ambiguity arising from the clash of opposing moral viewpoints never troubled Lee. In him the essence of the Episcopal religion blended with the noblesse oblige of his class to render "every problem of his life into right and wrong."[7]

Freeman finds Lee so perfectly self-sufficient that he defies analysis. "Those who look at him through the glamour of his victories or seek deep meaning in his silence labor in vain to make him appear complicated. His language, his acts, and his personal life were simple for the unescapable reason that he was a simple gentleman." Freeman portrays Lee as impregnable against modern assaults upon the wholeness of his person. Investigators using psychology or psychoanalysis, Freeman implies, will find no gaps. "Robert Lee was one of the small company of great men in whom there is no inconsistency to be explained, no enigma to be solved. What he seemed, he was—a wholly human gentleman, the essential elements of whose positive character were two and two only, simplicity and spirituality."[8]

In an age when Americans were rapidly learning how fragmented their individual and social lives actually were, Lee was summoned as the figure of stasis. He was preferable, as hero, to competing figures of modern man. Dreiser's Clyde Griffiths, for example, flew apart because of hormonal storms and unstable family and economic circumstances; his demise enacted man's nonheroic fate in a determined universe. Steinbeck's Joad family might have survived waves of economic hardship, but not for one instant did they see the face of their oppressor. Lee stood for the simple, the positive, and the whole that would abolish the bewilderment of modern man as victim. Life was not a dark corridor in which individual or nation blundered from one disaster to the next. The hero had returned to show us how to live a life in perpetual light. Southerners, Virginians especially, had known this truth in their cultural marrow for two centuries and generously stood ready to donate once again to national salvation.

7. Douglas Southall Freeman, *R. E. Lee: A Biography* (New York, 1934), I, 452; IV, 503.
8. *Ibid.*, IV, 501, 494.

Freeman stresses the outreaching power of the heroic figure. He insists that from the surface inward, Lee is consistent and clear. The clarity radiates outward as well, for Lee's character was "naturally sociable."[9] The heroic self requires and sustains the subsidiary bodies of society that orbit about him. This heroic gravitational field is a staple of nineteenth-century southern narrative, where it vies with battlefield action for pride of place in narrative structure. Freeman's *R. E. Lee* adds confirmation, if it is needed, that this belief in the hero's socially unifying presence is an integral part of the southern myth of cultural preeminence in modern times. Slurs of medievalism, which Tate and other modern southerners fought off, are not, from this perspective, simply gratuitous. The pattern of heroic behavior prominent in southern narrative and biography was last seen in medieval times, and readers attuned to such patterns will readily acknowledge the direct bloodlines from Chevalier Bayard to the eternal southern hero.

Freeman, like all of Lee's biographers, devotes a great deal of space to Lee's forebears. The closer one reaches the splendid past, the stronger is one's case for natural heroism. The heroic figure is not an accident in history, tossed up randomly from a chaos of genetic and environmental factors. He is necessary; his very existence is a token of meaning in the universe and a symbol of what Simpson calls "the value of cultural wholeness." Lee, on his mother's side, was connected with the Carter clan of Virginia—"the best endowment for greatness that he could have had in the Virginia of his day." The Carters not only had a tangible fortune, they possessed the treasure of pure blood. "Kinsmen were joined in marriage until the lines are at some points confused. The prime family characteristic of geniality and friendliness seemed to be accentuated with each new generation. The size and endogamy of the Carter tribe made it socially self-contained. Every true Carter liked everybody, but most of all he liked his kinspeople." A similar purity and social consistency marked the Lees. "Back to Richard the immigrant, whose wife's family name is unknown, there was not one instance in which a direct progenitor of Lee mated with a woman of blood and sta-

9. *Ibid.*, IV, 500.

tion below his own. His line was not crossed in a century and a half with one that was degenerating."[10]

The heroic figure is stamped with relentless familiarity. The pattern of endogamous mating is stressed in nineteenth-century southern narrative, even when there is little or no fictional necessity for it. Freeman lends the pattern the authority of history, for it already bears the conviction of myth. Lee's existence witnesses the primacy of myth over history through the actuality of the hero.

Freeman approaches the brink of arguing that Lee is the model of proper eugenics. He boldly claims in the biography that "eugenically, his [Lee's] career is perhaps, above all, a lesson in the cumulative effect of generations of wise marriage." In an address on the occasion of the dedication of Lee's home, Stratford, as a public memorial, Freeman echoed this theme.

> Bound up with this cornerstone of family here at Stratford was the second, essential to its support, the cornerstone of wise marriage. Two years ago, the hope was expressed on this very spot that Stratford most properly could include a library on genetics, as distinguished from genealogy, for there is no home in America where the value of wise mating is better exemplified than here. In the annals of the Lees for three centuries there was only one marital scandal and, so far as I know, not one divorce. For six generations after the emergence of the Lee family in America there were not more than two or three instances where it could be said that the Lees married persons who were not of equal blood and station with themselves. The result was the steady maintenance of the physical stamina and intellectual vigor of the stock for generations until its perfect flowering in one of the greatest human beings of modern times, Robert E. Lee.[11]

Wise mating is, Freeman implies, both a mark and an obligation of the heroic figure. The hero is a husband in a double sense. Literally, he marries a woman of his station and becomes husband to her. Figuratively, he is husband to a cumulative treasure of genetic accomplishments and features. He carries this

    10. *Ibid.*, I, 26, 25; IV, 425.
    11. *Ibid.*, I, 164; Douglas Southall Freeman, "The Cornerstones of Stratford: An Address at the Dedication of Stratford [October 12, 1935]" (MS in Freeman Papers), 7.

cultural treasure as the Ark carried the word of Yahweh. The
hero's person is culturally sacred, for it iconologically figures the
people's holy self-image, the promise of purity and perfect familiarity. Everything that can happen in such a heroic world is already known in the hero's genes. The wise-mating argument
maintains that heroes exist only if and as they are bred by vigi-
lance and monitored over generations. In the end, Freeman
holds that America will be saved by just this heroic figure and the
inward and outward patterns of control that radiate from him.

As a specimen of selective breeding, Lee is as near to physical
perfection as the hero can be. At age twenty-two, when he grad-
uated from West Point, Lee was five feet ten and one-half inches
tall—a few inches above the average height for American males
well into the twentieth century. "His hair was ebon and abundant, with a wave that a woman might have envied." He bore
himself with dignity and restraint. Freeman quotes from a contemporary description of Lee, "evidently [by] a fellow-cadet,"
that matches the heroic silhouette so often found in the iconology of nineteenth-century southern narratives: "His personal
appearance surpassed in manly beauty that of any cadet in the
corps. Though firm in his position and perfectly erect, he had
none of the stiffness so often assumed by men who affect to be
very strict in their ideas of what is military. His limbs, beautiful
and symmetrical, looked as though they had come from the
turning lathe, his step was elastic as if he spurned the ground
upon which he trod." [12]

The figure of the hero pivotal to earlier narratives is clearly
visible in the flesh-and-blood Lee, resurrected for modern homage by Freeman. This particular heroic figure functions significantly in a pageant in which history has brought us to the ultimate failure of a romantic-democratic image of the self and of
the doctrines of progress, science, and industrialism. We are
"dissociated" men, as Tate would have it. The figure of the
southern hero has the power to banish this malformation, modern man, but only if it is firmly lodged in the popular mind and
heart. Evidently the people craved the icon, for the four volumes
of R. E. Lee sold astonishingly well for such a massive work.

12. Freeman, R. E. Lee, I, 84–85, 68.

There was little dissenting criticism about Freeman's image of Lee. There had, in fact, been little dissent about Lee since the attempts of Federal propagandists to stigmatize him as a self-serving slaveowner. What dissent there has been seems to run in the channel carved by T. Harry Williams' critique of Freeman's accomplishment soon after the latter's death in the early 1950s. Williams, a historian of empirical rather than mythic stripe, faulted Freeman for being too much like his subject: both were Virginians and Christian gentlemen. This identification, Williams pointed out, induced Freeman to be more forgiving of Lee than the facts might have warranted. Facts, however, have never been potent charms in the presence of the heroic.[13]

Allen Tate, who did not discover until he was thirty that he had not been born in Virginia, did not fault Freeman for his identification with the epitome of all Virginians and of all white, Christian warrior-heroes. He acknowledged Freeman's work as the definitive life of Lee.[14] This was not an empty compliment, for Tate had begun a biography of the greatest southern hero in 1930, soon after the publication of his book on Jefferson Davis. The work on Lee was never completed, however; Tate more or less abandoned the manuscript in the late summer of 1931. But he did not soon stop thinking about the southern heroic and its implication for the modern age. As Simpson pointed out, the heroic attempt to recover the historical and mythic South was a major part of Tate's lifework.

Tate's extraordinarily adept intellect provided him with a steady supply of provocative insights into the historical and cultural significance of southern heroic images. In fact, so fertile was Tate's mind on that subject that the one fault he did locate in Freeman's *Lee* was the Virginian biographer's "lack of historical imagination." He gave Freeman praise for standing high and mostly dry above the Pagean tide of "genteel defeatism of the Reconstruction generation." But merely avoiding one problem was not enough to satisfy Tate's insistent mind. Freeman should

13. T. Harry Williams, "Freeman, Historian of the Civil War: An Appraisal," in *The Selected Essays of T. Harry Williams* (Baton Rouge, 1983), 185–94.

14. Allen Tate, "The Definitive Lee," *New Republic*, December 19, 1934, p. 171.

have correctly gauged the political and economic echoes of the war, not only its mythic and religious import. "The South fought against rising capitalism," Tate explained, "and risen capitalism, crushing both agriculture and its own labor, creates the crisis today."[15] In other words, Tate's "times," the period of American history with which he felt most fully engaged, spanned an age that saw the demise of the hero as man of action and awaited the hero as man of letters. The hero that Tate would eventually represent in his own life and work would be an amalgam of the southern hero of the narrative tradition and the modern man of fragmentation. The ideological certainty upon which Freeman stood for his contemplation of Lee and the southern heroic figure had vanished from Tate's geography; his "Ode to the Confederate Dead" is aimed at the moment when this grounding irrevocably vanishes. Yet the form of this consciousness remains, in memory and in the models of history. The modern hero as man of letters shuttles between both poles; his normal state is a passionate tolerance of incompleteness. Tate forged the hero as man of letters out of this ambivalence and thus made a bridge from his vision of the South's past to his vision of its fate in the maw of the modern.

Stonewall Jackson: The Good Soldier (1928) and *Jefferson Davis: His Rise and Fall* (1929) were Tate's first steps toward "the true source of the South's history in the ancient heroic society." *Stonewall Jackson* is further subtitled *A Narrative* and is notable for Tate's experimentation with a point of view coincident with Jackson's own. Tate wrote to Davidson, a true believer in the empirical recovery of the past, explaining the nature of his biographical technique: "If I were intending to write a literal, technical account of Jackson's career, I wouldn't write it! . . . I am going to try to give it the unity of a novel by passing it through Jackson's own mind."[16] From Davidson, who had been to the recent war in Europe, Tate borrowed the particulars of the battlefield. The central objective, however, Jackson's own mind, was to be won through Tate's own unassisted imaginative drive. If that mind

15. *Ibid.*, 172.
16. Simpson, Foreword, Tate to Davidson, May 13, 1927, both in Young and Fain (eds.), *The Literary Correspondence of Davidson and Tate*, xviii, 203.

could be known, the abyss between a dead past and the unstable modern present might be spanned.

Jackson is, then, lean on historical analysis and rich with authorial technique. The motif of Jackson's "fierce revery," for instance, is repeated several times to stitch the narrative into a whole cloth. For the larger elements of Jackson's character, Tate accepts material at hand. Jackson was formed by his uncle's "English yeoman" outlook, as decorated by visions of heroism limned by Weems's life of Washington and other colonial Virginian models. Psychologically, Jackson was, as were all antebellum southern males, a unified man. Tate mocks the modern's attempts to fathom the depths of a man such as Stonewall: "Perhaps he had an inferiority complex; perhaps his glands needed attention; it was likely that some of his religious ideas, under psycho-analysis, would reveal very, very significant complexes. It was certainly a quaint idea that, above all other earthly ends, the independence of Virginia stood first. . . . So the talk ran." [17] This Jackson is not reducible to his parts; he sends the fashionable modern on his way. He is a figure of integral consciousness; in him, idea is one with gesture. He leaves no shadows. Tate dwells on what he considers to be Jackson's ability to see the world as a whole. This hero had visions, not thoughts, and his visions omitted nothing they might encompass; like Arnold's cultural hero, he always saw life whole. The absence of thought in Jackson's mind left Tate the biographer little to do, so he devoted several pages to heroic figures with ideas: Calhoun, Jefferson Davis, even—at this distance—Lee. Jackson, as a literalist, ultimately rests in Tate's work as a primitive man. He is not the vehicle that the heroic man of letters can steer toward and over the abyss of dissociation.

In *Jefferson Davis,* Tate fully exercises the ideological possibilities of Confederate biography in modern America. In this work, Tate uses the southern figure to carry the man of letters toward his "engagement with modernity." Tate sees Davis as an ideologue suffering from the modern plague, a strain of the "dissociation of sensibility" that Tate and many who shared his convictions saw as the besetting modern disease. Davis suffered from the separa-

17. Allen Tate, *Stonewall Jackson: The Good Soldier* (New York, 1928), 111.

tion of his intellect from his feeling. Tate sees him, therefore, as a prototype of the modern southerner, "emotionally undeveloped," unable to connect with his land and people on the immediate level of the blood. To have been an integral human person, Davis would have had to enjoy the holistic consciousness Freeman described in Lee. In such a person, action is automatic and socially infallible; no gesture disturbs inward or outward equilibrium. But Davis "had not gained any discipline over his feelings, for this comes by adversity or by long training to a traditional ideal," neither of which were a part of Davis' background.[18] So Davis could have been, and according to Tate was, ripped apart by the power of the *idea* of Union on one hand—affection for which made Davis a good U.S. senator, Tate says—and the supraconscious concrete local fact of land and birth and lineage on the other. Virginians, like Lee, possessed both as a sort of birthright. Others, like Calhoun, miraculously achieved the welding of the two through intellectual power. But Davis, the image of the modern wayfarer, could not accomplish the fusion. He could never find his place in the southern paradigm and so was an ineffective leader. Tate finds Davis' wanderings in the last twenty-four years of his life (1865 to 1889) the perfect image of an anticlimactic life that could only fall into fragments and fail to close.

Davis represented for Tate the perfect example of the creeping mentality of industrialism that, by the 1930s, had a death grip on Western civilization. The symptoms were evident in the restlessness of Davis' father, who moved from Fairview, Kentucky, to the larger and richer lands in the Natchez territory. For a person of Tate's acutely Agrarian mentality, the lesson teaches itself. Westward expansion in the first decades of the nineteenth century, glamorized as the pioneer spirit, is actually no more than the progressive, acquisitive spirit of industrialism described by Ransom in "Reconstructed by Unregenerate," his contribution to *I'll Take My Stand*. A deeply self-divided and dissociated mind, such as Davis', was a more suitable metaphor for the modern malaise than was Jackson's. So Tate used Davis for a thorough discourse on the trends in modern industrial consciousness that

18. Allen Tate, *Jefferson Davis: His Rise and Fall* (New York, 1929), 12, 68.

had brought on the Civil War and were still operating in nefarious and ill-omened ways.[19]

The challenge, as Tate imaged it in "Ode to the Confederate Dead," is for the modern to project himself into the seamless consciousness that predates the hegemony of industrialism and alienation, specifically the communal mind of those who never knew what Davis knew, who never knew the restlessness, who saw their lives as insignificant before the altar of land and people attended by the order of priests under Lee. These people charged up Cemetery Ridge to certain death because life bereft of that order of reality was no real alternative. They could not stand outside themselves and watch the historical forces that had snared them. As fruitful as the work on Davis had been, then, embracing that consciousness was embracing one's own mind. Davis was a modern. To understand him still left the man of letters barred from heroic knowledge.

There was something Promethean in Tate's attempt to write about Lee's life. Diverted from the titular subject of *Jackson,* Tate had shown signs of interest in "one of the great men of all time." The Lee he saw from the distance of the Jackson work was "almost God," a hero whose chief gift was "Godlike omniscience" that paradoxically made him less viable as a soldier than were subordinates such as Jackson and Longstreet, who were great warriors but not also great men.[20] To write the biography of God is to snatch the divine fire, and Tate determined to risk it. If he could accomplish an understanding of Lee, who understood the reasons for the war and simultaneously made a perfect choice for Virginia, the concrete local fact, and against the abstraction, the Union, he could show the way out of the modern dilemma.

His friends cheered him on with something more intense than the usual encouragement for newly undertaken work. Late in July, 1931, when Tate's energy for the heavenly ascent was flagging, Davidson prodded him: "But I won't hear to your letting-up on Lee; no matter what torture, you must do that

19. Paul Buck, "American Heresies," *Hound & Horn,* VI (January-March, 1933), 357–67. Buck points to Tate's obvious debt to Christopher Hollis, *The American Heresy* (London, 1927), which figures prominently in the epilogue to *Jefferson Davis.*
20. Tate, *Stonewall Jackson,* 254.

book." Other friends—Warren, Ransom, Mark Van Doren—wrote that summer begging for news. As early as June, 1931, however, Tate had confessed to John Peale Bishop that "the Davis book was relatively a success, but the Lee is a failure."[21] It was something more than a failure of interest; Tate knew that he had reached a limit to the modern's imagination.

Many circumstances contributed to the failure of the work on Lee. One element of the mosaic was Tate's discovery of an ideological abyss between himself and the font of southern heroic. Focusing on this difference enables us to view the tradition from an angle that throws light backward into the previous century of literary productions as well as forward, not only to Tate's own novel, *The Fathers*, but beyond, to the writers who followed. "With Lee," Bishop wrote, "you have a most difficult subject. There seems to be no drama, no conflict within the man. Of course, I don't know the material as you do, in fact, know it but slightly. And then, our attention has always been fixed on Lee in his maturity and age. There must have been a conflict necessary to achieve his apparent success (in fulfilling his form) and even in maturity he must at moments have revealed the incompletion of his character." Bishop carried on probably the fullest correspondence with Tate on Lee and the process of writing the biography. Write the life of Lee, Bishop argued, as Renan wrote the life of Jesus: set aside factual history and the rule of objectivity. "So, if you write the life of the Southerner (yourself, myself, all of us) in terms of Lee so much more it will be than a life of Lee."[22] Bishop and Tate agreed that writing about Lee was writing not biography but autobiography and was not so much personal as communal. Bishop, in effect, counseled Tate to allow himself to respond to the heroic presence in a pattern deeply inscribed in southern narrative. Tate's willingness or capacity to make that surrender is the crucial point.

21. Davidson to Tate, July 29, 1931, in Young and Fain (eds.), *The Literary Correspondence of Davidson and Tate*, 264; Allen Tate to John Peale Bishop, n.d. [early June, 1931], in Thomas Daniel Young and John J. Hindle (eds.), *The Republic of Letters in America: The Correspondence of John Peale Bishop and Allen Tate* (Lexington, Ky., 1981), 26.
22. Bishop to Tate, June 24, 1931, n.d. [October 19–26, 1932], both in Young and Hindle (eds.), *The Republic of Letters*, 38–39, 65.

For Tate, the difficulty became personal and social, historical and timeless.

> You are right about the problem of Lee. I have worried about it in precisely the terms you speak of it in. I have a few gray hairs behind my ears which even now begin to show in the prevailing blondness. I am not really concerned about the effect of the book on our sensitive compatriots, except that I should vaguely hope that it might do them good. The whole Southern incapacity for action since 1895 is rationalized in the popular conception of Lee. It is time this was broken down. . . . Lee did not love power; my thesis about him, stated in these terms, is that he didn't love it because he was profoundly cynical of all action for the public good. He could not see beyond the needs of his own salvation, and he was not generous enough to risk soiling his military cloak for the doubtful salvation of others. I personally feel very much this way; but then I am not at the head of a large army and I have no political position. You know Lee pretended all along that he had no connection with politics—a fiction that won him applause because it seemed to mean that he was above intrigue; but no man should be above the right kind of intrigue. This is what I feel about Lee. Yet is it true? That is what keeps me awake at night. I can't "prove" a word of it. Of course the facts do not in the least prove the current notion of him: they don't prove one thing or another. But the facts have got into an emotional association with a certain conception of his character which will be very difficult to break down. That brings up a formal problem. To be most effective my treatment should be direct and cumulative, not argumentative; yet I am obliged to show that the popular notion is not inevitably true. I can't just assume that it is false. But I could go on forever. And I always ask: Is it true? On what ground do I think so? I can't answer that, and it worries me.[23]

Tate found himself faced with a hydra of questions: the nature of the fact in history, the enormous esteem with which Lee was cherished by his region, the cynical side of the supremely social and integral man that Lee seems to have been in the orthodox southern paradigm. Add to these the personally supercharged significance of the project. Letter after letter reminded Tate that

23. Tate to Bishop, October 19, 1932, *ibid.*, 64–65.

people he knew and respected were awaiting his retrieval of the essential ideas of southern history in times of crisis. It is little wonder that Tate lost sleep.

Like almost all biographers of Lee, Tate retreated to the ancestors for the beginning, for in the generations that preceded the southern Arthur (in the acts of generation themselves, *pace* Freeman) were the sources and conditions that made him. Tate does not share Freeman's literal assumption that breeding made Lee, but he does argue that a legacy of closely defined kin and kind was Robert Lee's birthright. Seventeenth- and eighteenth-century Virginian concepts of property and wealth seem to Tate to be the deep soil that nourished Lee at the time of the crumbling of the stable agrarian order in the nineteenth. Working still on the political and economic theses he had advanced in *Jefferson Davis,* Tate speculates that for Richard Lee, the immigrant, capitalism had not yet polluted property or the idea of ownership. "Order and stability and repose were the chief values of Richard Lee's society, and except for the Scotch traders who later built the towns of Alexandria and Fredericksburg, Virginian property existed not primarily for profit, but secondarily for that ·purpose, so that in the first place property could be enjoyed."[24]

In Tate's view, property, like Adam, was at one time innocent and morally untainted. Ownership had not always corrupted man, as Faulkner would argue in *Go Down, Moses.* Furthermore, the property of this early, premodern Lee was also, perhaps even primarily, metaphorical. Just as its boundaries were stable, its surfaces in repose, its outlines orderly, so also was the idea of the life the early Lees led. Richard Lee's estate "was to be carried on intact, not as source of abstract profits, but as an undivided whole for the protection and enjoyment of his descendants. This is the foundation of the Southern tradition, for which the greatest of all the Lees fought."[25]

Placing property and wealth beyond the reach of any system involving profit served the immediate needs of the Agrarian manifesto. If, as Tate believed, this reactionary theory of prop-

24. Allen Tate, "Lee" (MS in Allen Tate Papers, Princeton University Library, Princeton), 10.
25. *Ibid.,* 10–11.

erty were correct, a man of Richard Lee's time and station must have felt himself to be integral with his estate, free from the smoldering threat of acquisitiveness. Apropos of this point, Tate explains that in the Virginian's mind, there were two obligations toward one's property: to preserve it and to defend the system that enabled innocent possession. "No man," Tate argues, "was obligated to increase his estate."[26]

In the Agrarian scheme, land must be kept apart from the capitalistic system. Once it was metonymically linked with cash, hard goods, raw materials, and other mundane things as elements in an economy of history, land would be sapped of its saving mystique. That mystique produced the opposite of fragmentation, analysis, and dialectic. *Intact* is the key word in Tate's explanation. For Freeman, the intactness was transported in the blood of the Lees, but the idea is nevertheless the same. Both biographers placed wholeness at the empirical and abstract core of Lee's being.

Thus far, Robert E. Lee gives Tate little trouble. But a species of the problem that stymies the modern man in "Ode to the Confederate Dead" rises up to block the biographer. Tate adumbrates his dissatisfaction with the greatest southern hero:

> Could one but penetrate to the heart of the Lee family at this period [immediately after Lighthorse Harry Lee's death], one would see the beginnings of the almost inhuman impersonality [the word *personality* is crossed out in the manuscript] of the youngest son, who seems to have got out of his early life nothing but character, which seems less to live than to find infallibility its appropriate part. From the earliest trivial anecdotes of Robert's boyhood, we are struck by the fact that he never quite participated in any human situation, but rather moved in it untouched, and came out of it a living criticism of other men and, at his best moments, as we shall see, of all men. It is this quality, perhaps, that made Lee the most perfect and the most mysterious of men.[27]

Not surprisingly, Tate begins to view Lee as the type Davis could never be. Whereas the president of the Confederacy was

26. *Ibid.*, 23.
27. *Ibid.*, 27.

fragmented and incomplete, the commanding general of the
Army of Northern Virginia was an impregnable whole, a catalyst
in all human situations. The seamless selfhood of Lee, after
Tate's initial admiration dies down, becomes a barrier to successful biography. Tate tries to write himself across or through the
wall, but, as the following passage shows, he ultimately finds
himself on the outside, where he started:

> Lee had no parts, from the day he was born: he was born a per-
> fect specimen of human integration. And so it is impossible for
> any analyst to say that this influence did that with him, or this
> other threw him into a military career. All influences worked to-
> gether as one on a mind that constantly reformed and controlled
> them. He was so complete a character that his capacity for action
> mystifies us until we reflect that his repose and seeming passivity,
> his perfection in inactivity, was typical of him, was as much Lee, as
> The Wilderness Campaign. In whatever position he found him-
> self he was always completely Lee, and by an infallible instinct he
> avoided those situations that might make demands upon him
> which would take him out of his true character.[28]

What begins as Lee's laudable integrity and repose soon becomes his cold and impassable supremacy. So aloof does Lee
become, for Tate, that the biographer uses the word *inhuman* to
describe him. The word appears in the discussion of Lee's courtship of Mary Custis. Freeman, as we have seen, warmed up to the
subject of wise mating among generations of the Lee and Custis
clans. To Tate, however, the "formidable austerity" of the mating
custom afforded Lee and Custis nothing akin to human emotion. Freeman extolled the pure, controlled product of these
rigidly prescribed rites. But Tate more or less abandons Lee at
this point:

> It is possible that the whole sexual basis of marriage was in Lee's
> case too easily assumed; which means that the precarious basis of
> life in a vast background of contingency was shut out of his mind.
> He was a man who found himself completely in realizing the con-
> ventional forms, in purifying and raising their meaning; he could
> not, however great the need, betray his proper role. And so, in his
> courtship and marriage, he must have been tender and sympa-

28. *Ibid.*, 30.

thetic, but lacking in those little violations of self-control, of perfect demeanor, which distinguish a lover from an abstraction.[29]

A few pages later the biography terminates. Several of Tate's
correspondents urged him to continue, flattering him with claims
that if he were not to interpret southern character and history,
no one could do it adequately. Bishop suggested that Tate, with
the work on Lee behind him, "undertake a political and social
history of the U.S. . . . I don't mean, of course, a factual history;
but an account of the essential ideas and forces that have made
our life, a concentration on the important decisions, a revalua-
tion of the conventional historical values."[30] Time after time,
Tate's contemporaries told him that his intellect functioned with
unsurpassed agility and incisiveness. He alone possessed the
splendid gifts of intellect and style that would resurrect the
southern heroic, place the past before the present as its guide,
and reinstate the tradition of southern thought at the vanguard
of American culture. Perhaps this honorific burden contributed
to the physical and emotional fatigue that led Tate to cast his
manuscript on Lee aside unfinished.

Tate's dedication to the matter of southern heroic originated beyond the boundaries of "factual history"; he was never comfortable among mere documents. Indeed, the pieces of a life were
less important to him than its overall design, which is the matter
of Tate's essays, poetry, and *The Fathers,* the novel in which he sal-
vaged much from his failed biography of Lee. For example, the
distinction between character and personality that Tate had
drawn in his attempt to fathom Lee, resurfaces in the differences
between Major Buchan and his son-in-law George Posey. Character is the bloodless adherence to custom, type, and the past;
personality is its opposite, the pure concentration in the self and
the unblemished present, leaving the individual, George Posey
for example, utterly defenseless against the relentless barrage of
everything and everyone that is not the self.[31] The formidable

29. *Ibid.,* 43. Louis D. Rubin, Jr., arrives at a similar judgment in *The Wary
Fugitives: Four Poets and the South* (Baton Rouge, 1978), 301.
30. Bishop to Tate, August 25, 1931, in Young and Hindle (eds.), *The Republic
of Letters,* 48.
31. Published criticism of *The Fathers* begins with an analysis of the dichot-

austerity and lack of human feeling that Tate imagines in Lee's courtship is counterpointed in *The Fathers* by the implicitly rich sexual relationship of George and Susan and is mirrored in the character and behavior of the major, who does nothing legions of his ancestors had not done. Lacy Buchan is called to both models of the self. His confusion—moral, sexual, social, familial—is the modern's besetting confusion, the operative state of dissociation scarcely distinguishable from one of Dante's infernal circles.

Caught, like Tate himself, between a vast background of contingency that is the world and its history, and the austere, formal, and "intact" tradition of his father, Lacy relives the dilemma faced by the author of the aborted "Lee." For all the veneration due Pleasant Hill, the concrete local fact in the lives of the Buchans, there is for Lacy its clear associations with death (the funeral of his mother, with which the novel opens), hypocrisy (the tournament at which Langton is drunk and Broadacre offers Lacy the mulatto girl under the pavilion where the white ladies sit), and the fatal inertia of custom (the peeling paint on the house and the major's stagnant husbandry).

Lacy indeed faces irreconcilable alternatives, since meaning and tradition have failed as guides. For example, the guidance of the blood has failed; Yellow Jim, George's half brother, shows Lacy that wise mating is a polite fiction, not a cherished fact. The perfect mate for Lacy, his sister-in-law Jane Posey, is also the object of his brother Semmes's desire. Jane's first question concerns death, not love. Their "innocent" first kiss brings guilt and emotional turmoil; Lacy seizes Jane's slipper and a piece of his mother's petticoat at the same time, thus conflating the objects of his desire. Long, unbroken celibacy for Lacy puts an end to the line of the fathers and paradoxically leaves Lacy's unfathered progeny free to make meaning where we will, or can. Lacy, like

omy of values represented by Major Buchan and George Posey. See Arthur Mizener, Introduction to *The Fathers*, by Allen Tate (Denver, 1960), ix–xix; Radcliffe Squires, *Allen Tate: A Literary Biography* (New York, 1971), 123–46; Thomas Daniel Young, *The Past in the Present: A Thematic Study of Modern Southern Fiction* (Baton Rouge, 1981), 47–64; and Richard Law, "Active Faith and Ritual in *The Fathers*," *American Literature*, LV (1983), 345–66.

all moderns, lives a fine replica of hell, yet there seems to be no trace of his unmitigated mortal sin. The figure of Lee was far from an antidote to this lostness; his presence aggravated the pain.

Freeman, even though he acknowledged a few faults in his paragon, was not dismayed with the saint that Lee had become. At every opportunity, Freeman held up the galvanizing image of masculine, Christian dignity and mastery over the vast background of contingency. The icon would, Freeman pledged, quell the troubled national waters and the private soul in the decade between the Crash and World War II and would bring America back to its heroic senses. As individuals and as a nation we need not drift into the abyss.

Tate, exploring the realm of essential ideas and forces, could see only doubles and paradoxes. He could see himself positioning an image of Lee, never the actual man, in the place of the concrete fact. And so he asked himself each time he thought he had reached a possible conclusion, "Is it true?" There was never an answer. Suspense, then, is the mode in which the modern, necessarily making a home in the abyss, must carry out his life. There are to be no answers, even for the dedicated but homeless spirit of the "Ode" who asks,

> What shall we say who have knowledge
> Carried to the heart? Shall we take the act
> To the grave? Shall we, more hopeful, set up the grave
> In the house? The ravenous grave?

In "Narcissus as Narcissus," Tate admits that there is nothing but natural death, not even a return to an "ironic vision of the heroes." Survival on whatever terms is all there is.[32]

No matter how much he ransacked the empirical leavings of Lee's heroic life, or how fretfully he examined his own capacity to connect with the generation of the heroes, Tate could not make the southern Arthur live up to the modern situation. Announcing the demise of the manuscript on Lee was a sort of confession to patricide or worse, since Lee was God's southern surrogate.

32. Allen Tate, *Collected Poems, 1919–1976* (New York, 1977), 22.

Davis, however, lived on stubbornly if ingloriously in his hold on Tate's imagination. The first stanza of Tate's elegy for Davis describes his uniquely modern fate.

> No more the white refulgent streets,
> Never the dry hollows of the mind
> Shall he in fine courtesy walk
> Again, for death is not unkind.

The Eliotic, modern echo is clear. Davis lived into the world of the wasteland, the prototype of the poet's own world of the post-war twenties. The past had died, and the survivors, like Tate, were denied any vital connection: "Our gain's the intellectual sound / Of death's feet round a weedy tomb." And Davis, enduring a Dantean hell, toils in the "back chambers of the State," relieved by no familial nurturing, no living roots in a time and place: "He who wore out the perfect mask / Orestes fled in night and day."[33]

In the elegy for Davis, Tate mourns for a tragically ambivalent figure, a modern born too soon who was fated to direct the actions of classical heroes—most of them Virginians, and Davis a Mississippian from Kentucky—in a great enterprise that Davis could see clearly but not simply or heroically. Masks that served the heroes wore out on Davis, who was exposed, implicated, like Lacy, like Orestes, in a species of patricide.

33. Allen Tate, "Elegy, Jefferson Davis: 1808–1889," in *Collected Poems*, 176–77. "Elegy" closely resembles a shorter poem, "Euthanasia," dated 1919 in *Collected Poems*, which was published in slightly different form in *Double Dealer*, III (May, 1922), 262.

VI

Faulkner's Pierrotic Hero: Stranger in Yoknapatawpha

And would it have been worth it, after all . . .
—T. S. Eliot
"The Love Song of J. Alfred Prufrock"

The answer to the epigraph's question, in chorus, is no; the old heroic engines sputter, and Prufrock forfeits the name of action. The accumulated catastrophes of World War I account for a large measure of the cultural numbing that afflicts William Faulkner's heroes. For the writers, and aspiring writers, of the modernist period, the theme of inaction and the cultivation of numbness as an escape from the lessons of the trenches were common property. The Somme only confirmed, in a vivid and ghastly way, symptoms already visible in the previous decade and more of Western literature. In a universe of purely mechanical or biological processes, no action guaranteed meaning—the human race was trapped "in certain half-deserted streets" with no more than half a memory of the way out.

This is familiar, even trite, prologue. But to the apprentice Faulkner, about whom we read more and more, the modernist stance gave definition to the struggle against parents and ancestors whose traditions had become the self-defeating, self-confronting arguments of insidious intent. Quentin Compson escapes in suicide, as does Bayard Sartoris. Joe Christmas is likewise released in death. Only Isaac McCaslin lives a long, if not happy, life; at his end, however, he must confront himself as the image of his own evil grandfather.

Between the young Faulkner, born in 1897 and ambivalently

identified with the new century, and the social and narrative modes of his acting, heroic past there could be no commerce without a figural broker. This broker was Pierrot, a figure that Judith Sensibar has traced in its American—primarily Aiken-esque—manifestation in Faulkner's early poetry. It seems likely, however, that the young Faulkner had absorbed more of the pierrotic sensibility than the formal aspects he admired in Aiken's poetry and that Pierrot led Faulkner to more than the discovery of the unreliable narrator.[1] In Pierrot he found a literary figure malleable enough to endure both suicide and ironic survival. Faulkner partnered the *fin-de-siècle* Pierrot with the southern heroic, and that strange hybrid enabled the difficult continuity in Faulkner's work from apprenticeship to *Go Down, Moses*.

Given the momentum of this study, the reader can probably anticipate the significant elements of my beginning regarding Faulkner. The accumulated force of the southern heroic tradition played a role in shaping Faulkner's narrative technique. This role is not always central, nor always unmediated. Early in his writing career, before he took possession of Yoknapatawpha, Faulkner seemed determined to avoid native material. His youthful attraction to *fin-de-siècle* French romanticism, full of moon-glow, fauns, nymphs, Pierrots, and Columbines, seemed a rather flamboyant rebellion against the aesthetic, moral, and social consensus of his time and place. But, if Shreve McCannon is right in saying that the South is as theatrical as *Ben-Hur*, then perhaps Faulkner's aesthete phase is not unusual.

As studies of the early work of Faulkner, especially those of Sensibar, have shown, his residence in the literary milieu of Stephane Mallarmé, Paul Verlaine, Oscar Wilde, Aubrey Beardsley, Algernon Swinburne, and the weaker decadent lights was serious and concentrated. Nor was attraction to these writers and artists peculiar to Faulkner. A generation of American poets (including Hart Crane, T. S. Eliot, Conrad Aiken, and Wallace Stevens), who were likewise taken up in the cloud of the pierrotic aesthetic, bayed after Laforgue and his "pallid sect" of *poètes pierrotiques*.

1. Judith L. Sensibar, *The Origins of Faulkner's Art* (Austin, Tex., 1984), 195. Sensibar's discussion of the influence of Aiken is concentrated in Chap. 7.

The figure of Pierrot was and perhaps still is the gravitational center of a system of images, attitudes, allusions, and style that collided, in Faulkner's case, with the heroic aesthetic of his community and narrative tradition. This collision precipitated literary works with peculiar markings. James Branch Cabell's *Jurgen*, for example, gets its particular ironies from the clash of the traditional southern heroic and the irreverent, skeptical attitude the decadents made notorious. Faulkner paid homage to this temperament in *Mayday*, his own ironic quest tale.

The shock of modernism among southern writers took many forms in the 1920s, the decade when Faulkner made his first progress in literature. More, and increasingly intense, attention is being brought to bear on the young Faulkner in a concerted attempt to account for the great works in his earlier phase. Virginia Hlavsa posits a stylistic and structural theory: at a certain point that separates early from middle, romantic from modernist, Faulkner consciously chose the modernist fictional technique.[2] Other critics, such as Jay Martin, David Minter, and Judith Bryant Wittenberg, opt for a more psychological explanation: Faulkner was intermittently aware of a "dark twin" with whom he had to come to grips before he could be free to write his great work. Even after liberation, traces of the dark twin can be found; Faulkner's fiction is always divided against itself.[3]

Cleanth Brooks espouses a less elaborate view, stressing the accessible, positive aspects of Faulkner's early reading and writing. Brooks's young Faulkner was not so atypical as the one who harbored a dark twin. He had a great talent and some difficulty in dealing with it, but he emerged intact from the struggle. Cognizant of the variety of constructions put upon Faulkner's ap-

2. Virginia Hlavsa, "The Mirror, the Lamp, and the Bed: Faulkner and the Modernists," *American Literature*, LVII (1985), 23–43.

3. The phrase "dark twin" can be found in Faulkner's *Mosquitoes* (New York, 1927), 251. The context is a long conversation between Dawson Fairchild and the Semitic man on the nature of poetry and life. The phrase has also been used as the keynote of two recent psychobiographical interpretations of Faulkner's work: Judith Bryant Wittenberg, *Faulkner: The Transfiguration of Biography* (Lincoln, Neb., 1979), and David Minter, *William Faulkner: His Life and Work* (Baltimore, 1980). Jay Martin, in "'The Whole Burden of Man's History of His Impossible Heart's Desire': The Early Life of William Faulkner," *American Literature*, LIII (1982), 607–29, uses the concept of twinship but not the phrase "dark twin."

prentice work, Brooks has written: "Faulkner possessed a great natural gift. . . . But he definitely went through a period of growth and development which shows, among other things, a movement from a rather decadent Swinburnian romanticism to a robust acceptance of reality and a tough-minded appraisal of it." Brooks has named some of the forces that worked to bring Faulkner to health as writer and citizen. "His mythical county provided him with a social context in which what was healthiest in his romanticism could live in fruitful tension with his realistic and detailed knowledge of the men and manners of his own land."[4]

A close study of Faulkner's early period also discloses his attachment—healthy or unhealthy is for the reader to decide—to the pierrotic aesthetic. His first Yoknapatawpha novel, *Sartoris* (1929), is permeated with its figures and tonalities. Faulkner remained deeply concerned with elements of this aesthetic as late as 1942, when *Go Down, Moses* was published. Certainly Faulkner's fiction treats the social context of small towns in rural Mississippi; certainly he came to terms with his own family and his own tangled psyche through his fiction; and just as certainly, he accomplished none of these objectives without literary mediation from Pierrot.

Pierrot is the French version of the *commedia dell'arte* figure Pedrolino.[5] Pedrolino made his transition from Italian theatrical and carnival presentations to similar French appearances in the early eighteenth century. Watteau's "Italian Comedians" (*ca.* 1719) is one of the earliest pictorial representations of Pierrot in French art. Watteau's Pierrot is a mild, innocent, apparently defenseless male figure. Clad in his usual white blouse and baggy pants, Pierrot's blanched, saintly face stares with vacant benignity from Watteau's canvas. On Pierrot's left, a fashionable woman turns her face to Pierrot while her eyes hunt for the viewer. Beside her is another woman who gazes upward in curiosity at Pierrot. A male figure, from his costume and ebullient posture probably Harlequin, gestures as if to present Pierrot to the audience. On

---

4. Cleanth Brooks, *William Faulkner: First Encounters* (New Haven, 1983), 5; and *Toward Yoknapatawpha and Beyond* (New Haven, 1978), xi.
5. Robert F. Storey, *Pierrot: A Critical History of a Mask* (Princeton, 1978). My condensation of the pierrotic tradition is based in large part on Storey's study.

Pierrot's right, a figure strums a mandolin and lounges backward; assorted clowns smirk at Pierrot and compete for the attention of the audience. Farther to the right an amorous couple are just about to kiss. In Watteau's vision, Pierrot is the naïve, unmarked, perhaps stupid hub of a human universe that is particolored by folly, vice, and vanity, none of which, however, blemishes the white smock. Nor does disdain for his fellows crease the moonlike, placid face.

For several decades into the nineteenth century, Pierrot maintained this innocent or lunatic simplicity. (The success of Charlie Chaplin and the young Buster Keaton testify to the traditional Pierrot's popularity with twentieth-century audiences.) He never, or almost never, won the maid of his heart's desire, Columbine, nor was he ever justified in his gullibly high estimation of her virtue or character. Columbine, like the woman on Pierrot's left in Watteau's picture, always keeps an eye out for another admirer, another audience, while pretending to reserve her adoration for Pierrot alone. Columbine is not to be trusted, although she might be admired. She, like Defoe's Moll Flanders, is a lively survivor of the human shipwreck.

Toward midcentury, Théophile Gautier noticed a definite shift in associations emanating from the figure of Pierrot. The simpleton began to chafe at the insults and injustices of his role as victim and goat. In some plays, Gautier wrote, Pierrot gave the kicks instead of suffering them. "Pierrot, under the flour and the smock of the illustrious Bohemian, takes on an air of mastery and self-possession that is not customary for him; he deals out kicks and does not take any back; Harlequin hardly dares to beat him on the shoulders with his stick; Cassandra thinks twice before she slaps him."[6] Pierrot became formidable in midcentury. His former antagonists began to think twice before they cuffed him around.

As the generation of Mallarmé, Verlaine, and their younger confreres of the 1880s and 1890s took over French romanticism, Pierrot metamorphosed rapidly, assuming each nuance of the

6. Théophile Gautier, *Histoire de L'Art Dramatique en France Depuis Vingt-cinq Ans* (Paris, 1859), V, 25. Mentioned in Storey, *Pierrot*, 102. All translations of excerpts from Gautier are mine.

extreme romantic character. He became an alter ego for many artists, a kind of patron saint for their written works. Mallarmé, for example, saw the floured face as a blank sheet of paper, the receptive medium for whatever marks the poet was driven to make.[7]

With the French aesthetes, Laforgue foremost among them, Pierrot became notorious as a decadent. For his new wave of popularity, however, he paid with his former purity and innocence. Watteau's Pierrot would have blushed. In 1881, Paul Margueritte, Mallarmé's nephew, composed and performed a mime play called *Pierrot assassin de sa femme*, in which Mallarmé and a select audience watched Pierrot avenge himself on Columbine by tickling her to death. Columbine's offenses seem to have been less the actual charges listed in Margueritte's script—"She stole my money, drank my wine, beat my back, beat it hard; and as for my head . . . she furnished it with a little bit of hardware"—than Pierrot's revulsion at woman's sensual nature. At the opening of the play, before Pierrot enters, the audience sees a large portrait of Columbine, "fleshy, with naked breasts . . . laughing throatily."[8] Reenacting the murder, Pierrot is moved by "retrospective lust" for his wife. At the climax of Pierrot's psychotic remorse, Columbine's portrait comes to life and laughs at her victim. None of this highly seasoned misogyny was lost on Mallarmé, who was impressed by the symmetry with which Columbine dies in a spasm so much like the orgasm for which she lives.[9] *Pierrot assassin de sa femme* is an early manifestation of the misogyny, psychotic melancholy, and desperate trespass upon social mores that Pierrot was to carry out frequently at the end of the century.

J.-K. Huysmans and Léon Hennique also capitalized on the vogue for depraved Pierrots in 1881 with *Pierrot sceptique*, in which Pierrot, mourning for his dead Columbine, murders his tailor and flees with a shopwindow mannequin. 1881 was also the year that Verlaine, whose poems Faulkner translated, published *Sagesse*. Poem V of Book One opens with this stanza:

7. Stéphane Mallarmé, *Oeuvres Complètes* (Paris, 1945), 310.
8. Paul Margueritte, "Pierrot Murderer of his Wife," trans. Robert F. Storey, *Denver Quarterly*, XIII (Winter, 1979), 44, 41.
9. Jacques Derrida reads this in Mallarmé's *Mimique*. See "The Double Session" in *Disseminations*, trans. Barbara Johnson (Chicago, 1981).

Beauty of women, their weakness, and those pale
hands, which often do good and can do ill.
And those eyes where there's nothing animal, but
still enough to say "Enough" to the maddened
male.[10]

Suspicion and distrust of women, who entice men to sensual surrender only to leave them maddened and unfulfilled, is a dominant theme in *fin-de-siècle* poetry. The central relationship in this
theme, that of Pierrot and Columbine, forfeited most of its
rustic good humor in the poets Faulkner read. Most of these
poets saw the match of Pierrot and Columbine as woman's en-
trapment and betrayal of man, as man's servitude to a lesser creature, a being for whom animal imagery seemed suitable. Woman
stood for unreason and the natural cycle, extinguishable by
death; man stood for the vector of mind escaping the natural
into the immortality of art.

In the 1890s, Laforgue fashioned a pierrotic pattern of retreat from and hostility to "the social context." In Laforgue's
Pierrot fumiste, published posthumously, Pierrot forces Columbine to buy a pornographic magazine and then watch him per-
use it on their wedding night. Laforgue's Pierrot answers Columbine's sexual entreaties with high-browed impotence until, in a
whirlwind of passion that one critic has called "beefish lovemak-
ing," he finally consummates the marriage. The next day Pierrot
fumiste (con man) leaves Columbine and decamps for Egypt.
A. G. Lehmann has written of the symbolic extremes to which
Laforgue took Pierrot and conventional respect for women.
"Columbine—woman—is, to him [Laforgue], a relentless ma-
chine working out the laws of the Unconscious; Pierrot the fasci-
nated but entirely lucid victim, attempts both to participate and
to stand outside; to remain alive, 'a dupe,' and to stand outside,
'a dilettante.'"[11] The white pariahs named and led by Laforgue
resolved to overturn society and woman, for they worshiped artistic, not natural, ideals and sought a place in the essential realm
of the absolute idea, not in the cycle of womb and grave as thrall

10. Paul Verlaine, *Selected Poems*, trans. C. F. MacIntyre (Berkeley, 1948), 141.
11. Storey, *Pierrot*, 154; A. G. Lehmann, "Pierrot and Fin de Siècle," in Ian
Fletcher (ed.), *Romantic Mythologies* (New York, 1967), 217.

to the unconscious. Woman, to them, was the cycle of conception, gestation, birth, and death from which they fled in hor-
ror. As Faulkner's poems in *Vision in Spring* amply demonstrate,
the young poet had enlisted in the war against woman. Pierrot
would mockingly worship woman at every virgin's funeral, mo-
lest statues in the parks at night, profess love, and then whirl
away in a jig. His revulsion at Columbine ran deep.

> But ah, the fact that woman can
> Still take herself so seriously
> They cannot bear; they turn away
> Roaring with laughter like madmen.[12]

Young American poets of the new century worked "sous le
signe de Laforgue." Eliot, while an undergraduate at Harvard,
wrote "Humoresque" after him. Eliot's critics have commonly
recognized Prufrock as a version of Laforgue's Pierrot figure.
Malcolm Cowley, as commonsensical a man of letters as we have,
translated some of Laforgue's poems into English. Wallace Stevens used the pierrotic figure in poems such as "The Comedian
as the Letter C." Sensibar details Aiken's great debt to Laforgue.[13]

The literary and artistic atmosphere of the late nineteenth
and early twentieth centuries was saturated with pierrotic figures and sentiment. We have ample proof that Faulkner inhaled
the pierrotic air and found it invigorating. His illustrations for
campus publications at the University of Mississippi bear the
marks of Beardsley's influence; his translations of Verlaine and
Mallarmé testify to his familiarity with the French poets, even
though an inventory of his Rowan Oak library shows no titles by
either poet. His dream play, *The Marionettes,* written for the campus drama group of the same name, features the characters
Pierrot and Shade of Pierrot. Joseph Blotner has discovered
young Faulkner's favorable review of "Aria da Capo," a one-act
play by Edna St. Vincent Millay produced by the Provincetown

12. William Faulkner, *Vision in Spring,* ed. Judith L. Sensibar (Austin, Tex.,
1984), especially "The World and Pierrot. A Nocturne," 10–29, and "The
Dancer," 67–75; William Jay Smith, "The Clowns, by Jules Laforgue," *Poetry,*
LXXVIII (July, 1951), 210–15. These are translations of five of Laforgue's
poems under the group title "Pierrots" in *Poésies,* II (Paris, n.d.).

13. Storey, *Pierrot,* Chap. 6; Warren Ramsey, *Jules Laforgue and the Ironic Inheritance* (New York, 1953), Chap. 7; Sensibar, *The Origins of Faulkner's Art,* Chap. 7.

Players in their 1919–1920 season. "Aria da Capo" is a symbolic drama in which Pierrot and Columbine, gliding through foamy dialogue reminiscent of Anthony and Gloria in Fitzgerald's *The Beautiful and Damned,* rehearse a scene that is interrupted by Cothurnus, Masque of Tragedy. Cothurnus brings on two shepherds who proceed to quarrel in a decidedly unpastoral way over property and water rights. The shepherds ultimately murder each other, but Cothurnus orders that their bodies be left onstage under the table where Pierrot and Columbine resume their conversation about kisses and macaroons.[14]

The pierrotic aesthetic followed Faulkner away from Oxford. A handful of Laforguian poems appeared in *Double Dealer* in the early 1920s, when Faulkner was intermittently in New Orleans. Crane's translations of three poems by Laforgue appeared under the title "Locutions Des Pierrots" in May, 1922. The poems reiterate the sexual antipathy between Pierrot and woman. In the first poem, the poet addresses his "prodigal and wholly dilatory lady," who has withheld, out of "perverse austerities," the means to a "languor" Pierrot avidly desires. At the moment, now imminent, when that languor will flood Pierrot's soul, he knows the lady will look upon him with a face as "Bland as the wide gaze of a Newfoundland." He will have been duped by a female creature inimical to the fine, stylized, and artistic fulfillment to which he aspires.[15]

In the second poem, Pierrot again importunes the lady to grant him favors that a double entendre in the first two stanzas makes fairly clear.

> True, I nibble at despondencies
> Among the flowers of her domain
> To the sole end of discovering
> What is her unique propensity!
>
> ——Which is to be mine, you say?
> Alas, you know how much I oppose
> A stiff denial to postures
> That seem too much impromptu.[16]

14. Joseph Blotner, *William Faulkner's Library—A Catalogue* (Charlottesville, Va., 1964), 90–98; Edna St. Vincent Millay, *Three Plays* (New York, 1926).
15. Hart Crane, "Locutions Des Pierrots," *Double Dealer,* III (May, 1922), 261.
16. *Ibid.*

Stiff, the crucial word in the double entendre, is Crane's rendering of Laforgue's *formel,* which can mean "strict" or "formal" but lacks the sexual connotation of the English *stiff.* Crane uses Laforgue's Pierrot to explore the double victimization of Pierrot: woman scarcely needs the fulfillment the male desires, and Pierrot's own flesh unequivocally betrays his need by opposing a stiff denial to woman's unique propensity.

The third poem follows the same pattern. Pierrot begs favor from the lady, here called "Eve, Gioconda, Dalila." Should woman still withhold her favors, the supplicant, frustrated by the coy and cold female, will spill his seed in onanistic protest:

> Oh, by the infinite circumflex
> Of the archbeam of my cross-legged labours,
> Come now—appease me just a little
> With the why-and-wherefore of Your Sex.[17]

The Pierrot of Crane's translations of Laforgue stands, or sometimes sits, in murky awe and repressed hatred of woman. The personal "I" is reserved for the male, while the female is a type (Eve, Gioconda, Delilah) denied subjective ego. Woman is indifferent to the passion of the male and withholds or ignores the pleasure of sex with canine impassivity. Since he cannot control or even influence woman, the relentlessly natural force, Pierrot designs a relationship that cancels equality and intimacy. He flees into solipsism and narcissism—unhealthy and antisocial traits in a world where realism reigns.

Two other poems "sous le signe de Laforgue" illuminate the high-pitched sexual relationship of the Pierrot and the woman. These poems were written by Allen Tate. In "Euthanasia," a solitary male lies in "the white refulgent streets," a suicide. The cause is woman.

> The graceless madness of her lips,
> Who was the powder-puff of life,
> Cannot rouge those cheeks nor warm
> His cold corpuscles back to strife.

17. *Ibid.,* 262.

No one can say what the dead lover gained or lost, the poet says, but subsequent lines assert that "death is not unkind" when the alternative is the ambiguous love of woman.[18]

"Elegy for Eugenesis" is much more hostile to the "Lady." She has died in childbirth, and the poet refuses to mourn. Her widower, the poet cruelly remarks, "is heartbroken—he said so / Winking at his cocktail, talking dollars carefully." The best the poet can do, having duly noted that the lady died at twenty-six "giving us an homunculus with bald head," is to wish her no memory and a quick fade back into protoplasm.[19]

This brief survey of poems suggests that poets who invested in pierrotic estrangement from the much too solid world of Columbine simultaneously acquired a pained ambivalence toward woman and more than a cursory fascination with death—usually suicide. Their adulation of Eve, Gioconda, Delilah, and Cynthia, goddess of the moon and all sublunary creatures, is dyed with darker emotion; they welcome the woman's death, deny her subjective life, and view her sexual nature as, at best, a sort of involuntary spasm and, at worst, a weapon of torture.

Whether he knew it or not, young Faulkner, the Swinburnian romantic and tricky personality of the 1920s, inhaled pierrotic air with his first literary breath. Whether it ever completely exited his imaginative system is impossible to say. Early works such as *The Marionettes*, his poems to Helen, *Mayday*, *Vision in Spring*, and a few reviews show strong traces of pierrotic suspicion of woman and a hypnotic fixation on death. In *The Marionettes*, for example, the Spirit of Autumn watches as a youth and a nymph return from straying (like Stevens' nymphs in "Sunday Morning") into a wood. Clearly, Autumn notices, fleshly passion has not united them. The youth moves off, ignoring the nymph's call, and launches himself vertically (a direction emphasized by Faulkner's repeated illustrations of poplars) toward the Absolute. The Spirit of Autumn comments, "Ah, he goes on, his young eyes ever before him, looking into an implacable future." The youth, of course, falls, like Icarus. His body, used up in the quest

18. Allan Tate, "Euthanasia," *Double Dealer*, III (May, 1922), 262.
19. Allen Tate, "Elegy for Eugenesis," *The Fugitive*, I (October, 1922), 92.

for the Absolute, plummets to earth, splashing into the pool where the nymph casually lounges. Only the reeds by the edge of the pool register any "sorrow" for the dead youth.[20]

Male youth tries to pierce the Absolute and is rewarded with oblivion. Both the world and woman survive, but woman's survival is lived out in confusion. "I desire—what do I desire?" Marietta asks more than once after Shade of Pierrot deserts her to strum his mandolin within the encircling outline of the full moon.[21] She is never vouchsafed an answer, and the last illustration in *The Marionettes* shows Pierrot staring at his image in a mirror while the corpse of Marietta lies before him.

Love and death, of course, are not new companions in literature. The pierrotic aesthetic, however, links them through male and female figures that Faulkner seems to have found all but obsessively commanding. His early fiction serves heavy doses of Eros and Thanatos in the figures of symbolic drama. *Soldier's Pay,* which concerns dying World War I veteran Donald Mahon and several women who would like to save him, attaches love and death like Siamese twins. *Mosquitoes,* disjointed and garrulous as it is, is unified most effectively by the themes of sex (love) and death (art); all the talking accomplishes little of the former (devoutly wished-for consummations are few) but some of the latter, for Gordon's sculpture seems to be the sole creation in the novel impervious to the corruptions of time and flesh.

We must look, though, at *Sartoris,* the novel that most critics have positioned at the point of Faulkner's transition from apprentice to master. In *Sartoris,* the pierrotic system accomplishes its most "fruitful tension" with a realistic world. Most of the criticism of *Sartoris* shows us future greatness foreshadowed in a flawed novel. Considerably less criticism shows us *Sartoris* with its literary tendrils reaching back. Faulkner made *Sartoris* out of what he had acquired up to the mid-1920s, not out of what he was yet to learn.[22]

Among the abundant literature of the late nineteenth century from which Faulkner absorbed the pierrotic images of treach-

20. William Faulkner, *The Marionettes* (Charlottesville, Va., 1977), 32, 33.
21. *Ibid.,* 45.
22. *Sartoris* is not an easy novel to read; nor has the publication of *Flags in the*

erous moonglow and Columbine, cultic worship of suicide, and stylized ennui in a banal world is a short play by Albert Giraud, *Pierrot Narcisse,* published in 1887. There is no evidence that Faulkner ever read Giraud's play or encountered any of his several pierrotic poems. *Pierrot Narcisse* is important, however, for the sharp fix in the pierrotic constellation that it gives to *Sartoris.* Lacking such a focal point, we could not see how Faulkner brings the southern heroic into the postheroic twentieth century in *Sartoris.*

Giraud's play is written in five scenes. The chief characters are Eliane, the young and attractive daughter of Cassandre (a civil official); Arlequin, a boisterously healthy youth who is loudly in love with Eliane; Messetin, a hypochondriacal hanger-on; three Abbés, who pursue the life of the palate rather than the soul; and, of course, Pierrot, about twenty-five and dressed in the traditional white costume.

Pierrot, then, is about the same age as Bayard Sartoris. Born in March, 1893, under the sign of Aries (determined astrologically to war), Bayard is twenty-six when the action of *Sartoris* takes place. The coincidence of age is, perhaps, more than slight; both Pierrot and Bayard may be expected to be beyond callow adolescence. Their suffering, therefore, claims serious attention. Each might be expected to move toward a reconciliation with history and the social context. Neither does.

Bayard also shares a self-destructive, narcissistic temperament with Giraud's Pierrot. When Pierrot is first seen in the play, he is "ivre-mort" (dead drunk), determined to drink himself into oblivion. Oblivion, however, is slow in coming. Bayard toils under a similar obsession with liquor as anodyne; he spends a good deal of his time trying to pass out, without notable success.

The pain that Giraud's Pierrot wishes to alleviate is consciousness itself, for there is nothing in the world of which he wishes to be aware. As snow falls around him, token of the icy vacancy of

---

Dust in 1973, the manuscript presumably as Faulkner submitted it to Horace Liveright in 1927, made the reading any easier. *Sartoris* is, nevertheless, the novel as it existed throughout Faulkner's lifetime. I will adopt Michael Millgate's reasoning and deal principally with *Sartoris.* Michael Millgate, "Faulkner's First Trilogy: *Sartoris, Sanctuary,* and *Requiem for a Nun,*" in Doreen Fowler and Ann J. Abadie (eds.), *Fifty Years of Yoknapatawpha: Faulkner and Yoknapatawpha, 1979* (Jackson, Miss., 1980), 91.

reality, Pierrot greets it as a redemptive blankness in which he sees himself successfully effaced.

> It [the snow] is a fantasia, it is the flourish
> Of this banal world, flat and stale:
> The snow is my semblance, and I am its kin.[23]

Melville had found whiteness more powerful than black as a symbol for nullity; the pierrotic poets found their patron's floured face a reflection of the banality of the world. Both nature and history were so blank as to make no imprint on Pierrot.

Young Bayard is similarly depressed by his existence within stale and flat reality. After nearly sustaining a concussion by falling from a runaway horse and then spending a night drinking and serenading, Bayard finds himself on a jailhouse cot, cold and regretfully conscious, still burdened with "that body which he must drag forever about a bleak and barren world." His soliloquy echoes that of snowbound Pierrot. "'Hell,' he said, lying on his back, staring out the window where nothing was to be seen, waiting for sleep, not knowing if it would come or not, not caring a particular damn either way. Nothing to be seen, and the long, long span of a man's natural life. Three score and ten years to drag a stubborn body about the world and cozen its insistent demands. Three score and ten, the Bible said. Seventy years. And he was only twenty-six. Not much more than a third through it. Hell."[24] Bayard's *de profundis* echoes Verlaine's Pierrot.

> This no moonstruck dreamer from the play
> who jeered at pictures of his dead grandsires;
> his light heart, like his candle, has lost its fire—
> his thin transparent ghost haunts us today.

Verlaine's Pierrot is "one about to die," obsessed with death as the root and blossom of self-consciousness. That his body is a bur-

---

23. Albert Giraud, *Héros et Pierrots* (N.p., 1928), 117. All translations of excerpts from Giraud are mine, unless otherwise noted. Charles Beaumont Wicks, *The Parisian Stage* (University, Ala., 1979) records no stage production of *Pierrot Narcisse* for the years 1876–1900.

24. William Faulkner, *Sartoris* (New York, 1964), 138, and *Flags in the Dust*, ed. Douglas Day (New York, 1973), 169.

den, too, gives Bayard's lament literary precedent: "Poor flesh!
So helpless and so much chastised!"[25]

Giraud's Arlequin, Pierrot's ancient antagonist, is brashly untroubled by his flesh or any other *memento mori*. He enters the
play vociferously proclaiming his love for Eliane, singing Whit-
manesquely of his sinews and bones and their part in love. Pierrot is immediately aggravated; he grabs a mirror, stares into it,
and faints. Later, in a soliloquy, he elaborates upon his objection
to Arlequin's high spirits.

> Oh this bully Harlequin, I think I envy him!
> Harlequin though is nothing more than life itself,
> Nothing more than youthfulness . . . Alas, nothing more than that!
> Nothing more than that!

Confronted by Arlequin, Pierrot tries to strip him of his joy in
life by reducing life—as Bayard does in his cold cell—to nothing
more than slow death by inexorable aging. Arlequin swears that
he will not grow old; he would sooner kill himself. "To grow old?
To die a little bit day by day? I'd rather / Grow old in one instant
by the blast of a rifle!" Pierrot mocks him: "Bravo, Bravissimo!
Bayard! But Columbine? / But Eliane?"[26] *Fin-de-siècle* poets saw
the traditional antagonism between Pierrot and Arlequin as
something too serious for the pratfalls and brickbats of farce.
Pierrot's allusion to the Bayardic ideal (demoted to the swagger-
ing figure of Arlequin), to the woman, and to death over life indicate the general outlines of his objection to human mortality.
Life seems a sentence, not a gift; the traditional model of the
hopeful, heroic, affirmative life—Chevalier Bayard—has become an anachronism.

Faulkner imagined the antagonism between the flesh's dogged
will to live and the mind's trajectory toward the immortal in the
inseparable twinship of the Sartoris boys: one of light, the other
of darkness; John as Arlequin, Bayard as cynical Pierrot. He
gave their relationship a violence and passion that verge on incest and homosexuality. If Laforgue's pallid sect could assault

25. Verlaine, *Selected Poems*, 173, 165.
26. Giraud, *Héros et Pierrots*, 129, 132.

public statuary, Faulkner would go them one better by aiming "the arrow of his [Pierrot's] life" at society's unmentionable secrets. Faulkner's devotion to the pierrotic aesthetic makes this more than gratuitous sensationalism.

On his first night home from France, Bayard sits in his room, "treacherously illuminated by the moon," besieged by memories and emotions that defy the healthy order of the social context.

> And then he sat quietly in the room which he and John had shared in the young masculine violence of their twinship, on the bed where he and his wife had lain the last night of his leave, the night before he went back to England and out to the Front again, where John already was. Beside him on the pillow the wild bronze swirling of her hair was hushed now in the darkness, and she lay holding his arm with both hands against her breast while they talked quietly, soberly at last.
>
> But he had not been thinking of her then. When he thought of her who lay rigid in the dark beside him, holding his arm tightly to her breast, it was only to be a little savagely ashamed of the heedless thing he had done to her. He was thinking of his brother whom he had not seen in over a year, thinking that in a month they would see one another again.[27]

Taking Columbine to the sacred chamber looms as an act of treason against a higher love, the love between masculine twins consecrated to heroic action. Bayard agonizes over his temporary but unatonable lapse from the ideal of Aries, the fine desire that the other, the dead, twin had kept intact. In the pierrotic code, Bayard has fallen from grace by loving woman; in the Bayardic code, he has sinned by deserting the battlefield to begin a domestic life. Bayard has, in effect, betrayed his name. His twin is always there, like Pierrot's image in a mirror, to echo the sin. Caroline White Sartoris and the child in her womb died that same year; they merit only a simple entry in the Sartoris Bible.

Caroline had to die, of course, for woman spoils the pierrotic dream of the Absolute by diverting it toward a natural process. What Bayard cannot endure, the point of his repeated confiteors for the death of John, is that he did not uphold the absolute standard, did not, like John, put an end to life in the instant of its

27. Faulkner, *Sartoris*, 53–54, and *Flags in the Dust*, 48–49.

brightest purity. John had always dwelt in light; he had soared into the Absolute and lived to tell about it. He had gone up in a balloon and come down in a parachute, had known a "desire so fine" that possessing it set him apart from all men.[28] John, the true hero of the twins, lived an immediate and impulsive life, untroubled by reflection. He always took a trinket to the MacCallum's Mandy and lived in the MacCallum lore as vividly as if he had never died. John, like Giraud's Arlequin, was nothing but youth and life, and Bayard envies him the more he (Bayard) slips into ordinary, day-by-day life.

Repressed hatred gnaws at Bayard. He tries to repeat John's angelic life, but Narcissa Benbow knows he is now brother to the cold and blank—the snow that Pierrot claims as his cousin. Bayard, nevertheless, allows Narcissa to call him back from oblivion a second time, after he is dragged from his swamped car and patched together. He impregnates her, compounding "the heedless thing" he had done to his first wife, and enters again the natural cycle of the earth he hates. Nothing, the narrator avers, could have been more destructive to Bayard than this dream of oneness with the earth. "Without being aware of the progress of it he had become submerged in a monotony of days, had been snared by a rhythm of activities repeated and repeated until his muscles grew so familiar with them as to get his body through the days without assistance from him at all. He had been so neatly tricked by earth, that ancient Delilah, that he was not aware that his locks were shorn."[29] The Old Testament allusion touches both Giraud's play, where Arlequin lives with little or no sense of his own mortality, rather boasting of the apparent immortality of his ebullient youth, and Laforgue's "Locutions," in which woman is typed as Delilah. Faulkner's "notorious and by no means unconscious misogyny" surfaces in *Sartoris* as a "controlling, selective influence."[30] To function as a selective influence, however, the misogyny—the dark twin of the earth mother imagery—must be mediated by an orderly array of images, allusions,

28. Faulkner, *Sartoris*, 73.
29. *Ibid.*, 205, 171, and *Flags in the Dust*, 229–30.
30. Albert J. Guerard, "The Misogynous Vision as High Art: Faulkner's *Sanctuary*," *Southern Review*, n.s., XII (Spring, 1976), 215.

and themes. Faulkner found that order in the literary constellation of Pierrot, the chief articulated system in his early reading
and imagining.

Woman, as we have seen, does not fare well with Pierrot.
Faulkner is not generous with Narcissa in *Sartoris;* he is even
more severe in *Sanctuary* and the short story "There Was A
Queen." Belle Mitchell leaves a smell on Horace Benbow that is
not perfume. The pierrotic repulsion felt toward woman is sanctioned by the myth that woman is not a conscious being, is in fact
inimical to the conscious (logic, reason, will, art) by virtue of the
involuntary ebbs and flows that control her life. Man pursues the
antithesis of woman in art or science or the angelic fraternity of
war and is denied fulfillment by her intrusion. Columbine, who
basks in the moon and moves in natural cycles, negates reason
and will. She might be the eternal feminine or just as easily Ver-
lain's Columbine,

> whose eyes, green
> as a cat's and obscene
>   (she has cause
> to guard her full-blown
> charms), cry: "Keep down
>   your paws!"[31]

Pierrot, then, may murder Columbine, degrade her, rejoice in
her death in childbirth, or—as Bayard behaves toward his two
wives—treat her heedlessly and then flee, like Pierrot *fumiste.* In
all cases, though, Pierrot claims as his alibi a deeper, more authentic, more authoritative grasp of reality. This chaste knowledge causes his suffering, and that very suffering draws Columbine to him. The cycle of attraction and doom is unending, part
of Pierrot's sorrow. Giraud's Eliane pleads with Pierrot:

> I would be both your mistress and your sister,
> Pity! . . . I have seen you pale, melancholy,
> Suffering the obscure hurt of being unloved.

The obscure hurt that draws Narcissa to Bayard is not his plainly
cracked bones but her sense of him as "so utterly without any

---

31. Verlaine, *Selected Poems*, 81.

affection for anything at all."[32] Narcissa follows the path worn smooth by many a Columbine. At the end of the path is Pierrot's revulsion, his denial of her love, and perhaps even bodily insult.

It is clear in *Sartoris* that for Bayard to marry any woman is to renege on his vow to his twin, to betray the purer ideal for the sullied representative of the natural, woman. Denying rather than enabling the social context, as old Bayard had seen with his father and Drusilla, is an inescapable part of the heroic context. There is and can be no accommodation. In young Bayard, Faulkner found the breaking point for the southern heroic narrative. It had outlived its usefulness for community building. The hero showed himself, to Faulkner, to be solipsistic and death dealing; yet figurally there was no alternative, no new fable. No wonder Faulkner has so many doomed and divided heroes.

Woman cannot appreciate this condition; she is oblivious to all but her own cycles. The nymph-Marietta figure in *The Marionettes* cannot accompany the youth-Pierrot. Gordon keeps his distance from Patricia Robyn in *Mosquitoes* and sculpts a female figure that can neither speak, grasp, nor flee. Animal imagery, that of Verlaine's feline Columbine, suits the woman. Like an animal she cannot but twitch at a given stimulus; like life she cannot but move toward death. Only if she can be made to exist in a condition both near and untouchable can a relationship be supported. That, of course, courts ancient taboo, but Pierrot revels in such peril.

This paradoxical knowledge wearies Pierrot. Woman will never understand; her approach will always be from the land of the living where the moment is always the present. Giraud's Pierrot explains to Eliane why he can neither live nor love.

> Listen: there are two races,
> As old as the azure and limpidity [of the sky]:
> The one enamored of activity and reality,
> Handsome, lusty, heroic, entranced
> By the splendid banality of life.
> And this race is that of the happy ones.
> The other is the race of dreamers, or visionaries,
> And of those who, born under Saturn's sign,

32. Giraud, *Héros et Pierrots*, 139; Faulkner, *Sartoris*, 205.

Have a rising star [of Fate] in their taciturn hearts.
That is the sullen and mild race of jokers,
Who trail through the world a longing to be elsewhere
And who are forever being killed by the chimerical desire
Of living greedily and of observing life.
It is the race of those whose wearied dreams
Die of regret once they are realized.
The one is full of joy, the other of rancor;
The one comes from the sun, the other from the moon.[33]

Pierrot's grave dissertation illumines the central dichotomy of the pierrotic sensibility of *Sartoris,* and it even adumbrates Faulkner's as-yet-unwritten works. John Sartoris is full of joy, Bayard of rancor. John flies to the sun in balloons and Sopwith-Camels; Bayard moves in the tricky light of the moon for most of the novel. John is happy, Bayard a sullen joker.

The only redemption for the pierrotic hero is a good death. He suffers Hamlet's paralyzed fascination with self-slaughter. Bayard's preliminary attempts at suicide are stymied short of apotheosis. There is no refuge for him, not even at the Mac-Callum retreat. There, Bayard sees that no gesture he can make will even approach the purity of John's entire life. Like so many *fin-de-siècle* Pierrots, Bayard suffers from cold sweats and insomnia. He stumbles out of bed and makes for the door, for a breath of free air. "He knew where the door was and he groped his way to it on curling toes. It was fastened by a wooden bar, smooth as ice, and fumbling at it he touched something else beside it, something chill and tubular and upright, and his hand slid down it and then he stood for a moment in the icy pitch darkness with the shotgun in his hands."[34] That thing is both the shotgun and the phallic urge, mocking Bayard in this machined incarnation. This is the urge that woman indifferently teases and that Pierrot would abolish. It is also the "carabine" that Arlequin would not hesitate to put to his head.

Bayard does not kill himself that night as the cold rain falls on MacCallum's. But suicide is his ultimate goal. In Giraud's play, Pierrot, in the penultimate scene, hurls himself at a mirror,

33. Giraud, *Héros et Pierrots,* 143–44. This is Storey's translation of Pierrot's speech, *Pierrot,* 137, n. 77.
34. Faulkner, *Sartoris,* 259, and *Flags in the Dust,* 369–70.

desiring consummation with his own image. The glass shatters, slices Pierrot's flesh, and leaves his white costume spattered with blood. In the next scene, Pierrot pauses before he dies to tell his own epilogue (there being no Horatio): "Yes, I've put an end to myself: But how am I going to live!"[35] Once a narcissist, always a narcissist. After speeding through the world too fast to notice any connection with it, Bayard passes—according to his self-proclaimed apotheosis—into the realm of the Absolute, where he will not be burdened with this weary flesh. But his aircraft, the offspring of a loony inventor, much as the blind, deaf, and scentless puppies are Jackson MacCallum's unwanted gift to the world, only gains about two thousand feet, hardly more than a horizontal trajectory. Bayard is like neither Icarus nor the youth of *The Marionettes* who perishes in doomed flight.

Sartoris is consistently, if too obviously, ordered by the pierrotic aesthetic Faulkner absorbed in reading and translating *fin-de-siècle* poets. This scaffolding, more or less consciously erected for his first attempt at the matter of the southern heroic, was gradually dismantled or incorporated into the structures of his subsequent fiction.

Judith Sensibar, who has done the most detailed study of the Pierrot figure in Faulkner's art, concludes that the pierrotic hero evolved into Faulkner's failed men (for example, Horace Benbow and Gail Hightower) and that Faulkner was consciously drawn to the figure because its divided voice (for example, those of Quentin Compson and Joe Christmas) was convenient to his artistic desire to break the single voice into polyphony. Sensibar argues that the discovery of the unreliable narrative voice essentially ended Faulkner's full-time need for the Pierrot.

In the context of southern heroic, the career of Faulkner's Pierrot is more diverse. Elements of the collision of Pierrot and hero did not entirely depart Faulkner's creative system as the matter of Yoknapatawpha expanded; the pierrotic aesthetic remained a diminishing but influential generator of images, allusions, and themes. It would be safe to argue, for example, that Quentin Compson wears the white smock and floured face. He

---

35. Giraud, *Héros et Pierrots*, 168.

displays the incapacity to connect with the world that marks the *fin-de-siècle* Pierrot, especially in *The Sound and the Fury*. Byron Bunch echoes an earlier Pierrot, the innocent fool at the service of Columbine. Flem Snopes, with his face as plain as uncooked dough and his unchanging white shirt, reflects a sinister facet of the universal human type of the "ordinary." [36]

Faulkner retained a clearly pictorial representation of Pierrot to accompany and buttress the thematic associations of failure, betrayal, and reprehensible ignorance of life. In *Light in August*, Gail Hightower is an advanced Pierrot, still contending, like Bayard, with a heroic past but too distant from the sign of Aries ever to hope for actual participation in heroic endeavor. Hightower's death is stubbornly protracted and ordinary, no flashy suicide. [37]

Faulkner provides a posed and painterly vision of Hightower as decrepit Pierrot. "Hightower is asleep. Upon the swell of his paunch, where the white shirt (it is a clean and fresh one now) balloons out of the worn black trousers, an open book lies face down. Upon the book Hightower's hands are folded, peaceful, benignant, almost pontifical. The shirt is made after an old fashion, with a pleated though carelessly ironed bosom, and he wears no collar. . . . Again light, the reflection of sky beyond the mulberry leaves, glints and glares upon the spectacle lenses, so that Byron cannot tell just when Hightower's eyes open." [38] The August light catches Pierrot's costume and demeanor. The ballooning white smock, the benign but obsolete pose of peace and innocence, the "lunettes" popular on Pierrot in the decades after World War I, signify a regrettable failed vision. Those who have eyes to see, if they are Pierrots, never see.

Hightower's obsessive grip on the heroic past, like Bayard's, disqualifies him from useful action in the present. Ironically, within the pierrotic context, the single action in which he believes he participates is the birth of Lena's child. Thus is aging, paunchy Pierrot conscripted into the service of the natural, the woman. Hightower is acted upon in all other situations that call for heroism.

Faulkner brought the pierrotic to Hightower for the muted

36. Storey, *Pierrot*, 73.
37. William Faulkner, *Light in August* (New York, 1932), 343.
38. *Ibid.*

but rich irony he could turn upon the southern heroic. In *Light in August,* the relevance of the heroic order to the current lives (and deaths) of men and women is a feeble, ignored flicker. Percy Grimm is the new uniformed knight; with no real war to blood him, he is merely a civilized psychopath.

Faulkner bade an ironic farewell to Pierrot in *Go Down, Moses.* Ike McCaslin is a late encounter with the original Pierrot, of whom Gautier, also seeing the demise of the original, wrote in 1859: "Pierrot, pale, spindly, draped in those wan clothes, ever starving and ever thrashing about, the slave of old, the proletarian of today, the outcast, the passive and disinherited who abets, dejected and unwittingly, the orgies and follies of his exploiters."[39] Ike, Pierrot from puberty to four score, is the antique, disinherited (by his own act), passive being who (unwittingly, for most of his life) assists at the orgies and follies of his hunting fellows. Rereading *Go Down, Moses* with particular attention to the pierrotic, we see how the violent early figure metamorphoses in Faulkner's work, losing much of its aggressive symbolic quality but retaining, even in dilapidation, the crucial function of gauging heroic action.

Watteau's "Italian Comedians" and Gautier's summary sketch of Pierrot describe the older figure from which the notorious Pierrot of the *fin de siècle* emerged. In Watteau's painting, no peripheral character touches Pierrot, and he glows (like Hightower) with a reflected radiance that he does not impart to any other corner of the canvas. Gautier, correspondingly, describes a sad Pierrot who conspires in his own victimization. Ike's connection with the world is similarly pierrotic and pathetic. He repeatedly fails to comprehend the reality he ceremoniously resolves to control. He is Pierrot *comique* or *drôle,* not Pierrot *narcisse;* yet Faulkner does not write him a deed to all our sympathy. If Ike is a victim, he is implicated in his own ruin, and we are not approached to shed a tear for him. Faulkner plays with the farcical elements of the Pierrot tale, showing Ike in a series of mistaken or ill-timed gestures that culminate in his realization that he has never been a part of the procession he wants to redeem. Ike's disjunction begins before his birth.

39. Gautier, *Histoire de L'Art Dramatique,* V, 24.

Critics have maintained that "Was" is funny only so long as we forget that it concerns various forms of barter in human beings. Tomey's Turl, the human quarry of Buck McCaslin and Cass Edmonds, is Buck's slave half brother. Hunting him is depicted with the hilarity of a Marx Brothers farce, but Tomey's Turl is a human being and even shares the hunter's own blood. Sophonsiba's plight is no less poignant. To the male world in which she lives, she is unattractive and past her prime; her brother Hubert tries to dump her as one would an unwanted dog. To her sorrow Sophonsiba jingles like a dog or like a slave in chains; the jewelry she wears to attract a man only warns him of her approach. Finally, she snares Theophilus McCaslin and succeeds in bearing a child, Ike. Narratively, the disjunction of farce and tragedy produces Ike. Figurally, he is a patriarch, yet he dies childless. Faulkner places him, already aged, as an epigraph to "Was," the story of his conception. "But Isaac was not one of these [who had actually seen the action of "Was"] . . . [he] owned no property and never desired to since the earth was no man's but all men's, as light and air and weather were."[40] Ike wears renunciation like the blanched smock while the characters of "Was" crowd around him in the contortions of folly and vice.

"The Old People" inaugurates Ike's entry into the world of reality, symbol, and the cult of the connecting gesture. His tutor is Sam Fathers, but the lesson defies language. Sam's instruction in hunting is ambiguous: "Now . . . shoot quick, and slow." Whatever meaning lurks in that paradox, Ike claims to have learned it, and his elders in the hunting party acknowledge that he has, better and earlier than any of them. Mystery is a substance without traits. Ike is a gnostic seer. He carries nothing as concrete as Lucas' undetonated cartridge to remind him of the hard-edged world of contingency. Cass, as true a knight of the mystic order of the big woods as a descendant of the distaff and a man of property can hope to be, lectures Ike on the mystery of life the night after Ike sees but does not shoot *the* bear. Their exchange is similar to that between Sir Galwyn and the jaded figure of time in *Mayday*. Life, Cass says, is the use of life, and he leaves the

40. William Faulkner, *Go Down, Moses* (New York, 1942), 3.

loophole of the contingent in case Ike should want to escape the rigors of his ideal system.

> "And the earth dont want to just keep things, hoard them; it wants to use them again. . . . Besides, what would it want, itself, knocking around out there, when it never had enough time about the earth as it was, when there is plenty of room about the earth, plenty of places still unchanged from what they were when the blood used and pleasured in them while it was still blood?"
>
> "But we want them," the boy said. "We want them too. There is plenty of room for us and them too."
>
> "That's right," McCaslin said. "Suppose they dont have sub- stance, cant cast a shadow—"
>
> "But I saw it!" the boy cried. "I saw him!"[41]

For Ike, the world of essence overcomes contingency; for Cass, there is nothing necessary under the sun. Ike is a being from an earlier time, the innocent Pierrot marooned in a skeptical, postmythic age. The elaborate genealogy of *Go Down, Moses* re- inforces Ike's anachronistic position; he is always mismatched with a subsequent generation, even when his chronological age coincides with the other. He is out of sync with time, the peren- nial handicap of Pierrot.

"The Bear" traces Ike's various attempts to compress time into a single, stable present and to fire the arrow of his life at the enigma in time's heart: the ledger entries that Buck and Buddy had interpreted fifty years before. These serial acts of inter- pretation attempt the unification of time, or so it seems to Ike. When, at twenty-one, he discovers incest, miscegenation, suicide, and paternal denial in his disordered past, he sets out upon a quest to match inherited evil with a present willed good and thus expunge the record, untell the story, restore the virginal white- ness to his pierrotic character. He does not see, as Bayard does with a fatal shock, that the heroic tradition is the realm of death. Cass tries to dissuade him, but Cass's worldly irony makes no mark on Ike. Like Sir Galwyn, Ike sets out.

Ike's quest is doomed, but not by dragons or even by circum- stances wholly external to himself. Like the Pierrot of Watteau,

41. *Ibid.*, 163, 186–87.

he wears the smock of innocence while around him transactions of survival continue in the shadows. There is the bequest of old Carothers McCaslin to deliver, the ritual to complete. Ike cannot locate James Beauchamp, who vanished on his twenty-first birthday in 1885. Fonsiba, second inheritor, has gone off to Arkansas. There, on a run-down farm near the town of Midnight, Ike tries to make a proud black man, her husband, whose spectacles have no lenses, "see" the exploitation he has willingly taken upon himself and Fonsiba. "Dont you see," Ike cries, that the whole South is cursed by the compounded sins of land ownership and slavery and that Ike's act is the first step toward atonement? But the man rejects Ike's view, claiming that the "curse" has been lifted and that a better time is at hand. Getting nowhere with the husband, Ike turns to Fonsiba, who stops him by saying, "I'm free."[42]

Ike then makes an elaborate gesture by which he contributes to his own negation. He goes to Midnight after hearing of the "banker" who handles the husband's pension check, and he deposits with that same man, "a translated Mississippian who had been one of Forrest's men too," the gold that Fonsiba has inherited. It is to be doled out at three dollars a month for nearly twenty-eight years. The banker, whom Ike should not trust (Forrest's lot, the same group Ab Snopes found congenial, do not carry a reputation for probity in Faulkner's fiction), "promises" to deliver Fonsiba's monthly payments. The symbolic act complete, Ike leaves the real details to fallible agents. The true Pierrot prefers the unsullied fiction of his atoning act. Cass would have been a better trustee; money has real meaning in his world.[43]

Later, Ike renounces his birthright, a gesture that to him intends final release from old Carothers' sins. He marries a woman who assumes that she will occupy one of the county's finest farms. The news that Ike has renounced the land precipitates his traumatic fall into an abyss that echoes the woman's laughter, the sort of taunting Margueritte's Pierrot suffered after he murdered Columbine.

42. *Ibid.*, 278–79, 280.
43. *Ibid.*, 280.

Ike's wife comes from the mold of Faulkner's sexually manipulative and yet indifferent women, traced from the pattern of
the *fin-de-siècle* Columbine. Ike's Columbine is no sweet, buxom
country wench but the Other who arouses men's passion even
though, like the woman in poem XI of *Vision in Spring,* she
"hates" the man she leads to bed. Ike sees his wife naked only
twice. The second time, she declares an end to their sexual relationship. Ike is the naïve victim, partially implicated in his own
shame. For Pierrot *fumiste* and *narcisse,* the rule of the game is to
strike before you are humiliated by the woman. But Faulkner
sets up Ike—the figure of an earlier, innocent Pierrot who has
not yet heard of the varieties of sin—for seduction and humiliation. He sins nevertheless, like his precursor Hightower, and
also like Hightower lives the life of a relic in the midst of his
changing community.

Ike takes to the woods with the only objects he owns, "the nar-
row iron cot and the stained lean mattress" that refute conjugal
life and affirm the equivocal ideal of the anchorite. That world
dies when Ben, Sam, and Lion die after the big hunt. Ike continues to insist that the mystique still lives in the woods, even
though the era of "harmless" and redeemable human use of the
wilderness is over. Termination is clear when Ike beholds the
frenzied figure of Boon pounding the dismembered barrel of
the gun he holds in his lap "with the frantic abandon of a mad-
man."[44] The spectacle of mechanization, mad and frustrated
onanistic passion, and man's repellent and savage claim to own
the living energy of nature are left, at the close of "The Bear,"
without comment by or on behalf of Ike. Pierrot watches in silence. How much can the floured visage countenance?

The answer to how much Ike knows of the world he tries to
give up is pronounced in "Delta Autumn": more than he admits.
By the time Ike reaches four score, he has lost touch with his
own myth. He can no longer remember how many deer have
fallen before his rifle; he now kills from ingrained habit. He
hunts with younger men—the dissolute progeny of Walter Ewell
and Cass Edmonds—who do not even pay lip service to the code

44. *Ibid.,* 3, 330, 331.

of the hunt. The hunting party, aged Pierrot included, has run through ritual and come out on the far side where there is no meaning.

Ike still argues for a hopeful human destiny. He claims that there is an Omega point for human beings, male and female, when "the two of them together were God."[45] Does Ike remember his own marriage when he says this? He knows nothing of Roth's affair; he is the last member of the party to catch the double entendre of the words *doe* and *meat*. "Delta Autumn" repeatedly poses Ike as one who represses or lies. Innocence seems impossible. A false light surrounds him while darkness engulfs the real world.

Ike is wrapped in confusion; every gesture he has made in the hope of restoring innocence has compounded evil and guilt. His renunciation of McCaslin land to Edmonds has led to Roth's desperate, cynical "love" affair, the repetition of old Carothers' sin of incest and miscegenation. Having turned on his grandfather, Ike turns into his grandfather, for it is his hand that picks up Roth's money and thrusts it at the woman, just as old Carothers had designated money in place of his paternal acknowledgment. The signs that appeared at Ike's beginning in "Was" prevail at his end. The woman's indictment negates all of his philosophy. "'Old man,' she said, 'have you lived so long and forgotten so much that you dont remember anything you ever knew or felt or even heard about love?'"[46] What Ike can claim to know about love is minimal, perhaps null and void. With the blanket pulled up to his chin, he acts out the passing of Pierrot, the demise of the fiction of holy innocence and the recovery of hope. Like Pierrot in the final sketch for *The Marionettes*, Ike lives in death and in life, able to contemplate his own passing and the futility of his long life.

The figure of Pierrot was deeply inscribed in Faulkner's imagination as the figure of aspiration toward action that is doomed from the start to be swallowed up in contingency, in the ordinary. This figure appeared in several other manifestations, each

45. *Ibid.*, 348.
46. *Ibid.*, 363.

one a part of a running cultural and literary commentary on the heroic formula for meaning and action. Critics of the tradition of Pierrot have commented on its adaptability to the kind of dissenting commentary Faulkner's harsh and defeated Pierrots signify. "The plasticity of the role is—potentially—without limit: on a white ground all shades can be reflected; but it is to be feared that the white peasant's blouse and floury contenance, old images of innocence, denote in the surviving comedies nothing better than stupidity."[47] Nearer the actual origins of Faulkner's own inhalation of the pierrotic air is Mallarmé's observation that the blanched face of Pierrot is the blank page on which anything might be written, any character inscribed. It bespeaks a blankness that is the original and inescapable state of being into which all gestures, heroic or common, inevitably descend. There is no recovery once the mark is made, the action taken. Even more to the point of the *volte-face* of the heroic figure in the pierrotic context is Sensibar's arresting discovery that, in *Sartoris,* Faulkner infused his faun-Pierrot into the stature of the old colonel, thus subverting the heroic totem.

Faulkner artistically and temperamentally recognized early in his writing career the adaptability of the figure of Pierrot. The frequency with which he sketched in line and sentence the figure of "a higher pitch of delicacy" or the figure that meant a more violent rejection of the social context attests to his attachment to the figure and its importance in a great range of his work. When he turned to the local, personal, and southern matter of Yoknapatawpha, he brought the pierrotic aesthetic along. Pierrot, of course, would be comfortable in the host organism—southern heroic in narrative and in male behavior—but rejection also made Pierrot convenient for a writer who was a transient in his hometown. Faulkner prized failure in other writers and esteemed his own works by the magnitude of his failure in them, and he saw the human race as a *commedia dell'arte* troupe in which only Pierrot could believe, or act as if he believed, in heroism, the purity of motive, the truths of the human heart.

47. Lehmann, "Pierrot and Fin de Siècle," 210.

VII

The Percys: The Hero as the
Extraneous Man

It is so grievous living past the prime
And looking back for all one's glimpse of glamour.
                                    —William Alexander Percy
                                         "Enzio's Kingdom"

Under cover of philosophical and theological problems, Walker
Percy's heroes attempt to resolve the problem of heroic action
that had stymied many, including Percy's "Uncle Will." The figural hero of vision is significant in the narrative and heroic tradition that both Percys bear. William Alexander Percy felt extraneous, most of the time, to his civilization—a feeling shared by
Walker Percy's heroes, who try earnestly if ironically to perform
some action worthy of the name.

Walker Percy filters the heroic predicament that he learned
from William Alexander Percy, whose own father is the flesh-
and-blood hero of *Lanterns on the Levee: Recollections of a Planter's
Son.* LeRoy Percy never doubts his identity, his social or historical
footing, or the meaning of his actions. The story of his son—in
William's recollections and poetry—is a constant search for a
place to brace himself for action in a post-Christian, postheroic,
and now "postsouthern" world.[1] A constant theme in his writing
is the uncertainty of heroic action as a possible, let alone prescribed, response to the disintegration of the world order of the
past. He feels outside the pageant of meaning in the past, es-

---

1. Simpson, *The Brazen Face of History,* 255 ff. Robert H. Brinkmeyer, Jr., in
Three Catholic Writers of the Modern South (Jackson, Miss., 1985), places special
emphasis on Walker Percy's survival strategies in a post-Christian era.

tranged from the degraded present, forever excluded from the circle of heroes where contingency never undermines the purity of action and where bravery is unmixed with "the business of being brave."

Walker Percy continues the theme in an ironic key, for each of his heroes searches for a mode of action, nominally philosophical or theological but structurally consistent with the history of the heroic figure. The sought-for mode of action *should* be no different in kind from the heroic action of the fathers, for tradition means nothing if it does not mean continuity over time. But a succession of the Percys' heroes finds the footing, like the levee itself, deeply undermined. The new, amnesiac order is hostile to heroes. The heroic LeRoy Percy—lawyer, senator, civic leader— barely knew such a common, everyday world. His son lived through the twilight of the old world and saw the dawn break insipidly over the wasteland. He seemed, in his valediction, almost glad to be leaving. Walker Percy has made the apocalyptic American present the milieu of his heroes' quests for meaningful action. After Binx Bolling's modest start at the close of *The Moviegoer*, Will Barrett proclaims the restoration of a Christian heroic order, purged of death-dealing self-centeredness, in *The Second Coming*. Both Percys follow the route of the heroic in southern narrative.

The validity of heroes in Western history and a longing for their return were popular concerns in the late 1930s, when William Alexander Percy began to write his recollections. Europe was crumbling under Hitler and the social experiments of Soviet Russia. Stalin, Hitler, Chamberlain, Mussolini, and a long roster of so-called leaders challenged belief in the hero in history. Too many weak or evil men patently influenced the course of events, usurping the hero's place and prerogative. Sidney Hook responded in 1943 with *The Hero in History*, a study that reaffirmed the definitions of man and society cherished in Western, liberal democracies—the societies LeRoy Percy would have acknowledged, the civilization his son defended in World War I.

Although many of Hook's assertions seem embarrassingly chauvinistic in the post-Vietnam era, one of his observations is pivotal to understanding the crisis of belief in heroic action as

William and later Walker Percy viewed it. Torpedoing social phi-
losophies that would lock man into any sort of deterministic
model, Hook claims that man must, and can, act to order his
world; he is not and must not be extraneous: "If there is any
ethical imperative valid for all historical periods it is awareness
and action."[2] At all times and in all sets of historical contingency,
man must be aware of his situation and must also act to align
contingency with rationally discoverable and defensible democratic principles. Failure to do so is not the fault of circumstances; failure is always due to ethical shortcomings in the individual. If dictators run amok, we can blame only the inaction
and cowardice of men who knew right but failed to act. If a heroic father's order does not survive in the generation of the son,
the son can blame only himself. His failure amounts to patricide.
If America is drifting into chaos, and vines are sprouting in the
walls—as Dr. Thomas More sees in *Love in the Ruins*—it is because the hero has defaulted. A way toward action that would
banish this anxiety and guilt is the quest of the Percys' writings.

One of the most frequent figures in William Alexander Percy's
poetry is the young man who lives after an age of heroic certainty and conviction. He looks upon distant sites and signs, as
does the persona in "Girgenti," knowing that the ground of his
own heroism has eroded. This extraneous man dwells upon heroes of memory; he is, in fact, immobilized by heroic precedent.
Such is the condition of the speaker in Percy's poem "The Soldier Generation."

> We are the sons of disaster,
> Deserted by gods that are named,
> Thrust in a world of no master,
> Our altars prepared but unclaimed;
> Wreathed with the blood-purple aster,
> Victims, foredoomed, but untamed.

Being barred from the possibility of heroism is also the plight of
the narrator of "An Epistle From Corinth." The speaker entreats
an absent Paul for a share of the eyewitness certainty of faith.

2. Hook, *The Hero in History,* 148.

> . . . Paul, Paul, I'd give
> My Greek inheritance, my wealth and youth,
> To speak one evening with that Christ you love
> And never saw and cannot understand.

But no transaction between the generation of faith and the latter age of less pitch and moment succeeds. The plea for certainty within a vast sea of contingency goes unheeded.

> . . . Christ, perhaps—
> But I was born too late and so miss all.
> I see no aim nor end. And yet myself
> Hopeless of aught of profit from the fight,
> Fight on . . .[3]

Not even Christ, the original of the figure of the hero, represents a guarantee. The supplicant languishes in a state in which all is possible but no single thing is necessary. One must act the hero but forever abide the fact that there will be no certification.

This state of feeling extraneous (Walker Percy would later call it the condition of being left over in the universe) is most fully explored in "Enzio's Kingdom." Enzio, the beloved bastard son of Frederick II, is lord of a prison cell by the time he tells his story. Taken captive by his late father's enemies, Enzio is kept "a tame pet prisoner" whose thoughts swing between the perfection of his father's former kingdom and the "long sleep" of death that looms before him. Young Enzio, bereft of promise by the victory of his father's enemies—the Vardamans and Bilbos of late medieval Europe—awaits death in the perpetual shadow of recollection.[4]

His father's kingdom had been ideal; Enzio's memory gilds it with all of the higher pleasures. The best, brightest, mightiest, and richest made their way into Frederick's presence.

> Ambassadors and pilgrims, knights and seers,
> Star-gazers, troubadours, philosophers,

---

3. William Alexander Percy, *The Collected Poems of William Alexander Percy* (New York, 1943), 192, 202, 204. Perhaps Percy would have been pleased to learn that Girgenti, the birthplace of Empedocles, reverted to its original name, Agrigento, in 1928. Sometimes events turn backward.

4. *Ibid.*, 302.

> The wise, the wisdom-seeking, the renowned,
> The race's best and foremost swarmed to him,
> As night-things to a streaming far-seen light.

Enzio basked in the reflected brilliance of his father, enjoyed his favor and respect. But Enzio had to blink at certain savage features of his father's heroic will. When the town of Bari stubbornly resisted a siege directed by Frederick's lieutenant, Pietro da Vigna, Frederick ordered his man to adopt foul means: "Bribe them: or feast their leaders at a truce / And poison them." Da Vigna bridled; Frederick seethed. Enzio shut his eyes "so that I might not see / My father's terrible anger boiling up."[5]

Enzio must eventually endure the defeat of his hero-father. Excommunicated and stripped of temporal power, Frederick ultimately succumbs to his foes. "Mankind in the mass," for whom Frederick harbors undisguised contempt, overwhelms his splendid order. The "all-drowning ignorance" and "tatterdemalion unsorted world" of random arrangements rise up and erase the heroic ego. Enzio is left with images of his father's splendor and his rage, his magnificence and his wrath, the unthinking loyalty of cowed allies and the veiled treason of envious peers. For Enzio, the polarities are crippling. "It is so grievous living past the prime," he muses, "And looking back for all one's glimpse of glamour." As young as he is—only thirty—Enzio faces only death.

> My living days ahead are all old age.
> Here is a crass unthoughtedness, a waste,
> A mere continuing that is not life,
> Miserable to me, to no man helpful.

His final words indict the world, not himself, and certainly not the heroic figure of his father.

> I only know that the grain was golden and
> The earth is culpable if there's no harvest. . . .
> Darkness; darkness; and for me no hope.[6]

Figures of the bewildered and numbed survivor of a heroic order of men surface frequently in Percy's poetry. It is not reck-

5. *Ibid.*, 305, 308.
6. *Ibid.*, 317–18, 340–41, 342.

less to suppose that he felt some special identification with the figure of Enzio, the supplicant to Paul, and the many "sons of disaster" who had inherited a world from which gods and heroes had been evicted. Throughout Percy's poetry he uses, as emotional grounding, the conviction that all "thoughted" men are estranged, imprisoned by their recollections of heroes, and denied any direct means of imitating them.

It is this suspicion of being extraneous to meaning and action, and a consequent self-deprecating irony, that gives body to *Lanterns on the Levee*. Published in 1941, just months before Percy died, *Lanterns on the Levee* tests the effectiveness of heroic action and consciousness in "a new order unsure of itself and without graciousness."[7] The heroic age had maintained a crucial distinction between civilization and mere continuing. Percy found little of the former, except in recollection, and a surplus of the latter.

The son who records his recollections in *Lanterns on the Levee* plays Enzio to his father's Frederick II. He is given to "looking back for all one's glimpse of glamour," convinced that his world fails to meet the standards set by the hero-father. He can be caught blinking at what appear in retrospect to be unfair and imperious liberties taken by his father. These lines of similarity make *Lanterns on the Levee* a multilayered record of the personal as well as cultural impact of the diminishing heroic tradition on one southern male left over in its passing. The shadow of the past extends from Enzio to the planter's son and on toward the heroes of Walker Percy's novels.

William Alexander Percy, like his creation Enzio, cherishes an Arnoldian pessimism about the state of civilization. "Behind us a culture lies dying," he writes; "before us the forces of the unknown industrial world gather for catastrophe." To stave off certain oblivion, Percy invokes the generations that have made him. The luminous presence in the gathering gloom is LeRoy Percy, whom he calls Father, a title of awe and love and fear. Father is the archetypal hero of Christian civilization.

> He read *Ivanhoe* once a year all his life long, and *The Talisman* almost as frequently. Because of or in spite of Don Carlos [a Percy

7. William Alexander Percy, *Lanterns on the Levee: Recollections of a Planter's Son* (1941; rpr. Baton Rouge, 1973), 9.

progenitor] he was kin to Hotspur and blood-brother to Richard
Coeur de Lion, and looked the part. No one ever made the mistake of thinking he wasn't dangerous, and to the day of his death
he was beautiful, a cross between Phoebus Apollo and the Archangel Michael. It was hard having such a dazzling father; no wonder I longed to be a hermit. He could do everything well except
drive a nail or a car: he was the best pistol-shot and the best bird-
shot, he made the best speeches, he was the fairest thinker and
the wisest, he could laugh like the Elizabethans, he could brood
and pity till sweat covered his brow and you could feel him bleed
inside. He loved life, and never forgot it was unbearably tragic.

Next to a father who belonged with the heroes on the west portal
of Chartres, there was little room for the son.[8]

The problem of action asserts itself early in the son's memoirs—what can the succeeding generation do when Father has
absorbed all meaning associated with the culture's ideal figures,
when he has starred in all the cultural epics from *Hamlet* to *Para-
dise Lost?* The son can never expect to revive an old gesture or
make a new one, yet he must act. As if to gloat over his sovereignty, Father appears on a pediment of the Parthenon as dawn
rises and the ambitious son hastens up the Acropolis, hoping to
beat Father to the ground where important events have trans-
pired. Father's laugh, certainly Jovian and generous at the moment, is also latently cruel. In the episode of the meeting at
the Parthenon, Father possesses both literal and metaphorical
ground, making the son extraneous.

Nevertheless, the heroic imperative motivates William Alexander Percy's choices. He hopes, for example, that his work with
the Commission for Relief in Belgium will be "a trifle heroic."[9]
The paternal course—law and public service—does not hold
much real promise of success for the son. He spends his years at
Harvard Law School as Will Barrett does at Princeton, trying to
figure out the code that enables action and, while that code re-
sists cracking, observing those around him from a safe distance.

War rescues the son; in *The Moviegoer,* Binx remembers that
war had rescued his father from melancholia. Although William
Alexander Percy is not enthralled with the common civilization

8. *Ibid.*, 24, 57, 74.
9. *Ibid.*, 159.

at risk in 1914, he is anxious to serve. Martial circumstances thrust him into action, and he no longer feels so acutely extraneous. One of his letters from the front speaks of the "great privilege . . . to be allowed to go forth with the heroes." If that phrase smacks a little of self-directed irony—especially after the son has detailed the many mundane jobs the army found for him—his own account of the actions for which he is decorated is consciously held below epic pitch.

> Suddenly over the crest a company broke and I saw their Colonel single-handed trying to rally and direct them. So I joined him and took over the company. A fine young chap by the name of McSweeney (General Farnsworth's aide) joined me. It was a vivid, wild experience and I think I went through it calmly by refusing to recognize it was real. You couldn't bear to see men smashed and killed around you and know each moment might annihilate you, except by walking in a sort of sleep, as you might read Dante's *Inferno*. The exhilaration of battle—there's no such thing, except perhaps in a charge. It's simply a matter of willpower.[10]

For Walker Percy's heroes, the exhilaration of real action, unclouded and immediate and vivid, also comes like this: under fire. Dodging the sniper's bullet in *The Second Coming* or in *Love in the Ruins*, safely away from a crashing skylight in *The Last Gentleman*, Percy's heroes are absolved, momentarily, of their goofiness. Time and being in time are one and the same, if only because being in time seems about to be terminated. Under the shadow of annihilation one's particular contingency undergoes a simplification. One acts as an organism fully attuned to context; thinking continues, but "in a sort of sleep," liberated from self-consciousness and memory. William Alexander Percy, like Enzio returning to his father flushed with victory over his father's enemies, tastes heroism briefly under the special circumstances of war.

Unlike the hero-father, however, the son is not capable of domesticating the great pitch and moment of heroism. The armistice turns to Percy the false face of peace: "The physical relief, the absence of apprehension, brimmed us with ease and thanksgiving, but for each of us our bliss and serenity were only the

10. *Ibid.*, 201, 205–206.

superstructure over a hidden tide of desolation and despair."
Daily life loomed before the son as it did before Enzio—a long
descent to death. Only the short time in battle remained real.
"That short period of my life spent in the line is the only one I
remember step by step—as if it moved *sub specie aeternitatis*. Not
that I enjoyed it; I hated it. Not that I was fitted for it by temperament or ability, I was desperately unfitted; but it somehow
had meaning, and daily life hasn't: it was part of a common endeavor, and daily life is isolated and lonely."[11]

The hero that dominates Percy's universe is a man of action
instantaneously fitted to circumstances. For the extraneous man,
action is always already compromised by the example of tradition, and vision is divided between the present and the past. He
can never be heroic but only strive to imitate an earlier and unat-
tainable heroic pattern. He can never be one with his life; his
lack of fitness for life blocks the conviction of reality. Before he
can stop the process, an idea of life will have displaced life itself.
Irony, then, is his grammar.

Irony dominates *Lanterns on the Levee*. After the war, Percy returns to daily life in Greenville and to events so monotonous he
scarcely mentions them. After the wild and vivid purity of the
forward lines, daily life is dull. Father, however, is still steadily
capable of heroic action. The Ku Klux Klan infiltrates the town,
sowing its particular brand of ignorance and hatred, and the son
defers to the father to best the KKK's champion in single combat. At a public confrontation, the former senator rises to speak
against the KKK representative and so utterly demolishes him
that the audience all but bears the hero-father away on their
shoulders. It is indeed a "triumphant" event, the son recalls; yet
he also admits that in spite of the father's heroic victory in words,
the KKK still made inroads into town and country, still corrupted the pristine nature of the Percy kingdom.

The son's turn comes a few years later when the 1927 flood
covers the Delta. The danger is indeed real and the events far
from melodramatic, as Richard Wright's story "Down by the
Riverside" illustrates. William Alexander Percy is selected to
head relief efforts by virtue of his family ranking and experi-

11. *Ibid.*, 223.

ence with the Commission for Relief. He seizes contingency and straightens it into action.

His first decision is to evacuate the whites. One of his next moves, there being too little dry ground and no tents, is to evacuate the blacks as well. The barges are at the levee when, Percy reports, "the Negroes announced they did not wish to leave and a group of planters, angry and mouthing, said they [the Negroes] should not and could not leave." The son is furious at the rebels when Father meets him on the levee. In this scene, the son possesses the high ground and the privilege of action. But the father, as he had on the Acropolis, outflanks the son, cancels his practical and moral actions, leaves him groundless. "I explained the situation and he agreed I should not, of course, be intimidated by what the planters said, but he suggested that if we depopulated the Delta of its labor, we should be doing it a grave disservice. I insisted that I would not be bullied by a few blockhead planters into doing something I knew to be wrong—they were thinking of their pocketbooks; I of the Negroes' welfare." [12] Nevertheless, Percy bows to his father's suggestion that he consult his relief committee one more time before taking final action. The committee, which already approved the younger Percy's policy of evacuating the blacks, changes its collective mind at the subsequent meeting. Percy argues for hours but cannot budge them. In the end, the order to evacuate the blacks is rescinded. Fortunately, the weather clears the next day and tents arrive.

Not until his father was dead did Percy discover that, between the time he acquiesced to a recanvassing and the actual meeting of the committee, his father had lobbied each member to change his vote. Father, Percy writes, was a natural gambler who had no qualms about wagering his son's moral and ethical capital. What the son does not say in the narrative is important; he refuses to link his father with the dissenting planters who opposed the evacuation. While the hero-father lives, and even after his death, he controls the son. He was first to the Parthenon; he is first in changing the plans to evacuate the Delta blacks. It is the son alone who must endure the scathing denunciations of the Chicago *Defender*.

12. *Ibid.*, 257.

"The Flood of 1927" shows us the son undermined, his actions annulled by the hero-father, his authority and will usurped. He is still extraneous to his own life. If Percy was correct in assessing the moral bankruptcy of the blockheaded planters, his father must be tainted with the same crime. But the deep-rooted images of heroic worship borne by the father (cavalier, archangel, god) dwarf the hunched ego of the son.[13]

Later in the same chapter, when the blacks refuse to off-load supplies, Percy must face them alone. It is useful to juxtapose this episode of single combat by oratory with the earlier victory of the father over the KKK. The ironic reversal that faces the son surfaces clearly in the narrative. Percy must use blandishments to quell the exploited race; to his father came the privilege of striking blows against bigotry. The hero-father and his peers glide honorably into memory as the son sinks into ironic confusion and special pleading.

William Alexander Percy's recollections and poetry continually focus on the figure of the extraneous man, the hero crippled by recollections of an ideal order and an eminent father but impotent in realizing heroic actions and figures in his own life. This figure is not unique to Percy; Tate's Lacy Buchan and Faulkner's Isaac McCaslin are members of the same celibate and thwarted fraternity.

In the chapter "For the Younger Generation," Percy has only the wintry comfort of Stoicism to bequeath. "I had no desire to send these youngsters of mine [the three orphaned cousins he had adopted] into life as defenseless as if they wore knight's armor and had memorized the code of chivalry."[14] The well-tempered manners and morals the son had witnessed in the hero-father were moribund. The postheroic man had an empty testament. Perhaps the heroes had always been more ordinary than perfect, and the son, like Enzio, had shut his eyes to the aberrations, the clues to the real nature of heroic action. But Percy,

13. For an example of the sort of recollections that the son did not include, see William F. Holmes, "William Alexander Percy and the Bourbon Era in the Yazoo-Mississippi Delta," *Mississippi Quarterly*, XXVI (Winter, 1972–73), 71–87. Without muckraking, Holmes discusses some of the political actualities omitted from the chapter "A Small Boy's Heroes."

14. Percy, *Lanterns on the Levee*, 312.

the jackdaw in his own garden, hoards his beliefs, and his heroes retain their honored reputations. The Percy icon, the brooding knight, still stands, even though he is no defense against modern life.

Concluding his essay on the continuity from William Alexander Percy's to Walker Percy's work, Lewis A. Lawson speculates that "it may be the vision of such a noble man's failure has been the single most powerful stimulus to Walker Percy's continued writing." [15] Lawson makes a strong case for continuity based on commonly held ideals of public behavior and literary themes to be found in William Alexander Percy's poetry and memoir, and the first three novels of Walker Percy. We can take Lawson's analysis beyond these works, for Walker Percy's more recent novels have continued to reflect the issues and themes of the elder Percy's work—the nature of heroism, the possibility of action, the unsteady footing of the extraneous man in the twentieth century— even if they do not affirm them. In searching for alternatives to fatal inaction, Walker Percy reimplements the staples of southern heroic narrative. His usage of familiar, some might even say hackneyed, narrative structures is not peripheral to his fiction. Since these narrative elements have long been prominent in southern narratives treating the nature of the hero, his peculiar form of action, and the cause of cultural survival through narrative form, Percy might not have been able to avoid using them. Percy, however, defamiliarizes the forms just enough to exploit their potential for generating irony in his post-Renascence, self-conscious, even postsouthern literary tradition.

Walker Percy's fiction seeks to reimplant the hero at the center of a world order, revoke the feeling of being extraneous that has hampered him, and assert his necessity once again. To this end Percy returns, consciously or unconsciously, to several of the familiar structural components of traditional southern heroic narrative: the appearance of the hero, the challenge to arms, the quest for the ideal mate. [16] More often than not, Percy's use of

15. Lewis A. Lawson, "Walker Percy's Southern Stoic," *Southern Literary Journal*, III (Fall, 1970), 30.
16. See Simpson, *The Brazen Face of History*, 253. Simpson points to the ironic

these narrative elements is ironic. Except for the ending of *The Second Coming*, Percy never seems to steer his narrative toward the sort of closure these structural ploys presume. Yet they retain such residual power, by Ziolkowski's law of the conservation of cultural energy, that they function almost autonomously.

The coordinates of the route through Percy's fiction appear even before *The Moviegoer*. Lawson identifies Percy's 1956 *Commonweal* essay, "Stoicism in the South," as an important bridge between the southern heroic and the modern American moment. Lawson concludes that Percy's essay is a gentle but total refusal to accept the stoic philosophy espoused by his adoptive father.[17] It is important to note the younger Percy's reasons for declining to accept the model.

Walker Percy could see that the world necessary to support the stoic hero in the South had, like Enzio's kingdom, vanished. "The fact is," he writes, "that neither the ethos nor the traditional world-view of the upper-class white Southerner is any longer adequate to the situation." The situation, of course, is the recognition of the bottom rail on top and the release of the southern black from the paternalist bondage of the high-minded southern aristocrat. The southern order had become a democratic community. The "hierarchical structure" on which the old order had been predicated, Percy continues, "could not survive the change" to a definition of civilization in the mass rather than in the few. The southern stoic affected a "characteristic mood [of] poetic pessimism [and] took a grim satisfaction in the dissolution of [his] values—because social decay confirmed one in his original choice of the wintry kingdom of self." Apart from the vagaries of politics, then, the flaw in the heroic order lay in the impulse toward self. Enzio had seen this in Frederick II, but he preferred to tolerate it. Walker Percy announces that he will not serve the stoic end, yet he avoids militant rejection of the fathers' way.[18]

Walker Percy's ideological stance before *The Moviegoer* sug-

figural repetition of the hero of George Tucker's *The Valley of Shenandoah* in Lancelot Lamar.

17. Lawson, "Walker Percy's Southern Stoic," 13.
18. Walker Percy, "Stoicism in the South," *Commonweal*, July 6, 1956, p. 343.

gests that he saw in his elder's world view a permeating fatal flaw—egotism. Whereas Enzio spoke his valediction by indicting the "earth" and not the human actor, Walker Percy exonerates the earth, the ground of reality, and locates the flaw in the self. We can, then, see the headwaters of one thematic current in Percy's fiction and philosophy. What exists prior to man's tampering, the world before man's knowledge of it, is good; the extraneous man—extraneous because he has tampered with the world or because he suffers the effects of tampering by others— seeks reconnection with the original world.

The route of the heroic search is not inward but outward into the world and others. Following that route, of course, means coming to terms with the problem of contingency, a move the southern hero has been loath to make. Binx inaugurates this renewed search when he realizes, in a hotel in Birmingham, that he must search horizontally. The vertical search into the realm of closure—the feared angelism of Tom More—makes man a leftover. Binx explains:

> The greatest success of this enterprise, which I call my vertical search, came one night when I sat in a hotel room in Birmingham and read a book called *The Chemistry of Life*. When I finished it, it seemed to me that the main goals of my search were reached or were in principle reachable, whereupon I went out and saw a movie called *It Happened One Night* which was itself very good. A memorable night. The only difficulty was that though the universe had been disposed of, I myself was left over. There I lay in the hotel room with my search over yet still obliged to draw one breath and then the next. But now I have undertaken a different kind of search, a horizontal search. As a consequence, what takes place in my room is less important. What is important is what I shall find when I leave my room and wander in the neighborhood.[19]

The horizontal search is an antidote to the solipsism of the vertical search; it offsets the self-absorption of the stoic model. Binx finds himself on a search that runs counter to Aunt Emily's interpretation of life; she speaks for vertical, hierarchical, heroic arrangement. Walker Percy's relation to the narrative structures of

19. Walker Percy, *The Moviegoer* (New York, 1962), 68.

the southern heroic is analogous to Binx's attitude toward the world order summed up in Aunt Emily's speech. Both novelist and hero are enabled by a prior tradition they must use in order to evade or renew. Little wonder that irony is the Percy manner.

The crucial encounter in *The Moviegoer* is not between Binx and Aunt Emily but between Binx and his cousin Kate. Using the traditional narrative component of the search for the mate in close circles of kinship, Percy adjusts the cultural fix with a series of fine moves. One move is to leave the partnership of Gable and Colbert in *It Happened One Night* in the narrative memory to counterpoint the pairing of Kate and Binx. Another is to give Kate, early in the novel, a vital part to play in the examination of the heroic ethic and its relation to power over life and death. Kate says that she would have made an excellent soldier, the role Aunt Emily had pressed on Binx after the death of his brother. The role shift is ironic. "How simple it would be to fight. What a pleasant thing it must be to be among people who are afraid for the first time when you yourself for the first time in your life have a proper flesh and blood enemy to be afraid of. What a lark! Isn't that the secret of heroes?"[20]

William Alexander Percy had found that war was indeed the secret of heroic action. Thrust into battle, the sides clearly marked, one could breathe more easily. One was not likely to find the father on the other side, undermining personal decisions on which were staked moral and ethical identity. Kate's problem is that, as a woman in the Percy cosmos, no heroic role is open to her. She has, implicitly, the more difficult part—enforced inertia. Colbert could show up Gable, but that was in a Capra movie. War had cured Binx's father of melancholia and was the occasion of his own discovery of the need for the search, but Kate, denied clean combat, falls into a drifting, passive state. For her, as for all of Percy's women, there is no heroic action; she must wait for the male to rescue her and tell her what to do.

Binx's destination is Kate, the ideal mate according to the traditional narrative scheme. Making love to her on the train to Chicago certifies him in reality. In the midst of a thriving traditional heroic order—the order, say, of Robert E. Lee or the nar-

20. *Ibid.,* 57.

rative order of the antebellum novelists of the South—claiming a bride from among cousins would have brought joy to the circle of kin. In "the great shithouse" of the present day, Binx's action sets off few positive lights. Percy's heroes seem to lug about the residual cultural meanings of a dead time without knowing much about them. For the southern hero of the classical narrative pattern, finding the appropriate mate is as crucial as conquering the barbarian at the outskirts. For the hero of *The Moviegoer,* however, marrying Kate is ambiguous: she might know truth he cannot discover on his own; she might be a safe alternative to a real horizontal search into the neighborhood.

For Binx, it is not only sex that certifies, for the simplest daily gestures into the void help recreate the step-by-step world that Uncle Will had found in the front lines. As the ideal mate, Kate accepts the hero's sovereignty. Her surrender to Binx enables him to act. She tells him, "But I think I see a way. It seems to me that if we are together a great deal and you tell me the simplest things and not laugh at me—I beg you for pity's sake never to laugh at me—tell me things like: Kate, it is all right for you to go down to the drugstore, and give me a kiss, then I will believe you."[21] Binx pledges to do as she asks. *The Moviegoer* ends with the scene of Lonnie's death balanced by the scene in which Binx tells Kate to run a simple errand into New Orleans as if she were crossing enemy lines on a mission impossible.

The Moviegoer seems to affirm action, but not without irony. The hero of the novel gains no clear-cut success in reestablishing his regime. One might, for example, see the final scene as "Binx's most successful communion,"[22] Gable and Colbert, however, made a much smoother couple, and from the long perspective of the southern heroic narrative we might just as easily question, as Ellen Glasgow might, whether Binx's one-way instruction to Kate diminishes her more than it helps. In the search for real action, Binx as hero does not allow women equal status. Nor does his formula for going on resonate with great scope and depth. "There is only one thing I can do: listen to people, see

21. *Ibid.,* 214.
22. Jim Van Cleave, "Versions of Percy," *Southern Review,* n.s., VI (Autumn, 1970), 1010.

how they stick themselves into the world, hand them along a
ways in their dark journey and be handed along, and for good
and selfish reasons." He had been particularly uncomfortable in
an earlier scene in which Nell Lovell, another cousin, had tried
out her simple formula for living: "To make a contribution, however small, and leave the world just a little better off." This news
had pressed Binx to the brink of a "tremendous defecation." His
own rule of life, albeit phrased a bit more stylishly than his
cousin's, is not substantially different. On the lips of the hero,
however, even banality rings with significance. *Lanterns on the
Levee* offers a corresponding example. Ironically for William Alexander Percy, his father's prescription for life, when finally fer-
reted out of him, seemed rather prosaic: "I rather think it best to
draw a bead on something that you have a chance to hit. To keep
any part of Mississippi clean and decent in these days, is a job
that no man may deem too small."[23]

It may be that the hero, in fact rather than in vision, actually
does prosaic deeds on the world's time and the world's terms.
What but Enzio's fervent memory keeps Frederick's career from
being the ordinary tale of savagery and assassination, treachery
and egotism? Binx's peaceful, rigidly parsed life in Gentilly keeps
him away from the field of heroic action and vision; he allows
movies to shift his references and leaves the idea of life to Aunt
Emily and her ilk. The Little Way is as much a defense against
the sort of heroic redefinition that had made his uncle feel extraneous as it is a deliberate pursuit of virtue and peace and truth.

It is clear from the beginning of *The Last Gentleman* that for
Will Barrett the road to action has turned uphill instead of
down. "Over the years his family had turned ironical and lost its
gift for action." The great-grandfather had carried a gun and
had even called a member of the Ku Klux Klan out to the street
for a shoot-out. The grandfather "seemed to know what was
what but he was really not so sure. He was brave but he gave
much thought to the business of being brave." The father, Will's
immediate model, "wished to act with honor and to be thought
well of by other men. So living for him was a strain. He became

23. Walker Percy, *The Moviegoer*, 213, 96; William Alexander Percy, *Lanterns
on the Levee*, 152.

ironical." Will himself is so bewildered by the "business of being brave" that he makes a fetish of inaction—watching. He is
trapped in absurdity of his own making, "always on the look-
out for chance happenings which lead to great discoveries,"
but blind to the fact that it is the nature of chance not to be
looked for.[24]

Will's problem with action arises when he tries to reconcile the
imperative to heroic gesture implanted in him by generations of
forefathers with the immense self-consciousness connected with
the business of heroic action. In the democratic ethos of a postsouthern dispensation, Will is a lost soul. A chance rotation, such
as the crash of a skylight, will momentarily suspend democratic,
common reality and appear to thrust Will alone to center stage.
But the thrill is transitory; soon he is awash in everydayness
again. He is out of step with his time precisely because his model
of behavior is southern and heroic, and he is consecrated or
doomed to the search for meaning in that order of reality. Even
when the Percy hero appears to junk the heroic model, he actually retains its essence.

The episodic structure of *The Last Gentleman*, clearly evident
once Will hits the road, repeats the familiar pattern of hero confronted with alien foes. The antiquity of the pattern, set against
the modernity of the content, produces Percy's tone of irony. At
Mort Prince's suburban seat, Will faces an obviously ironic version of the enemy knight. The burly man in the alpine hat (mock
helmet), whose northeastern accent underscores his loony other-
ness, seems to present the eager hero with the proper foe. Will
scents nascent identity, a breakthrough to the fathers. "'Sir, I
don't believe I like your tone,' said the engineer [Will], advancing
a step with his good ear put forward. Perhaps the time had come
again when you could be insulted, bear it aright, and have it out
then and there as his grandfather used to have it out. But there
must be no mistake. 'You were speaking to me?' he asked again,
straining every nerve to hear, for nothing is worse than being an
honorable deaf man who can't be certain he is insulted." The
situation is farcical, and the engineer, crippled also by hay fever,
advances toward the villain only to be punched in his clogged

24. Walker Percy, *The Last Gentleman* (New York, 1966), 9, 5.

nose by a woman bystander. If the father had fallen into irony, the son is doomed to slapstick heroic. Will's groping toward certainty ends with the typical episode turned on its head: he is sucker-punched by a woman, a knight's nightmare of shame.[25]

His entire quest is thwarted in similar ways. He blows up a GAR plaque at Princeton, but nobody had known it was there in the first place. Back home in Ithaca, in the Delta, Will experiences one of the most ironic déja vus. The engineer finds himself in a hometown bar in the black section of town with a few people from a movie crew. Beans Ross, a town deputy (a realistic redneck version of the Shakespearean deputy of "The Ku Klux Klan Comes and Goes" in *Lanterns on the Levee*), enters the bar and barks, "Where's the poontang." He flattens the bartender, Sweet Evening Breeze, simply because he is black, and then advances on the booth where the Hollywood folk are sitting. He snaps his fingers at Will's fly, and the engineer feels one of his most vivid emotions of the novel—humiliation. Then Ross makes a menacing move at Mona, and Will acts to defend the Hollywood damsel. "The engineer had time to straighten himself and to brace his foot in the corner of the jamb and sill of the front door. For once in his life he had time and a position and a good shot, and for once things became as clear as they used to be in the old honorable days." He floors Ross with a single punch and then calmly tells the Hollywood folk exactly what to do and where to go to make their rescue clean.[26]

Action is cathartic for Will, as it had been on a smaller scale for Binx. Yet action is predicated upon a clarity and certainty seldom known in the age of the superseded hero. In the old honorable days Will's great-grandfather had beaten foes in the Klan. Now Will decks an officer of the law. In the old honorable days of LeRoy Percy, the sheriff was one of "our" people, a lowercase aristocrat. Will operates in the days of vulgarity. Certainty of action and integrity of character within a social order are accessible only in the printed page; he reads *The Murder of Roger Ackroyd* for narrative closure and Freeman's *R. E. Lee* for the well-wrought model of heroic character in man.

25. *Ibid.*, 137, 140.
26. *Ibid.*, 312.

Percy uses other traditional heroic narrative gestures in *The Last Gentleman* to set Will ironically in a universe where his actions and intentions seem garbled. In the quest for the ideal mate, Will is entangled in the cords of a postheroic sexual relationship. The traditional hero of southern narrative knew the right lady and moved confidently to possess her. Many of Percy's heroes hope to do the same, but their success is confounded. Will senses the difference between right and wrong mates, and between right and wrong sentiments in sex, but nobody else, including Kitty, seems to care.

Early in *The Last Gentleman*, Will recognizes the ideal mate, the woman who, if not actually close kin, is definitely not Other. Spying a girl through his telescope, Will falls in love at first sight, at a distance of two thousand feet. "It was not so much her good looks, her smooth brushed brow and firm round neck bowed so that two or three vertebrae surfaced in the soft flesh, as a certain bemused and dry-eyed expression in which he seemed to recognize—himself!" Kitty Vaught, whom he will later meet formally in a New York hospital, strikes the engineer as minimally different from himself and therefore appropriate. Mating with her would not throw his already unstable world further off its axis. Securing Kitty would also absolve Will of responsibility for the wider, horizontal world. He could complete a significant pattern of action. Like the hero of old narrative, he would find his true love at home, and the kinship mystique would restore meaning.[27]

There are impediments to the marriage of like with like. The rival for Kitty's hand is, ironically, another woman. Rita blocks Will's mating ritual by her physical intervention. Once, in the ironically named "service room" at a Virginia motel, Rita interrupts Will and Kitty. Again, when Will and his maiden are alone in a camper, Rita's knock rattles the hero-suitor out of his erotic purpose. Rita's interference goes beyond the physical. Her name and chilling presence crop up so often in Will's quest to possess Kitty's charms that he dreams of her as a witch who has cast a spell over the lovers.

Although Will might have temporarily possessed Kitty's favors in a Central Park grotto, he never possesses her person. Because

27. *Ibid.*, 7.

she reappears in *The Second Coming* as a strident bourgeoise, most readers sigh with relief at Will's lucky escape. But the effect of Percy's narrative play in *The Last Gentleman* is far-reaching. Will, striving semiconsciously through remembered patterns of action to be the orthodox hero of the southern narrative model, feels motivated to find a mate from near kin or kind. He fails in that aspect of his obligation, just as he fails to identify and smite the enemy of his people. He is the twice-thwarted hero—extraneous to his people as he was and is extraneous in the larger world.

Sutter seems a Vergil to lead Will toward the light. Rita and Kitty claim that Sutter is twisted because he "can only love a stranger"—perhaps, so goes the word on Sutter, too many strangers too often.[28] But the "pornographic" thesis of Sutter's new way back into the world would move Will out of the mirror chamber of family and into living, and out of the murk of thinking about the business of living. Sutter's way might leave the young man free from irony. It might also leave Will free from everything else, obliged to make a virtue of his feeling of being extraneous if he cannot abolish it. At the close of *The Last Gentleman,* Will is still pursuing the Sutter enigma. The tantalizing question posed by the narrative is whether Sutter is a reversion to a lower order of life, a retreat from the world, or a new prophet of a problematic breakthrough from the transcendence of the old heroic order to the immanence of here and now. Was Sutter the last gentleman before Will to discover the limits of heroic living? Is a return, as Dr. Thomas More speculates in *Love in the Ruins,* in the offing?

"We look in vain," writes Walter Sullivan, who has responded to Percy's implicit and explicit questions about the once and future heroic order, "for the heroic action around which to organize the past and by which to measure the present." Percy's novels *Love in the Ruins* (1971), *Lancelot* (1977), and *The Second Coming* (1980) begin with the frustrating look in vain but conclude with the declaration of a restored heroic order that has been rebuilt along the familiar lines of "the classical-Christian ground of

28. *Ibid.,* 175.

Western civilization." In these three novels, Percy's vision of history, the hurt that history has received in the breaking of the Christian heroic model, and the return of the hero constitute an ironic affirmative epic of loss and recovery. The narrative of southern heroic, always useful in times of cultural stress, serves Percy well, if ironically, in the latter days. He does not tell his stories without it.[29]

Dr. Thomas More gazes upon cultural twilight that is as ominous as the darkling plain that broods over *Lanterns on the Levee*. *Love in the Ruins* opens in "these dread latter days of the old violent beloved U. S. A. and the Christ-forgetting Christ-haunted death-dealing Western world." The cure is action, for the malady is excessive abstraction, the sort of creeping sickness that ruined Will Barrett's father. It has spread to all sectors of the population. Ted Tennis, one of the victims of angelism, "has so abstracted himself from himself and from the world around him, seeing things as theories and himself as a shadow, that he cannot, so to speak, reenter the lovely ordinary world." The sickness reaches its incurable nadir in Art Immelman, a man so abstracted from himself and barred from the lovely ordinary world that he actually discusses with equanimity the genocidal potential of MOQUOL and takes More literally when he calls him a son of a bitch. Art must eventually be exorcised by a prayer to St. Thomas More.[30]

Hovering over *Love in the Ruins* is the model of the Renaissance hero-saint who, amid a welter of differing constructions of truth and reality, found a path of action and followed it even though it took him to the chopping block. To the present Tom More, the heroic ancestor was a "gentle pure-hearted knight for our Lady and our blessed Lord and Savior," and those nostalgically simple traits of gentleness and purity of heart—reminiscent of the "sweetnesse" Will Barrett prays for—are the earmarks of the hero. Tom More struggles to possess them, but not without stumbling.[31]

Heroism in the dread latter days is rare; perhaps, so say re-

29. Walter Sullivan, *A Requiem for the Renascence* (Athens, Ga., 1976), 54; Simpson, *The Brazen Face of History*, 255.
30. Walker Percy, *Love in the Ruins* (New York, 1971), 3, 34.
31. *Ibid.*, 169.

searchers, it is pathological. Even the passionate intensity of
early days seems to have departed the world of good men. Ban-
tus and liberals alike are led by conceptualizers—men with theories of behavior rather than simple hands upon the ordinary
world. Whenever Tom is depressed by this thought, he recalls
auto trips with his late wife and Sunday mass in forsaken places.
"The stove-up bemused" priests bore, in Tom's eyes, the tangible
mark of continuity with a holy past. Yet they were undeniably of
the present moment. What his wife "didn't understand, she
being spiritual and seeing religion as spirit, was that it took religion to save me from the spirit world, from orbiting the earth
like Lucifer and the angels, that it took nothing less than touching the thread off the misty interstates and eating Christ himself
to make me mortal man again and let me inhabit my own flesh
and love her in the morning." Sutter was not all wrong; he just
could not see religion as the real and successful merging of spiritual and mundane. Transcendence and immanence, angelism
and bestialism, are not mutually exclusive. Descartes is the villain
of the piece.[32]

Of course the mysteries of religion are not the only catalyst
to bring Tom More into coincidence with his own flesh in the
present. Being shot at also erases the split between mind and
body. At the ruined Howard Johnson's with Monica, as automatic
weapons fire pings around them, Tom becomes a pure man of
action, a hero. "'Here's what we're going to do,' I tell her," and
together they do it. This specific pattern of action emerges often
in Percy's narratives—when nothing but action is possible, action
will redeem.[33]

The mystique of declarative talk and pure action seems attain-
able only in war because war is the only *sub specie aeternitatis* condition of the secular world. All of Percy's heroes know this. Not
only does war make heroes possible, war makes action possible.
One will act because failure to will cause one's death. One need
not think. In peacetime, any or no action is possible and equally
noncommittal of meaning. In war, any action taken becomes un-

32. *Ibid.*, 254.
33. *Ibid.*, 266.

ambiguous. One is thereby rescued from the curse of nonmeaning, drift, everydayness.

Religion, as Percy's novels show, is the analogue of war, because the certain, original Christian vision of a real God and a real and present Satan renders all action always *sub specie aeternitatis*. Action is revived, by the sacred guarantee, and heroes are possible again. Percy's evolving heroic type transfers the southern heroic, gone to seed in the postsouthern world, to a philosophical-religious sphere. Although *Love in the Ruins* can be viewed through its religious windows, we cannot overlook the effect Percy achieves by tinting those windows with southern heroic.

The figure of the hero in Tom More seems to answer the need felt by many critics for the reestablishment of action in literature of the postheroic era. Walter Sullivan sees the death of the southern Renascence as the direct result of the confusion of sacred and secular heroes and narrative.

> Heaven and hell still got their due on Sunday; the doctrine of salvation was resurrected at revival times; but the final appeal to moral authority was made more often to the family and to mythical Southern heroes such as Lee and Jackson and Forrest than to God. . . . There were forces working against the survival of such a culture. As we have seen, it was short on the sacred dimension, the mysteriousness in the true sense; there was no real way even to make the heroes transcendent, larger than life as are Beowulf and Roland. They remained flesh and blood, worshipped though they were, and therefore, though they resisted mightily, they were ultimately to fall victim to the erosion of time.[34]

Sullivan takes an overly pessimistic view of Percy's vision. (To be sure, he wrote this appraisal before *The Second Coming*.) In all of Percy's fiction, and explicitly in *Love in the Ruins*, the erosion of the secular heroic is manifest and the bondage of the sacred to literal minds seems to be final. Although Percy, until *The Second Coming*, stopped short of infusing the mysterious and sacred into the mundane, he does leave his endings ajar for just such an unexpected visitation. Sullivan's reading of the rage is correct; the

---

34. Sullivan, *A Requiem for the Renascence*, 19.

affirmation in *The Second Coming* is wrought in precisely the terms of restoration of the truly sacred he had requested.

Lancelot, the novel that, like the anti-Christ, comes just before the parousia, is, as Percy's epigraph makes clear, the answer to the questions of how deeply one man can sink into the secular and how bad his suffering is there. Lewis Simpson has expressed the urgency of answers to this battery of modern questions in terms of the history of cultural and literary self-consciousness; he sees Percy as the modern Jeremiah. Percy, Simpson writes, is a "self-conscious survivor of history and a highly self-conscious Christian, [who] has followed the prophetic inclination into apocalyptic eschatology." Lancelot Lamar, to borrow Simpson's language from another context, is a victim of "the closure of history in a post southern America." Bearing the names of southern mythical, religious, and military heroes, Lancelot still mangles the world and perverts action because, as Cleanth Brooks states, Lancelot believes that "man the creature is not responsible for the evil in which he finds himself . . . [and that] man's salvation depends upon his own efforts." Lance is, in a single word, a gnostic. In the context of Percy's view of the demise of southern heroic into the vortex of self, gnosticism is as low as one can go. Any and all attempts to justify his murderous actions, even to crown him as a hero armed against an aggressively tawdry modern aping of culture, simply continue the gnostic fallacy.[35]

To Simpson's question as to what survivors of history do without an infallible map of the past and present, *The Second Coming* supplies an answer. Binx is acting at the end of *The Moviegoer,* but how far his way will take him and Kate toward a new order is not clear. Will is trotting after Sutter's Edsel with questions. Tom More is primed for a return with the lapsometer. And Percival leaves Lancelot with an unequivocal answer to a series of cryptic questions from the inmate. The end of *The Second Coming,* however, is anything but cryptic. Percy leaves no doubt that Will Barrett has found the will and the way to restore the universe to a wholeness it has lacked since the departure of God.

35. Simpson, *The Brazen Face of History,* 248, 255; Cleanth Brooks, "Walker Percy and Modern Gnosticism," in *The Art of Walker Percy: Stratagems for Being,* ed. Panthea Reid Broughton (Baton Rouge, 1979), 264. Many have mistakenly tried to find redeeming significance in the figure of Lancelot, including myself.

The conclusion of Percy's fifth novel echoes with convinced Christian vision. The earlier phases of Will's quest for the certainty of unequivocal action, however, show him untangling the strands of secular heroic that have fallen like a net upon him from his enigmatic father, who, like Hamlet's father, calls to the son from the depths of the earth and paralyzes action with guilt. The puzzle of honor and guilt seems less fatal to Will in *The Second Coming* than it was in *The Last Gentleman*.

> And I was never so glad of anything as I was to get away from your doom and your death-dealing and your great honor and great hunts and great hates (Jesus, you could not even walk down the street on Monday morning without either wanting to kill someone or swear a blood oath of allegiance with somebody else), yes, your great allegiance swearing and your old stories of great deeds which not even you had done but had just heard about, and under it all the death-dealing which nearly killed me and did you.

Will has finally seen honor and death as the two heads of a male totem that he, now in North Carolina, in a world growing "more senseless and farcical with each passing day," is unwilling to worship.[36] Percy's hero approaches the iconoclastic vision of Ellen Glasgow's women of the early years of the century and more particularly of Eudora Welty's Dabney Fairchild in *Delta Wedding*, who views the male code of heroism and blood violence as only tangentially relevant to the better ends of life.

The problem, Will perceives, is that "these days" people are scarcely more than 2 percent themselves. People act in trances of expectation and ordinariness. Will, on the other hand, is beset by dreams of being extraneous; his earliest and most potent dream is to fall down in a "leftover" patch of land with Ethel Rosenbloom, a girl from his childhood. It is, however, the unforeseen—the crashing skylight or the ambush—that makes the hero totally coincident with himself. Ewell McBee's errant rifle shot ricocheting around Will's garage brings him to life and makes him 100 percent himself, giving him an early taste of wholeness he does not duplicate until he finds Allison and a way to action through love for her.

36. Walker Percy, *The Second Coming* (New York, 1980), 72, 3.

The solution to the decenteredness of secular identity is fairly simple, although no one, especially the doctors, knows what it is. Allison moves directly and serenely toward it. The cure for the 2 percent self is to find the center outside the self. Seeking mistakenly in the angelic orbits of abstraction or the technological orbits of drugs and machinery will not bring man back to himself. Will's spelunking for God is likewise flawed. Fortunately, he blunders back to his center when he breaks through to Allison.

The relationship of Allison and Will, with its faint but rescinded suggestion of incest, evokes the relationship of Kate and Binx, the relationship between hero and mate central to the heroic narrative. Will requests that Allison do what he tells her to do, and she, like Kate, readily agrees. The path to action seems bright. We see Kate doing only the simplest of errands; her relationship with Binx works in only one direction, and not far at that. Allison, however, does the "hoisting"; Will allows himself to be lifted. Action, these curious negotiations seem to tell us, is bipartisan. No hero of the old days and ways ever acted that way; perhaps, as Percy has revised the heroic tale, the ill lay in the fact that no hero ever shared the privilege of action.

At stake in this example of genuine intersubjectivity is the reinstatement of, first, individual centering and, second, the righting of the entire cultural order. This order, or community, as most of Percy's critics have realized, is severely derelict. Percy's formula for redempton takes him close to the brink of simplistic romance, for the narrative pattern of old has been at home in romance. Allison is the first to voice the news of salvation, graceful rescue from self. Read without its full context, her testimony sounds very similar to the breathy prose of pulp romance. "'And will I for the first time in my life get away from my everlasting self sick of itself to be with another self and is that what *it* is and if not then what?' . . . She was moving against him, enclosing him, wrapping her arms and legs around him, as if her body had at last found the center of itself outside itself."[37] Yet Percy takes this risk for the sake of the affirmation long sought in all his fiction and adumbrated in his philosophical essays.

Curiously, memory does return to Will and even serves him

37. *Ibid.*, 257.

well when he forgets his heroic father and the failed past. The antigentleman Sutter seems not to have been the totally bankrupt secularist after all—not if the blessed Allison can share some of his traits. Will tells Allison, "You're Sutter turned happy," which is to say that Will sees in Allison's rejoicing in immanence the salvation that Sutter saw only darkly. Allison is free from the downward spiral of nihilistic self-concentration that negates Sutter. For Allie, immanence does not lead instantly back to the self. The rest of the population might be, as Will chants in the backseat of his Mercedes, "no different from the Jews at Buchenwald who did not give themselves leave to resist death," but Allison will hoist him back to life, and he will help. He will act like the holy heroes—Lonnie, Saint Thomas More, Percival—who decide to believe in something outside and beyond themselves in spite of having no evidence.[38]

Will not only becomes the rejuvenated attorney capable of plan and implementation in the secular world of writs and deeds; he also becomes a Christ, a Word, the holy hero. He reenters the "lovely ordinary world," the boon for which Tom More prayed in the wilderness, and bypasses the false Christs. Jack Curl, ironically bearing the initials that condemn him as a fraud, cannot bring salvation to anyone, for he himself is trying "to catch hold of his own life." Father Weatherbee, who looks upon Will as an aged John the Baptist might have gazed upon a messiah he had just about given up hope of seeing, compares Jack to a "dungbird" that follows the herd and sifts its excrement for food. But Will plunges forward, calls his disciples from among the halt and the maimed, and sets about developing a new order that heals the split between angelism and bestialism. "Could it be that the Lord is here, masquerading behind this simple silly holy face [of Father Weatherbee]? Am I crazy to want both, her [Allison] and Him? No, not want, must have. And will have."[39]

Will makes himself coincident with his intention, the linchpin in the meaning he announces as possible and, in fact, at hand. In proclaiming his and the world's good news, Will denigrates the stoic order that the old mole his father had handed down through

38. *Ibid.*, 263, 271.
39. *Ibid.*, 125, 360.

deed and memory. "What other end if you don't make the end? Make your own bright end in the darkness of this dying world, this foul and feckless place, where you know as well as I that nothing really works, that you were never once yourself and never will be or he himself or she herself and certainly never once we ourselves together." [40]

In the second coming of Will Barrett, the heroic tradition of action and the continuation of community—what Sullivan called organizing the past and measuring the present—is pushed out of its stoic stall and into an affirmative and risky redemptive Christian surge in which, by implication, each man becomes his own messiah and communicates his holiness to the rest. No more the reductive materialism of the old mole, who could see human life as no more than something expelled into the world from "between an asshole and a peehole." [41] In *The Second Coming,* Percy claims to have restored the sacred, mysterious element to life on earth. To critics of the earlier novels, who had accurately read his diagnosis of the present age as terminally "short on the sacred dimension," *The Second Coming* proclaims a visitation. To his own early view that history had metamorphosed into apocalypse, Percy gets a second and saving opinion. The darkness that enveloped Enzio is lifted.

40. *Ibid.,* 337.
41. *Ibid.,* 176.

Afterword

> In a way, the reception of the statements is more revealing
> for the history of ideologies than their production; and
> when an author is mistaken, or lying, his text is no less
> significant than when he is speaking the truth; the important
> thing is that the text be "receivable" by contemporaries, or
> that it has been regarded as such by its producer.
>
> —Tzvetan Todorov
> *The Conquest of America*

The paradigm I have proposed must, of course, be tested continually. Certain works, for example, seem to be clear affirma-
tions of the paradigm's usefulness. Robert Penn Warren's *All the
King's Men* is a study in figural heroes and their crusades against
contingency in history. Jack Burden, weighted down by the past
and by the heroic figure of the past in Judge Irwin, agonizes in a
state of spiritual and emotional paralysis. None of the preserved
heroic modes is open to him. He does not know whom to love or
whom to honor. Action is risky; sleep is better. Like Percy's Will
Barrett, Jack watches and reports the actions of others. Applying
himself to the challenge of attaining the ideal mate, he is also
frustrated, but not comically. Ann Stanton is eventually his, but
not before she is contingency's mistress, and not before Jack
must relinquish all dreams of controlling the future by mating
with his heroic image in woman. Willie Stark is the figure who
scrambles the neat heroic equation. Always moving, keyed to the
volatile whim of the people while Judge Irwin is still in the
shrine of the law, Willie is the eternal variable. Jack's entry into
"the convulsion of the world, out of history into history and the
awful responsibility of Time" is not merely a fine, orotund flour-

ish for the end of the novel.[1] In the ongoing, autonomous context of heroic narrative, the lexicon of time and history and the world stores up meaning as a dammed river stores up energy. Just writing the words sends out arcs of cultural charge.

Reynolds Price's *A Generous Man* features a hero, Milo Mustian, who is the secret sharer of the author's restive prowling of a literary cage that threatens to revoke the future for both author and hero. Milo conquers a python named Death and, in Tristan-like fashion, finds a mate, Lois Provo, whom dreams and ghosts and imperfect recollection would make his kinswoman. Selma Provo, Lois' mother, who shows Death at country carnivals and fairs, is convinced that Lois—her daughter by Tommy Ryden, who died in World War II—has fallen for Milo, the image of Tommy Ryden. And Price lets loose a romance in *A Generous Man* that runs off on the path well worn by writers in the heroic mode.

Milo later wrestles with the ghost of Tommy Ryden. Exorcising the figural father frees Milo from the succubus of the past, the suffocating mask of hero. Like Jacob, Milo earns a new name and the freedom to breathe. At the end of the novel, Milo and Lois separate; the closure of the romance plot is avoided. All Milo wants is rest—rest from the unchecked flood of experience and claims upon his young wisdom and generosity, rest from the cultural imperative to be a hero and fulfill all men and women.

Price himself attests to a certain degree of cultural sabotage in his plan for *A Generous Man,* for he too desires rest from what Percy's Will Barrett would later call the hates and hunts of the southern heroic consciousness. In "News for the Mineshaft," an essay written in response to wrongheaded and obtuse readings of *A Generous Man,* Price admits that writing the novel was a great pleasure for him, for it gave the opportunity of "guying . . . as many as possible of the sacred solemnities of Southern fiction." One target in particular is the ritual of the hunt—a ritual Percy also uses for demolition purposes in *The Second Coming.* Naming the python Death, Price writes, was his way of driving "one more nail in the coffin I was building for the great Southern hunt," of preparing the last rites for "The Bear" and all its

1. Robert Penn Warren, *All the King's Men* (New York, 1946), 464.

precursors and imitations in southern writing.[2] Price's guying of the staples of southern narrative and male heroism indicates a strong and perceptive literary intelligence determined to clear away the antiques of literary expression to make room for a new story, for a rejuvenation of the rite of storytelling. Milo Mustian is Price's *agent provocateur.*

The critical paradigm herein accommodates unrest in several ways and enables us to see aspects of southern writing usually out of the traditional line of sight. Price makes fun of the sacred narrative, knowing full well that it is in fact sacred, in the act of breathing life into it. Southern women writers, such as Ellen Glasgow, can also work from within the male-controlled cultural enterprise to overturn the heroic monolith. Eudora Welty's *Delta Wedding* focuses on the trials of the heroic figure—George Fairchild—as seen through the eyes of various women who maintain the culture by different but no less effective means. With the aid of the southern heroic paradigm, this aspect of Welty's novel comes to the fore, and the familiar aspects of "plantation school" writing move to the periphery.

A place for the black southern writer in the narrative tradition of southern heroic is difficult to imagine. From Simms's hero Gabriel Harrison to Styron's Stingo, the southern hero either enacts or embodies the enslavement of the black. Consider the example of Richard Wright. In "Big Boy Leaves Home," the figure of the white male hero, clad in military uniform, armed, charging to the supposed rescue of the maiden, is not a figure of cultural pride and affirmation—not the honored figure of Simms or even the ironically undercut figure of Glasgow. Nor can Wright settle for the more militant irony of Percy. The white hero is, on the contrary, the figure of death.

Wright's Big Boy kills the white hero, but his action does not confirm his social or kin group in a stable position in history vis-à-vis a competing people. Instead, family and social solidarity—love—fails, and the son flees. In other stories in *Uncle Tom's Children,* the black hero's position must be violently seized at the cost

---

2. Reynolds Price, "News for the Mineshaft," *Virginia Quarterly Review,* XLIV (Autumn, 1968), 644, 658.

of being lynched, castrated, immolated, or more commonly demeaned by the debasing epithet *boy*. If one were to read Wright through the mediation of the southern heroic paradigm, one would see clearer symbolic outlines for the violence that the races inflict upon one another as a matter of regular intercourse. In fearful defense of his group, the white hero senses that the black man is the ultimate threat to the cultural purity and order in history guaranteed by the mating of hero and female cognate. White male violence toward black males is never, therefore, without a psychosexual component of meaning, usually fear and paranoia. Wright's work bears out this interpretation, as does Ralph Ellison's *Invisible Man*. "Battle Royal," the first chapter of the novel, can be read as the black view of a white, male, ritual exorcism of the psychosexual fear of the black man that had accumulated over centuries of heroic attention to racial roles in the order of world history. William Styron's *The Confessions of Nat Turner* takes on that cultural and sexual paranoia; perhaps the storm of black protest against Styron's use of the black point of view is explainable as protest against a so-called liberal usurpation of the black cultural parole.

Black writers have, of course, known literature as a ritual reserved for the white male (infrequently for the white female) and denied to them. There is, understandably, nothing affirmative in the figure of the white male hero for the black writer or reader. Black American writers in the South have, at least since Charles W. Chesnutt, evolved more or less covert literary forms for overthrowing the white heroic hegemony. Their work has been as arduous as that of the women writers and perhaps more difficult in proportion, for they have been denied the tools of writing: a voice, an audience, a vocabulary, a narrative.

The test of a critical paradigm is, of course, the freshness and light it lets into the gallery of known and received texts. Airing can be done in several ways: by culling the canon, discarding or demoting works upon which familiarity has sired contempt; by admitting new or previously unreceived works (feminist criticism and scholarship operates this way); by re-viewing the familiar from a new angle of vision. I have taken the third route, re-viewing known works in the canon of southern narrative prose under the rubric of a heroic literary mode. Although there are several assessments of the historical span of southern writing, and several more for restricted historical periods, a study of the continuity (or discontinuity) of literary structure in southern writing is rare.

There is a clear and present need for a rearrangement of southern literary texts along structural lines. Recent studies by Richard King (*A Southern Renaissance*, 1980) and Michael O'Brien (*The Idea of the American South, 1920–1941*, 1979) give new readings to the cultural debate over the unique status of southern literary and intellectual expression. They isolate the period in southern literary history known as the Renascence (variously dated) from the continuum; the implicit claim in this strategy is that these decades of the twentieth century are the most crucial. King mixes criticism of literary works with studies of southern polemic; O'Brien deals primarily with polemic and the personalities of the people engaged in the debate. Both studies set southern writing and thinking within the context of an ongoing and triangulated cultural debate that yokes nation, region, and individual consciousness.

Daniel Singal's *The War Within* (1982) resembles Richard King's study in that Singal mixes literature and sociology. Singal's mixing usually means that literature (his primary example is Faulkner) is handled as if it were sociology. That is to say, Singal extracts from Faulkner's works those aspects that most closely approximate the data of case study rather than literature. Literature as data is more amenable to paraphrase in the language of social science. Singal's paradigm, then, functions upon a clear but unstated bias in favor of data. Herein I have worked just as clearly on a bias in favor of literature as the dominant currency, for a culture's sincerest dreams and preferences about itself, past and future, are expressed in the forms of its narrative. Narrative form is, in Reynolds Price's phrase, "the secret autonomous life of the story"—a life that does not negate authorial plan and intention but is nonetheless independent of both.[3]

The paradigmatic approach of Fred Hobson's *Tell About the*

3. *Ibid.*, 641. *The Cavalier in Virginia Fiction*, by Ritchie Devon Watson, Jr. (Baton Rouge, 1985), is a more recent example of the tendency to read narrative primarily as data.

South (1983) is powerfully persuasive because of the temporal range Hobson covers in the history of southern writing and the variety of writings (letters, diaries, chronicles, as well as published works in several genres) he studies. The wide applicability of his theory that apologia is the characteristic and unifying form of southern literary expression is thoroughly documented. Hobson also accommodates literature and polemic in his study. Like Singal, he stresses the commerce between the order of historical event and circumstance and the less public universe of writing. Hobson affirms the seniority of history and circumstance; that is, a writer such as Thomas Nelson Page or Donald Davidson is best understood (in both intention and reception) in the light of the contemporary context. What happened to and around the writer explains what he or she wrote. Hobson does find elements of a structural pattern in the works of his representative southerners, but only the manifest content of their writing bears genuine meaning in his eyes. He stops short of claiming that an accumulation of form influences what is perceived and what is written.

What I have tried to do is to complement these studies, and others that have preceded them, with a study of the formal elements of southern writing. Manifest content, for the time being, is held in abeyance. My models have already been cited. Edward Said's *Orientalism* provides a plausible model for the study of cultural relations as power relations in and through works of literature and criticism. It would be foolhardy for anyone to deny that historical events (votes in the Congress, changes in the world cotton or tobacco markets, slave insurrections, population shifts, defeats and victories in war) influence shifts in the relative power of regions or nations. Said shows, however, that immemorial forms of consciousness (fears, faiths, investments in reality) refract events. Refraction rather than reflection is Said's subject; it is mine as well.

Theodore Ziolkowski's studies of figural subtexts in literature suggest a way of viewing literature abstracted from its historical circumstances. His law of the conservation of cultural energy proposes that the primary set of relationships in any literature is that which covers literature and its written continuum rather than literature and its historical moment. In other words, Ziolkowski's attention is also drawn to refraction. He proposes that the study of figure in literature is the study of refraction.

Tzvetan Todorov sets up a more far-reaching scholarly and ethical paradigm. Todorov argues that history is always and everywhere subordinate to the refraction of human consciousness. He further proposes that the structures of consciousness and reality itself are not eternal but are culturally determined and housed in a culture's written documentation of its actions and motives. To Todorov, the imposition of one group's reality upon another is always a power play that seeks to obliterate the Other. His study of the "semiotic conquest of America," by which he means the eradication of Mesoamerican history and reality by the European order, goes further than this study of southern narrative. There are, however, parallel elements in our ideas of what happens in writing when cultures clash. My reading of the figure of the southern hero opposed by the Other of history and human heterogeneity is very similar in form to Todorov's vision of Montezuma (and the culture he epitomizes) and Cortés. And Todorov's conclusion that crossbreeding, genetic and cultural hybridism, and linearity in historical imagination are prints of the modern, while the opposites—genetic and cultural sameness and "repetitive time frozen in an unalterable sequence"—are the doomed characteristics of the Other, lends this study of the South's vision of its culture an eerie echo.[4]

4. Tzvetan Todorov, *The Conquest of America: The Question of the Other*, trans. Richard Howard (New York, 1984), 86–87, 101.

Bibliography

Manuscript Collections

Library of Congress, Washington, D.C.
    Freeman, Douglas Southall. Papers.
Perkins Library, Duke University, Durham, N.C.
    Lee, Robert E. Papers.
    Page, Thomas Nelson. Papers.
    Confederate Veteran. Papers..
Princeton University Library, Princeton, N.J.
    Tate, Allen. Papers.

Books and Articles

[Adams, Henry]. *Democracy: An American Novel.* New York, 1880.
Alter, Robert. *The Art of Biblical Narrative.* New York, 1981.
Anderson, Charles R. "James's Portrait of the Southerner." *American Literature,* XXVII (1955), 309–31.
Auerbach, Erich. "Figura." In *Scenes from the Drama of European Literature,* translated by Ralph Mannheim. N.p., 1959.
Bakhtin, Mikhail. *Rabelais and His World.* Translated by Helene Iswolsky. Cambridge, Mass., 1968.
Blotner, Joseph. *William Faulkner's Library—A Catalogue.* Charlottesville, Va., 1964.
Brinkmeyer, Robert H., Jr. *Three Catholic Writers of the Modern South.* Jackson, Miss., 1985.
Brooks, Cleanth. "Walker Percy and Modern Gnosticism." In *The Art of Walker Percy: Stratagems for Being,* edited by Panthea Reid Broughton. Baton Rouge, 1979.
———. *William Faulkner: First Encounters.* New Haven, 1983.
———. *William Faulkner: Toward Yoknapatawpha and Beyond.* New Haven, 1978.
Buck, Paul. "American Heresies." *Hound & Horn,* VI (January-March, 1933), 357–67.

————. *The Road to Reunion: 1865–1900*. Boston, 1937.

Caruthers, William Alexander. *Cavaliers of Virginia; or, The Recluse of Jamestown*. 2 vols. 1834; rpr. Ridgewood, N.J., 1968.

Cash, Wilbur J. *The Mind of the South*. New York, 1941.

Cooke, John Esten. *Hammer and Rapier*. New York, 1870.

Crane, Hart. "Locutions Des Pierrots." *Double Dealer*, III (May, 1922), 261–62.

Daniel, John Warwick. *Robert Edward Lee, An Oration Pronounced at the Unveiling of the Recumbent Figure at Lexington, Virginia, June 28, 1883*. Savannah, 1883.

Davidson, Donald. Introduction to *The Letters of William Gilmore Simms*, edited by Mary Simms Oliphant *et al.* Vol. I of 5 vols. Columbia, S.C., 1952.

Davis, Sara deSaussure. "Feminist Sources in *The Bostonians*." *American Literature*, L (1979), 570–87.

Derrida, Jacques. *Disseminations*. Translated by Barbara Johnson. Chicago, 1981.

Devlin, Albert J. *Eudora Welty's Mississippi Chronicle*. Jackson, Miss., 1983.

Farber, Bernard. *Conceptions of Kinship*. New York, 1981.

Faulkner, William. *Flags In The Dust*, edited by Douglas Day. New York, 1973.

————. *Go Down, Moses*. New York, 1942.

————. *Light in August*. New York, 1932.

————. *The Marionettes*. Introduction by Noel Polk. Charlottesville, Va., 1977.

————. *Mosquitoes*. New York, 1927.

————. *Sartoris*. 1929; rpr. New York, 1964.

————. *Vision in Spring*. Edited by Judith L. Sensibar. Austin, 1984.

Faust, Drew Gilpin. *A Sacred Circle: The Dilemma of the Intellectual in the Old South*. Baltimore, 1977.

Freeman, Douglas Southall. *R. E. Lee: A Biography*. 4 vols. New York, 1934–35.

Gautier, Théophile. *Histoire de L'Art Dramatique en France Depuis Vingt-cinq Ans*. Vol. V. Paris, 1859.

Gilbert, Sandra M., and Susan Gubar. *The Madwoman in the Attic: The Woman Writer and the Nineteenth-Century Literary Imagination*. New Haven, 1979.

Gilder, Richard Watson. "The Nationalization of Southern Literature: Part I—Before the War." *Christian Advocate* (New York edition), July 3, 1890, pp. 425–26.

————. "The Nationalization of Southern Literature: Part II—After the War." *Christian Advocate* (New York edition), July 10, 1890, pp. 441–42.

Giraud, Albert. *Héros et Pierrots*. N.p., 1928.

Glasgow, Ellen. *The Deliverance*. New York, 1904.

———. *The Descendant*. 1897; rpr. New York, 1900.

———. *Life and Gabriella: The Story of a Woman's Courage*. Garden City, N.Y., 1916.

———. *The Romance of a Plain Man*. New York, 1909.

———. *Virginia*. 1913; rpr. New York, 1938.

———. *The Voice of the People*. New York, 1900.

Guerard, Albert J. "The Misogynous Vision as High Art: Faulkner's *Sanctuary*." *Southern Review*, n.s., XII (Spring, 1976), 215–31.

Harwell, Richard, ed. *Margaret Mitchell's "Gone With The Wind" Letters: 1936–1949*. New York, 1976.

Hlavsa, Virginia. "The Mirror, the Lamp, and the Bed: Faulkner and the Modernists." *American Literature*, LVII (1985), 23–43.

Hobson, Fred. *Tell About the South: The Southern Rage to Explain*. Baton Rouge, 1983.

Hollis, Christopher. *The American Heresy*. London, 1927.

Holman, C. Hugh. *The Roots of Southern Writing: Essays on the Literature of the American South*. Athens, Ga., 1972.

Holmes, William F. "William Alexander Percy and the Bourbon Era in the Yazoo-Mississippi Delta." *Mississippi Quarterly*, XXVI (Winter, 1972–73), 71–87.

Hook, Sidney. *The Hero in History: A Study in Limitation and Possibility*. New York, 1943.

Howells, William Dean. "The Southern States in Recent American Literature: First Paper." *Literature* (London), September 10, 1898, pp. 231–32; September 17, 1898, pp. 257–58.

———. "The Southern States in Recent American Literature: Second Paper." *Literature* (London), September 24, 1898, pp. 280–81.

Hubbell, Jay B. *The South in American Literature*. Durham, 1954.

Jacobson, Marcia. "Popular Fiction and Henry James's Unpopular *Bostonians*." *Modern Philology*, LXXIII (February, 1976), 264–75.

James, Henry. *The Bostonians*. Edited by Irving Howe. New York, 1956.

Jones, Anne Goodwyn. *Tomorrow Is Another Day: The Woman Writer in the South, 1859–1936*. Baton Rouge, 1981.

Kelly, William P. *Plotting America's Past: Fenimore Cooper and the Leather-stocking Tales*. Carbondale, Ill., 1983.

Kennedy, John Pendleton. *Horse-Shoe Robinson*. Edited by Ernest E. Leisy. 1835; rpr. New York, 1962.

————. *Swallow Barn: or, A Sojourn in the Old Dominion*. Rev. ed. New York, 1852.

Kermode, Frank. *The Art of Telling: Essays on Fiction*. Cambridge, Mass., 1983.

King, Grace. *Memories of a Southern Woman of Letters*. New York, 1932.

King, Richard. *A Southern Renaissance: The Cultural Awakening of the American South, 1930–1955*. New York, 1980.

Laforgue, Jules. *Poésies, II*. Paris, n.d.

Law, Richard. "Active Faith and Ritual in *The Fathers*." *American Literature*, LV (1983), 345–66.

Lawson, Lewis A. "Walker Percy's Southern Stoic." *Southern Literary Journal*, III (Fall, 1970), 5–31.

Lehmann, A. G. "Pierrot in Fin de Siècle." In *Romantic Mythologies*, edited by Ian Fletcher. New York, 1967.

Lubbock, Percy, ed. *The Letters of Henry James*. 2 vols. New York, 1920.

Lukacs, Georg. *The Historical Novel*. Translated by Hannah Mitchell and Stanley Mitchell. London, 1962.

Mallarmé, Stéphane. *Oeuvres Complètes*. Paris, 1945.

Margueritte, Paul. "Pierrot Murderer of his Wife." Translated by Robert F. Storey. *Denver Quarterly*, XIII (Winter, 1979), 41–51.

Martin, Jay. "'The Whole Burden of Man's History of His Impossible Heart's Desire': The Early Life of William Faulkner." *American Literature*, LIII (1982), 607–29.

Millay, Edna St. Vincent. *Three Plays*. New York, 1926.

Millgate, Michael. "Faulkner's First Trilogy: *Sartoris, Sanctuary*, and *Requiem for a Nun*." In *Fifty Years of Yoknapatawpha: Faulkner and Yoknapatawpha, 1979*, edited by Doreen Fowler and Ann J. Abadie. Jackson, Miss., 1980.

Minter, David. *William Faulkner: His Life and Work*. Baltimore, 1980.

Mizener, Arthur. Introduction to *The Fathers*, by Allen Tate. Denver, 1960.

Nevins, Allen, ed. *The Diary of John Quincy Adams, 1794–1845*. New York, 1928.

O'Brien, Michael. *The Idea of the American South, 1920–1941*. Baltimore, 1979.

Page, Thomas Nelson. *Robert E. Lee: The Southerner*. New York, 1908.

Percy, Walker. *Lancelot*. New York, 1977.

————. *The Last Gentleman*. New York, 1966.

————. *Love in the Ruins*. New York, 1971.

————. *The Moviegoer*. New York, 1962.

————. *The Second Coming*. New York, 1980.

————. "Stoicism in the South." *Commonweal*, July 6, 1956, pp. 342–44.

Percy, William Alexander. *The Collected Poems of William Alexander Percy.* New York, 1943.

————. *Lanterns on the Levee: Recollections of a Planter's Son.* 1941; rpr. Baton Rouge, 1973.

Price, Reynolds. *A Generous Man.* New York, 1966.

————. "News for the Mineshaft." *Virginia Quarterly Review,* XLIV (Autumn, 1968), 641–58.

Propp, V. *Morphology of the Folktale.* 2nd. ed. Austin, 1968.

Ramsey, Warren. *Jules Laforgue and the Ironic Inheritance.* New York, 1953.

Ransom, John Crowe. *Selected Poems of John Crowe Ransom.* New York, 1945.

Raper, Julius Rowan. *From the Sunken Garden: The Fiction of Ellen Glasgow, 1916–1945.* Baton Rouge, 1980.

————. *Without Shelter: The Early Career of Ellen Glasgow.* Baton Rouge, 1971.

Ridgely, J. V. *Nineteenth-Century Southern Literature.* Lexington, Ky., 1980.

Rubin, Louis D., Jr. *The Wary Fugitives: Four Poets and the South.* Baton Rouge, 1978.

Said, Edward. *Orientalism.* New York, 1978.

Sensibar, Judith L. *The Origins of Faulkner's Art.* Austin, 1984.

Simms, William Gilmore. *Areytos; or, Songs of the South.* Charleston, 1846.

————. "Kennedy's Life of Wirt." *Southern Quarterly Review,* XVII (April, 1850), 192–236.

————. *The Life of The Chevalier Bayard.* New York, 1847.

————. *The Partisan. A Romance of the Revolution.* Rev. ed. New York, 1856.

————. *Views and Reviews in American Literature History and Fiction. First Series.* Edited by C. Hugh Holman. Cambridge, Mass., 1968.

————. *Woodcraft; or, Hawks About the Dovecote.* Rev. ed. Ridgewood, N.J., 1968.

————. *The Yemassee.* Edited by J. V. Ridgely. 1853; rpr. New York, 1964.

Simpson, Lewis P. *The Brazen Face of History: Studies in the Literary Consciousness in America.* Baton Rouge, 1980.

Singal, Daniel. *The War Within: From Victorian to Modernist Thought in the South, 1919–1945.* Chapel Hill, 1982.

Smith, William Jay. "The Clowns, by Jules Laforgue." *Poetry,* LXXVIII (July, 1951), 210–15.

Squires, Radcliffe. *Allen Tate: A Literary Biography.* New York, 1971.

Steiner, George. *Extra-Territorial.* New York, 1971.

Storey, Robert F. *Pierrot: A Critical History of a Mask.* Princeton, 1978.

Sullivan, Walter. *A Requiem for the Renascence.* Athens, Ga., 1976.

Tate, Allen. *Collected Poems: 1919–1976.* New York, 1977.

————. "The Definitive Lee." *New Republic*, December 19, 1934, pp. 171–72.

————. "Euthanasia." *Double Dealer*, III (May, 1922), 262.

————. *Jefferson Davis: His Rise and Fall*. New York, 1929.

————. *Stonewall Jackson: The Good Soldier*. New York, 1928.

Taylor, William R. *Cavalier and Yankee: The Old South and American National Character*. New York, 1961.

Todorov, Tzvetan. *The Conquest of America: The Question of the Other*. Translated by Richard Howard. New York, 1984.

Trent, William P. *William Gilmore Simms*. Boston, 1892.

Tucker, Beverley. *The Partisan Leader*. 1836; rpr. Upper Saddle River, N.J., 1968.

Tucker, George. *The Valley of Shenandoah; or, Memories of the Graysons*. 2 vols. 1824; rpr. Chapel Hill, 1970.

Van Cleave, Jim. "Versions of Percy." *Southern Review*, n.s., VI (Autumn, 1970), 990–1010.

Verlaine, Paul. *Selected Poems*. Translated by C. F. MacIntyre. Berkeley, 1948.

Warner, Charles Dudley. "Impressions of the South." *Harper's New Monthly Magazine*, LXXI (September, 1885), 546–51.

Warren, Robert Penn. *All the King's Men*. New York, 1946.

Watson, Ritchie Devon. *The Cavalier in Virginia Fiction*. Baton Rouge, 1985.

Weber, Max. *The Theory of Social and Economic Organizations*. Translated by A. M. Henderson and Talcott Parsons. New York, 1964.

Wicks, Charles Beaumont. *The Parisian Stage*. University, Ala., 1979.

Williams, T. Harry. *The Selected Essays of T. Harry Williams*. Baton Rouge, 1983.

Wittenberg, Judith Bryant. *Faulkner: The Transfiguration of Biography*. Lincoln, Neb., 1979.

Wolfe, Tom. *The Right Stuff*. New York, 1979.

Woodward, C. Vann. *The Burden of Southern History*. Rev. ed. Baton Rouge, 1968.

Wyatt-Brown, Bertram. *Southern Honor: Ethics and Behavior in the Old South*. New York, 1982.

Young, Thomas Daniel. *The Past in the Present: A Thematic Study of Modern Southern Fiction*. Baton Rouge, 1981.

Young, Thomas Daniel, and John J. Hindle, eds. *The Republic of Letters in America: The Correspondence of John Peale Bishop and Allen Tate*. Lexington, Ky., 1981.

Young, Thomas Daniel, and John Tyree Fain, eds. *The Literary Correspon-

dence of Donald Davidson and Allen Tate. Foreword by Lewis P. Simpson. Athens, Ga., 1974.

Ziolkowski, Theodore. *Disenchanted Images: A Literary Iconology.* Princeton, 1977.

———. *Fictional Transfigurations of Jesus.* Princeton, 1972.

Index

MIDDLEBURY COLLEGE